LAWRENCE JAMES gained a First Class Honours degree in History at the University of York. He did research in fifteenth century English History at Oxford where he obtained an M.Litt. He then taught History at Merchant Taylor's School and is now head of the History Department at Sedbergh School and Chief Examiner for one of the Boards.

D1825795

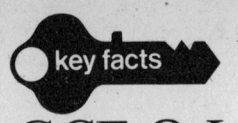
key facts

GCE O-Level Passbooks

BIOLOGY, R. Whitaker, B.Sc. and J. M. Kelly, B.Sc., M.I.Biol.

CHEMISTRY, C. W. Lapham, M.Sc., A.R.I.C.

ECONOMICS, J. E. Waszek, B.Sc(Econ.).

ENGLISH LANGUAGE, Robert L. Wilson, M.A.

FRENCH, G. Butler, B.A.

GEOGRAPHY, R. Knowles, M.A.

HISTORY, (Social and Economic, 1815-1939), M. C. James, B.A.

MODERN MATHEMATICS, A. J. Sly, B.A.

PHYSICS, B. P. Brindle, B.Sc.

REGIONAL GEOGRAPHY (British Isles), R. Bryant, B. A. and R. Knowles, M.A.

TECHNICAL DRAWING, P. Barnett, D.S.C., M.C.C. Ed., Adv. Dip. Ed.

GCE O-Level Passbook

History
(Political and Constitutional, 1815-1951)

L. James, B.A., M.Litt.

Published by Charles Letts & Co Ltd
London, Edinburgh and New York

This book is sold subject to the condition that it shall not, by way of trade or otherwise, be lent, re-sold, hired out, or otherwise circulated without the publisher's prior consent in any form of binding or cover other than that in which it is published and without a similar condition including this condition being imposed on the subsequent purchaser.

First published 1980 by Intercontinental Book Productions

Published 1982 by Charles Letts & Co Ltd
Diary House, Borough Road, London SE1 1DW

2nd edition, 1st impression
© Charles Letts & Co Ltd
Made and printed by Charles Letts (Scotland) Ltd
ISBN 0 85097 543 3

Contents

Introduction

All of us have an interest in our past. Fashions in clothes for men and women often quite deliberately copy the styles of a previous generation, films and television programmes draw much of their material from history, many more people buy antiques and bric-à-brac and even larger numbers visit ancient buildings. There are many reasons for this interest in the past. People like to have a sense of continuity, that is a feeling of belonging to and being part of a process. Maybe people are also a little frightened and uncertain of the future and therefore seek comfort in an escape to the past.

History is about people and part of our essential natures makes us curious to know about other people. Through history we can observe people thinking and behaving in ways which are very different from our own. We may also recognize human qualities such as courage, vision or dishonesty which are familiar to us in our own lives. Comfort can be drawn from appreciating achievement and equally important is the realization of the human ability to adapt and survive. History should be a pleasure since its raw material covers every aspect of human thought and behaviour. Through its study and understanding, we can sometimes become more aware of ourselves and our present world.

It is obvious that the ways in which we think and behave now are directly or indirectly the consequence of the past. At times the links are very clear. The ambitions and activities of men like Kruger or Rhodes have shaped present day southern Africa. The determination, purposefulness and sense of destiny which rightly or wrongly mark out and guide the Boers of modern South Africa were shaped by the experiences of the Great Trek and two wars with Britain. The conflict in Ireland is to a great extent the result of the failure of nineteenth and early twentieth century politicians to solve the Irish problem. The present problem can only be understood in all its complexity if it is related to Ireland's past. Other connections are less obvious but none the less exist. The part played by women in the working life of this country today is in part the result of two world wars when it was a matter of necessity that women took over the jobs of men required in the fighting forces.

We cannot be separated from our past, even when we would like to be. It is therefore useful that we attempt to understand our history. At CSE and O Level, a history course is designed to cover a period in a broad sweep so that the student can appreciate a general pattern of development, or trace movements of change. This book follows British political history from 1815 to 1951, a period bounded by Waterloo at one end and the Cold War at the other. This was a time of great change in Britain; it included the steady growth of democracy, the spread of state intervention in all aspects of life, the expansion of the British Empire, the beginnings of self-government for the colonies and two great wars.

When dealing with topics such as Liberal or Conservative ministries, this book has followed chronology, that is the sequence of events. With other topics, such as Foreign Policy, the Empire and Ireland, the subject is dealt with separately. This has been done so that a wider pattern can be discerned.

Acknowledgements

I should like to thank my wife Mary for her help, in particular with the chapter on the Labour Party, and encouragement. I should also like to thank Mrs. Richard Cann and Miss Lesley Hine for typing the manuscript.

Chapter 1
The Tories in Power, 1815-30

Introduction

From 1815 to 1830 the Tory party ruled Britain under the leadership of a succession of Prime Ministers, Lord Liverpool (1812–27), George Canning (1827), Viscount Goderich (1827–28) and the Duke of Wellington (1828–30). The beliefs of the Tories were varied. Political parties of the early nineteenth century were different from those of today in that Members of Parliament often voted according to their private feelings rather than as their party leaders dictated. Membership of a party did not mean that a man agreed with everything that the party leaders did and there would be occasions when he would vote against his own party. Quite often Members of Parliament, Tory and Whig, would go to the House of Commons, listen to the debate and then vote according to the quality and power of the arguments which had been put forward.

The Tories did however have certain beliefs in common. They believed in the monarchy, the Church of England and the traditional order of society. At the top of society were the landowners, the nobles and squires of the countryside, men of wealth whose duty it was to govern in the interests of all. The Tories were not stubbornly opposed to change, but they opposed changes which might overturn society or endanger the rights of men of property.

For some time, groups of men, loosely called **radicals** had been calling for changes in the way in which Britain was governed. Many wanted Parliamentary Reform (see p. 19) and called for a House of Commons which represented a wider section of the British people, in particular the middle classes. Some radicals went further and demanded a complete change in society, with an end to the dominance of the rich. Their views were expressed by the poet Shelley:

> Men of England, wherefore plough,
> For lords who lay ye low?
> Wherefore weave and toil and care
> The rich robes your tyrants wear?

After 1815 the radicals became more active and their demands more clamorous. The Tory government, dominated by Lord Castlereagh, the Foreign Secretary, Lord Sidmouth, the Home Secretary, and Lord Eldon, the Chancellor, became alarmed by the extent and violence of the reform movement. Liverpool had watched the outbreak of the French Revolution in 1789 when the masses of Paris attacked the Bastille. Like his colleagues he feared that what had happened in France would happen in England, and not without cause, for many of the more extreme radicals openly called for a rising of the masses and spoke loudly about the 'British Republic'. The Tories, fearful of revolution along the lines of that in France, were determined to defend the political and social system with stern measures. So, **from 1815 to 1822,** the **Tories ruled represssively.**

After 1822 when the fears of popular uprisings had died down, the government's policies changed. **New men, like Sir Robert Peel** who had replaced Sidmouth as Home Secretary, **came into prominence and with them came a willingness to introduce liberal measures of reform. This second period, which lasted to 1830, contrasted with the first, for it showed that the Tory party was prepared to make concessions to change and popular opinion.**

Unrest and repression, 1815–22

An economic recession was the root cause of the unrest after the ending of the Napoleonic Wars. There was a widespread slump in trade which coincided with rising prices of food and other necessities. A Lancashire weaver who had earned 26 shillings (£1.30p) a week in 1800 was receiving only 9 shillings (45p) in 1817. The fall in demand for manufactured goods led to lay-offs and unemployment, a problem made worse in some industries by the introduction of new machinery which meant that fewer workmen were required. The bad harvest of 1816 added to the difficulties of the poor by forcing up the price of bread.

The Corn Law of 1815 made matters worse. The end of the war had meant that large amounts of cheap foreign corn could be imported, so pushing down prices and bringing ruin to British farmers. Faced with possibility of farmers unable to pay their rents and an agricultural depression, the government introduced the Corn Law. This stated that no foreign corn would be imported until the price of British grown corn had reached 80 shillings (£4) a quarter (504 lbs.) This arrangement suited the farmers and the landlords, in particular the country squires who sat in the House of Commons and supported the Tories. On the other hand it helped to keep the price of bread at an artificially high level and so added to the burden of the poorly paid. **The abolition of Income Tax in 1815** and its **replacement by taxes on food and other commodities** similarly **increased prices.** As Sydney Smith pointed out there were 'taxes on the ermine which decorates the judge and the rope which hangs the criminal – on the poor man's salt and the rich man's spices – on the brass nails of the coffin and the ribands of the bride'. At a time of economic slump, unemployment and falling wages, the Corn Laws and new taxes added further misfortunes to the poor.

Discontent quickly broke into violence. In Cambridgeshire and Norfolk, ill-paid farm workers rioted and called for 'Bread or Blood'. There were riotous demonstrations against rising food prices amongst factory workers in the North and Midlands during 1816. Economic hardship gave the poor a common cause and made them take the only action they could, disorderly protests. Political agitators were quick to take advantage of the groundswell of popular unrest. Since the 1790s there had been groups working for political reform, in particular the reform of Parliament and the way in which Members were elected. In 1812 the **Hampden Club** had been formed under the direction of Major Cartwright and the Whig, Lord Brougham. Its objective was Parliamentary Reform and a House of Commons chosen from a wider electorate. After 1815 its activities increased and included public meetings and petitions to Parliament. **William Cobbett** a radical journalist who detested the new industrial society and the power of money, published a weekly paper, *The Political Register.* As it cost 2d (1p) it was within the means of the labouring man to buy and read, so this journal's influence and circulation grew. Other groups also flourished with wilder schemes for change, based upon the total overthrow of existing society. One of these, the **Spenceans,** who wished to take over all land, was behind a violent demonstration in London in 1816 during which rioters had threatened but not entered the Tower of London. London had also seen a large meeting at Spa Fields with speeches demanding Parliamentary reform and a banner which was called the flag of the 'British Republic'.

Rioting farm-workers, factory hands shouting for cheap food and massive public assemblies addressed by wild radicals together suggested **revolution. Or at least this was how the Tory cabinet regarded the events of 1816.** They were determined to scotch the troubles before they got out of hand and took firm measures, which in turn made them even more unpopular. **The East Anglian rioters were tried and hanged as an example and soldiers were sent to areas where unrest had showed itself.** There was no police force at this time and the government had to rely on limited numbers of regular troops and the volunteer cavalry (Yeomanry) whose ranks were drawn from the farmers and middle classes, officered by landowners. **Troops** of both kinds were widely used to protect property and control crowds. **Spies and informers** were also employed with orders to infiltrate radical groups and report back on their activities to the Home Secretary, Lord Sidmouth. To help local magistrates, **Sidmouth suspended the Habeas Corpus Act early in 1817** and so gave the authorities the power to imprison suspected persons without trial. (The Habeas Corpus Act insisted that persons under arrest had to be brought before a judge or magistrate within 24 hours of being taken into custody.) **Measures were also taken to ban public meetings.**

Agitation continued during 1817. North Country workers, known as **Blanketeers,** threatened to march on London but were stopped by cavalry. In Derbyshire, **Jeremiah Brandreth** led a ragged body of men armed with pikes and muskets to seize Nottingham Castle but was himself taken and hanged. The disturbances in northern England were in part the responsibility of a government agent, **Oliver the Spy,** who penetrated radical groups and urged them to commit desperate acts. He would warn the government which would take measures to arrest the plotters. Such underhand tricks aided the government's propaganda for they exposed the wild and blood-thirsty schemes of some of the would-be revolutionaries. The harvest of 1817 had been good and there were signs of an economic revival which led to a decrease in public unrest but **pressure for political reform continued** and expressed itself through a series of **mass meetings** up and down the country. This campaign alarmed **Sidmouth** who sent **circulars to the Lords Lieutenant of every county** with orders to keep Yeomanry squadrons in readiness and to take strong measures to keep public order.

In June 1819 a great meeting was held at **St. Peter's Fields in Manchester,** where the crowd was to be addressed on Parliamentary reform by **'Orator' Hunt.** Over 60,000 men, women and children turned up and the local magistrates, fearing a riot, summoned regular Hussars and the local and none too well trained Yeomanry. At the start of the meeting the Yeomanry were ordered to enter the crowd and arrest Hunt but these inexperienced horsemen got stuck and the Hussars were sent to rescue them. Sabres were drawn and used, and the crowd panicked. Eleven were killed and the incident was called **'Peterloo'** in scorn of the great victory of Waterloo. The country was horrified at the bloodshed but the government stood by the Magistrates.

Peterloo was followed by a resurgence of agitation. Seriously frightened, the government responded with the **Six Acts (1819).** These restricted public meetings, increased and extended the tax on newspapers (a blow to Cobbett's *Political Register*), gave wide powers to magistrates for the suppression of blasphemous or seditious (revolutionary) literature, controlled the sale of firearms and made private drilling of men illegal. These strong measures were apparently justified when government agents uncovered the **Cato Street Conspiracy (1820).** Led by an ex-Spencean, Arthur Thistlewood, a group conspired to murder all the Cabinet whilst they were having supper, cut off their heads and declare a republic. The plotters were arrested, tried for treason, found guilty and hanged. (As a token of a civilized age they did not suffer the full and frightening punishment for treason and so their bodies were not cut into quarters.) Agitation began to die down after 1820 but not until the radicals and London crowds had given noisy support for **Queen Caroline,** the wife of the new king, George IV. She had been separated from her husband for fourteen years but attempted to attend his coronation service in 1820. Denied entry amid some confusion (the door of Westminster Abbey was guarded by Cribb, an ex-prize fighter and champion of England) Caroline was later divorced by the King. An unpleasant case but it did serve to give the radicals the opportunity to voice their distaste for the King and his government.

Conclusion

The Tories had stood by their beliefs in the years from 1815 to 1822. Faced with widespread discontent and calls for reform, they chose to defend society and the system of government as they then existed. The bogey of the French Revolution had frightened them and they were determined to crush agitation and agitators. Their measures were successful but earned them widespread popular loathing. The crowds of London cheered the funeral procession of

Castlereagh, and Shelley, a radical and enemy of Toryism, portrayed him and his colleagues as tyrants:

> I met murder on the way –
> He had a mask like Castlereagh –
> Very smooth he looked, yet grim;
> Seven blood-hounds followed him;
>
> Next came Fraud, and he had on,
> Like Eldon, an ermined gown;
> His big tears, for he wept well,
> Turned to mill-stones as they fell.
>
> Clothed with the Bible, as with light,
> And the shadows of the night,
> Like Sidmouth, next, Hypocrisy
> On a crocodile rode by.

A grotesque picture of men who saw the state in danger and beyond that the social system which had given them power, and which, they believed, benefited the whole country.

The Liberal Tories, 1822–30

Peel and Huskisson

After 1822, the politics of the Tory government changed, largely through the influence of George Canning (see p. 45), Sir Robert Peel, Home Secretary from 1822 to 1830, and William Huskisson, Secretary of the Board of Trade from 1823 to 1827. The party's leaders had come to realise that slavish adherence to traditional values could, at times, be pointless and that they had a duty to make controlled and sensible changes if these could be proved to be in the interest of the country.

Sir Robert Peel, whose family had been cotton manufacturers who had risen into the ranks of the landowning gentry, was concerned with **changing the penal code.** During the crime-waves of the eighteenth century, governments had increased the number of crimes which could be punished by death. Hanging was the punishment for several hundred offences which included thefts, house-breaking, fraud and resisting a game-keeper. The *Newgate Calendar* (a contemporary record of crimes and punishments) records that in 1809 a forger of bank notes, a Chester man who stole salt, a clergyman's son who was a 'Notorious Burglar'

14

and two more house-breakers were all hanged for their crimes. Peel, under the influence of Samuel Romilly and other prison reformers, obtained the repeal of laws which had set the death sentence for over a hundred offences. There were, however, members of his own party who felt that he was going too far, and so sheep-stealing, counterfeiting coins and some kinds of forgery were punishable by death until 1832 (a forger was hanged in 1828 whilst Peel was Home Secretary). Peel had however established a principle which would be followed throughout the century and that was the replacement of harsh and often vindictive punishments by imprisonment. Most important of his reforms was the introduction in 1829 of the **Metropolitan Police** force in London. The new police or 'Peelers' as they were soon nicknamed were not popular at first but their value in the prevention and detection of crime was quickly apparent. Other areas followed the example of London and by the mid-1850s all areas of Britain had their local police forces.

William Huskisson's work at the Board of Trade saw the beginnings of **Free Trade,** the system by which goods came into and left Britain without paying duties. Huskisson, in response to pressure from manufacturers anxious for cheap raw materials, reduced duties on wool, silk and iron. Duties also came down on other commodities such as glass, books, wine, coffee and sugar. Another step towards Free Trade was **the alteration of the Navigation Laws**. These had been passed in the seventeenth century to protect and encourage British shipping. They had restricted the bringing of imports into Britain to British ships or those of the country where the imported goods had come from. Huskisson supervised the relaxation of these laws, extending shipping rights to European nations (the United States had been exempt from the laws since 1814). Whilst trade with British colonies still had to be carried in British owned vessels, foreign shipping was on equal terms with British.

Huskisson was also instrumental in securing the **repeal of the Combination Laws (1824).** These had been passed in 1799 as a measure to stifle unrest amongst working men and they had made illegal any association of workmen, designed to improve wages or shorten hours of work. It was therefore impossible for workmen to form Trade Unions and the removal of this restriction had been the objective of Francis Place, a London radical. He had been able to persuade Huskisson to assist him and the laws were repealed. The consequence was the immediate formation of a number of

Trades Unions, whose members demanded higher pay. A rash of strikes made the government amend the law in 1825 and Trade Unionists were made liable to prosecution if they molested either their workmates or employers during a strike. The result was that Trade Unionism was free to begin its slow growth without fear of the law.

The period of Huskisson's activities was one in which trade was again flourishing and there was industrial expansion. The country had abandoned paper currency in 1819 when the **gold standard** had been restored, so reducing inflation. The **Corn Laws** had also been altered in 1828 when a **sliding scale** was introduced which permitted foreign corn to be imported if British corn reached 73 shillings a quarter. Against this background of restored prosperity, the Tory government had introduced measures which softened the often brutal rigour of the law and paved the way for Free Trade. Concessions had been made to the manufacturing interests and to humanity.

Catholic Emancipation and Tory downfall, 1828–30

The programme of Huskisson and the foreign policies of Canning (see p. 46) **did not please many members of the Tory party**. A group which came to be called 'Ultras' were deeply suspicious of policies which involved concessions to popular or radical opinion. In 1826 Lord Liverpool found that the squires of Kent were 'sore and sulky' about Huskisson's programme and one peer predicted the 'liberality' would lead to the overthrow of the country's constitution. The resignation of Lord Goderich at the beginning of 1828 brought the **Duke of Wellington** into power as Prime Minster. A national hero, he had little sympathy with reform and he dismissed 'liberal' Tories from the cabinet, keeping only Peel.

Tory beliefs had always insisted that the Church of England and the state could not be separated. As one Tory, Croker, expressed it, 'Westminster Abbey is part of the British Constitution'. In many Tory eyes, those who were not members of the Church of England, could not be full citizens. Into this category fell Roman Catholics and Nonconformists (Methodists, Quakers, Baptists and Unitarians). These religious denominations had been excluded from government offices and positions of responsibility by the seventeenth century **Test and Corporation Acts**. These Acts stated that officials in national government and members of local corporations had to be members of the Church of England. These acts were repealed in 1828, a measure which reflected the spirit of Tory liberalism but angered many party supporters.

The repeal of the Test and Corporation Acts aroused the hopes of Roman Catholics who were banned from sitting in the House of Commons. **A movement for Catholic Emancipation** had grown up and spread in Ireland under the leadership of **O'Connell**. The agitation in Ireland had reached such a state (see p. 78) that the Duke of Wellington feared that it could easily break into open rebellion if Catholic Emancipation was not introduced. This view enraged many Tories. The King, George IV, an 'Ultra' Tory, reacted to the news that Wellington intended to allow Catholics the right to stand for election with the exclamation, 'Damn it, do you mean to let them into Parliament?' His words reflected the angry views of many other Tories. Wellington and Peel, convinced that the bill was necessary, managed to get it through the Commons and the Lords. The **Catholic Relief Act** became law in 1829. It left the Tories divided between the 'Ultras' who had bitterly opposed the act (one, the Marquess of Winchilsea, had fought a duel with Wellington over the issue) and the 'Liberals' who felt that the Duke had betrayed their cause earlier.

In 1830 George IV died, little regretted by his subjects, and a General Election was called, as was the custom on the monarch's death. The background to the election was tense. In France and elsewhere in Europe, liberal revolutionaries were rising against despotic governments and in Britain pressure was mounting for Parliamentary reform. A Birmingham Tory, **Thomas Attwood,** had formed the **Birmingham Political Union, a mass movement which intended to press for Parliamentary reform.** Across southern England there was widespread rioting and hayrick burning **(the Captain Swing riots)** by ill-paid farm labourers. The election result did not give an overall majority to the Tories but Wellington remained Prime Minister and stated that he saw no reason to reform Parliament. Lacking support, even from members of his own party, he resigned at the end of the year.

Conclusion

In 1830 the Tory party was divided. There were 'Ultras' who loathed reform of anything and saw little wrong in resisting any kind of pressure for change, seeing it as dangerous. The traditional order of society and the Constitution worked well enough and should not be tampered with. It was not surprising that in 1830 Wellington, a man out of sympathy with reform or change, prepared his house for a siege by the London mob and organised his Hampshire neighbours into a squadron of cavalry to ride down rioting farm labourers. On the other hand the ideas of the 'liberal' Tories, represented by the work of Peel and Huskisson, reflected a feeling within some Tory circles that the party could not turn its back on the changing needs and conditions of Britain. As members of a party which considered it the responsibility of certain classes to rule, they realised that they should govern in the national interest and not be deaf to advice, even from radicals. By 1830 there were men like Attwood and Oastler, a Yorkshire parson, who called themselves radical Tories and saw it as their duty to bring about reforms, especially of conditions of work in factories. In terms of policy, the Tory rule from 1815 to 1830 saw a shift from repression to concession. In terms of party ideas, it was a time of slow adjustment to new conditions.

Chapter 2
Parliamentary Reform, 1815-1939

Parliamentary reform was the subject of serious and passionate debate during the nineteenth and early twentieth centuries. Parliament lay at the heart of British political life. It made and unmade laws and the decisions it took affected the lives of everyone in the country. It was therefore natural that men, and eventually women should concern themselves with questions about how Members of Parliament should be chosen and by whom. The right to vote, or franchise, was seen as an important one which gave the owner a direct say in how the country was ruled. This was a weighty responsibility and not to be given or received lightly. There was also debate about the composition of Parliament which centred on which areas deserved to return M.Ps or in other words, whether certain places with large populations should have more M.Ps than those with less inhabitants.

The 1832 Reform Act

The Unreformed Parliament
In 1815 it was believed that Parliament should be chosen by, and reflect the opinions of men of property. This principle had been established in the Middle Ages, and then, as in 1815, the ownership of property meant the ownership of land. Land was wealth, and men who possessed land were considered to be well suited to rule the country. Their interests were those of stable and ordered government under which a man could peacefully enjoy the fruits of his property. Such a well-ordered and orderly government benefited all classes and encouraged the well-being of the whole community. **Men of landed wealth were also regarded as well-suited to rule for they had plenty of free time to devote to the tasks of government,** and their education, based on the Classics and the civic virtues of Greece and Rome, gave them a sense of **public responsibility.** So the Parliaments of 1815 to 1830 reflected the interests of the landed classes, the owners of noble houses, fine parks and broad acres. Such men and their sons made up the greater part of the members of Parliament, either in the House of Lords, or as elected M.Ps in the Commons.

There were 658 Members of Parliament in 1830 of which just under 500 represented English seats, and the rest Irish and Scotch seats. **These M.Ps. were chosen by a very small section of the population for the right to vote was confined to men of property**, although there were a handful of exceptions to this rule. **Each of the 39 English counties returned two members to the House of Commons elected by men who owned freehold (that is not rented) property worth 40 shillings a year.** In effect the county voters were squires and rich farmers. There was **no uniform qualification for the right to vote in the 465 boroughs of Britain and Ireland**. In some, like Westminster and New Shoreham (Sussex), all those who paid rates or owned a house could vote, giving large electorates. Elsewhere the right to vote was more strictly limited to local freemen or to members of the local Corporation such as the mayor, aldermen and councillors.

The **boroughs were of different sizes. Many had once been well-populated, thriving towns but over the years their importance and population had declined.** Camelford in Cornwall was one such town which, by the early nineteenth century, had only nine electors and Ilchester in Somerset was another, but with sixty. **In some instances the population had all but vanished.** Gatton in Surrey had scarcely more than 100 inhabitants, and of them the owners of six substantial houses possessed the vote. The local squire, Sir Mark Wood, lived in one house and paid the rates and taxes for the tenants of the other five. The result was that he was the only voter for the borough's two M.Ps. These boroughs with a mere handful of voters were called **'Rotten' Boroughs.** The Rotten Boroughs returned M.Ps. through the direct intervention of their landlords and they could often be bought and sold. Camelford, with its nine electors all living in the landlord's houses, was sold by the Duke of Bedford in 1812 for £32,000. With the property went the right to return two M.Ps. to Parliament.

Many other boroughs, often with quite large electorates, **were also in the pocket of the local landlord** – hence their name **'Pocket Boroughs'.** The 640 voters of Stamford (Lincolnshire) danced to the tune played by the Marquess of Exeter, a local landowner, whose great house, Burghley Hall, lay next to the small town. The great local landowners had considerable powers over the voters. **Corruption was normal** since the landlord could promise reduced rents, threaten eviction and offer bribes. **Voting was public and took three days.** Everyone knew how everyone else voted and so it was easy to offer cash or lavish entertainment to a voter for his support. The electors of Ilchester sold their votes for £60 each and true to the spirit of the age, a candidate in the Northumberland county election of 1826 assured his friends that carriages and coaches would daily take them to the George Inn, Morpeth, where 'all possible attention will be paid to their Accommodation'. A failure to provide food and brandy for the electorate was poorly regarded. One candidate at Aylesbury in 1802 spent nothing and got 6 votes whereas his less niggardly opponent who had promised £3,000 to his supporters obtained 271 votes. Where money failed, brute force could be employed. One candidate at a Hertfordshire borough raised a troop of London prize fighters, each of whom received money and as much gin as he could take, to browbeat the voters. His Whig rival replied by raising an equally terrifying and hard fisted company of bargemen from a nearby canal. The three days of voting ended in a riot.

Elections were noisy carnivals with drink flowing and blows given and received. Most contests were no-holds barred affairs in which every possible form of trickery, bribery and coercion could be used. A Northumberland poster of 1826 captures some of the flavour of a contemporary election. Mr. Bell, the Tory, was described as, among other things, a man whose 'conversation never rambles further than his Stables, his Kennel, or his Barnyard'. He had 'a defective mind' and 'His days have been spent in brewing Beer, and his nights in studiously trying the strength of it'. The freeholders were not put off by these alleged qualities, and Mr. Bell was elected.

Movement for Reform

To its enemies, the unreformed Parliament was a mockery. First, it was seen as **a product of corruption which ensured that power remained firmly in the hands of the landed classes.** In the past fifty years there had been **widespread changes within society** which had resulted in the **growth in the numbers and wealth of the middle classes.** This change was most noticeable in the increase of wealth gained directly from industry. The men who had got rich from the profits of the Industrial Revolution became convinced that their voice was excluded from Parliament. The landed interest, the interests of the India trade or the Sugar trade were all heard in Parliament, whilst that of Industry was rarely represented. **As producers of wealth, the middle classes felt that they had the right to play an important part in**

21

chosing M.Ps. so that Parliament would fairly represent their opinions and wishes. There had also been a **great shift in population as a consequence of the Industrial Revolution but this was not reflected in the distribution of Parliamentary seats.** The **new industrial towns, like Birmingham, had no M.Ps.,** whilst mere villages like Camelford or hamlets like Gatton returned members to Parliament. Further arguments for reform were put forward by radicals, men who wanted drastic change as the only means of putting right abuses. They argued that property should not be the only qualification for the vote. The work of Parliament affected the whole community and it was therefore right that everyone should have a vote.

After 1815 pressure for Parliamentary Reform increased. The Hampden Club, founded in 1812, spread the Reform cause throughout the country. The cause was also taken up by working men who thought that only by representation in Parliament could they gain settlement of their grievances about pay and working conditions. All of this agitation was outside Parliament where the Tory government was in power and determined to defend the old order or, as it was called in one particular song, 'Our Happy Constitution'. **The Whigs were more open to arguments about reform.** Like the Tories they were led by great landowners, but they also drew support from businessmen and were not unsympathetic to demands for middle class interests to be represented in Parliament. The Whig leadership also understood that it was better that reform was introduced by them and so remain under their control rather than be imposed by radicals backed by the mob. **It was better,** so the argument ran at the time, **to have ordered reform of Parliament rather than revolution from the masses.** So those who favoured reform were beginning to see the results of their speeches and pamphlets. The Whig party was committed to some form of Parliamentary reform and this measure was widely supported throughout the country.

The 1832 Reform Act

The passing of the Reform Act took place against a background of popular agitation, and in 1831, of rioting and disorder. It was a struggle largely because of the determination of many Tories to do all in their power to hinder or stop Reform.

After the Duke of Wellington resigned in 1830, the Whig Earl Grey became Prime Minister, backed by some liberal Tories (see

p. 14). In March 1831 his government proposed a Reform Bill which was narrowly defeated in the Commons. A general election followed and the Whigs were returned with a comfortable majority of 136 seats. **The mood of the country was clearly behind Reform and the Whigs introduced a second bill,** but in Octobet 1831 this was **rejected by the House of Lords.** The battlelines were drawn with the Lords facing the Whigs who had the backing of the voters as well as the hopes of the middle and lower classes. Popular indignation exploded. There were riots in Bristol, Nottingham and elsewhere, and the palace of the anti-Reform Bishop of Exeter had to be guarded by troops. A radical newspaper called upon its readers to save up their coppers to purchase a musket and *The Times*, also expecting a revolution, proposed the formation of 'Conservative Guards' to defend property. The Whigs produced a **third bill at the end of 1831** and when this was likely to be rejected by the Lords, Grey suggested that the King, William IV, create 50 new peers to swamp the Tory majority. William IV refused and Grey resigned.

Wellington could not form a ministry and Grey returned. **The King gave way and promised to create 50 new peers if the Lords continued to reject the Reform Bill.** The hard-line Tory peers and bishops gave way grudgingly and stayed away from the House of Lords whilst the Bill went through. In May 1832 the Reform Act became law.

The terms of the Reform Act were in two parts. The first concerned the **redistribution of seats.** 56 'Rotten' boroughs lost their seats and a further 30 small boroughs were left with only one M.P. 42 new boroughs were created including such industrial towns as Sheffield, Leeds and Birmingham which each received two M.Ps. The counties received 65 new seats so that the larger counties such as Yorkshire had more M.Ps than say Rutland. **The qualification for the vote was extended.** In the boroughs men with property worth more than £10 a year received the vote, and in the counties tenants with copyholds worth £10 or leaseholds worth £50 a year were also entitled to vote. The 40 shilling freeholders retained their votes.

Results of the Reform Act

The 1832 Reform Act **increased the number of voters by 217,000,** most of whom were members of the **middle classes.** Business and professional men (lawyers, doctors) in the towns now had the vote, as did tenant farmers in the countryside. The population of Britain in 1832 stood at 23 million, including women and children, although the voters were just 1% of the population. There was however a greater fairness in the distribution of seats and the needs of the industrial Midlands and North had been recognised. Nevertheless small boroughs remained, such as Totnes with its 214 voters. Many boroughs still remained under the thumb of the local landlord. Corruption in the form of bribery and 'treating' the voters was as common as ever it was.

There were other important changes. Whilst most M.Ps remained members of the **landowning classes, they were now forced to pay greater attention to the wishes of a largely middle class electorate.** Earl Fitzwilliam, who controlled the Yorkshire borough of Malton, had in the 1840s to do his best to secure a railway for the townspeople in order to keep their goodwill. The interests of industry now had a voice in Parliament. There were those who were disappointed by the Act. The working classes who had agitated, rioted and shed blood found themselves without a vote. Their disillusion gave rise to Chartism (see p. 35). Nevertheless it was argued at the time that the passing of the Reform Act did much to reduce the chances of a popular revolution in Britain. Change, however limited, had occurred and the very fact that it had taken place offered the hope that other changes would follow.

The 1867 and 1884–5 Reform Acts

Background

The 1832 Reform Act had followed the tradition of giving political power to men of property on the principle that they would use their power wisely and sensibly in the best interests of the community as a whole. Movements such as Chartism (see p. 35) had unsuccessfully challenged this principle but the Whig, **Lord John Russell,** favoured a further extension of the vote. His attempts to do this failed in 1854 because of the distraction of the Crimean War. Palmerston, who dominated political life from 1855 to his death in 1865, was satisfied with the existing system and unwilling to change it. There was however one important convert to the cause of Parliamentary reform in this period, Gladstone. **Gladstone** in 1864 **made public his sympathy towards extending the franchise to members of the working class.**

Such a step aroused controversy. At the centre of this debate was the question as to whether working men were sufficiently responsible or not to vote. Those who said they were not, claimed that a mass working class electorate would blindly follow leaders who promised to act in their interests. As a result the wider interests of the country would be neglected in favour of laws which concerned one class only. Those in favour of giving the vote to working men argued that these men were capable of thinking for themselves and in the national interest. The new Trade Unions of such skilled men as Carpenters and Engineers, had shown the sound sense of the working class. Working men by their labour contributed to the wealth of the country and many of them, through their sober lives and thrift endeavoured to raise themselves up. It was only right that such men should be entitled to a say in how the country should be run.

The 1867 Reform Act

Once Palmerston was dead, his party felt free to pass a Reform Act but one which was so carefully drawn up as to avoid swamping the existing electorate with new voters. With this in mind, **Lord Russell introduced a Reform Bill early in 1866. It was rejected thanks to the determined opposition of members of his own party led by Robert Lowe,** all of whom believed that such a bill would bring ruin to the country.

Russell resigned and the **Conservatives, under Lord Derby formed a ministry. Disraeli,** the Conservative leader in the Commons, saw his opportunity. He **wished to increase the popularity of his own party through bringing about a measure which was widely supported by working men in the country.** In purely political terms his party might benefit from the gratitude of the new electors. Like the Whig Reform Bill, the Conservative version contained balances to prevent the working classes from swamping the electorate. For instance Disraeli proposed that all tax-payers who paid more than £1 a year should have an extra vote. As this bill went through the House of Commons, there were various amendments made by pro-Reform Liberals such as Gladstone. As a result, all the balances vanished. **Disraeli stayed in power, as he wished, but the final Reform Act passed in 1867 was more far-reaching than he or his followers had intended.**

The **terms of the 1867 Act gave the vote to all householders and lodgers who paid more than £10 annual rent in the boroughs;** in the countryside all tenants of property worth more than £12 a year and to all leaseholders or freeholders whose property was worth £4 or more a year. There was also a redistribution of seats. This took one member away from boroughs with under 10,000 population and gave extra seats to such large towns as Liverpool, Manchester and Birmingham and to the more populous counties. In all 938,000 new voters were added to the electorate most of them members of the more prosperous working class in towns.

Results

For many, the phrase 'a leap in the dark' summed up the 1867 Reform Act, but the more alarmist fears of its enemies were not fulfilled. The new voters showed that they were satisfied with the policies offered to them by the main parties, the Liberals (as the Whigs came to be known) and the Conservatives. Both parties were able to adapt their policies to the satisfaction of the new voters. It was nearly thirty years before a party with policies designed specifically for the working man, the Labour Party, appeared. The nightmare of class politics in which one class struggled with another did not become reality. Nevertheless one radical Liberal, Chamberlain, was quick to show that the parties needed to embrace social reform measures in order to keep the loyalty of the new voters.

Ballot and Corrupt Practices Acts

The **Ballot Act of 1872** introduced a secret ballot and ended voting in public. The old system had been defended by men such as Palmerston on the grounds that every free Englishman should be able to proclaim publicly what he believed in and not have to cast his vote darkly in a corner. In reality this system attracted bribery and even intimidation. The electors of Grantham received an annual 5 shillings each (25p) from the Duke of Rutland and in 1853 Lord Fitzwilliam's agent found it necessary to pay the large sum of £6 15 shillings (£6.75) to get rid of a Peterborough voter on polling day. The Ballot Act and the **Corrupt Practices Act (1883)** ensured that all such payments and tampering with the elections ceased.

1884–5 Reform Acts

A measure to extend the vote to working men excluded by the 1867 Act was proposed by **Gladstone** in 1880 with the strong support of **Chamberlain.** He admitted that the old principle that the vote should be confined to men of property was no longer applicable with the words 'I take my stand upon the broad principle that the enfranchisement of capable citizens, be they the few or be they the many, is an addition to the strength of the State. The strength of the modern State lies in the representative system'. In other words all those whose lives were influenced by what Parliament did had the right to elect the members of Parliament.

A bill was introduced in 1884 which intended to give the town and the countryside the same franchise but the Tory majority in the Lords first insisted on a Redistribution Bill. In spite of some angry reactions from the radicals, Gladstone agreed and there were two Acts, the 1884 Reform Act and the 1885 Redistribution Act. The **1884 Reform Act** gave the vote to countrymen on the same terms as town dwellers. The property qualifications laid down in the 1867 Act remained, but they were not steep enough to prevent a further 2 million voters from being added to the electorate. The **1885 Redistribution Act** was a sweeping change for it divided the country up into equal electoral districts, each with one M.P. University seats (Oxford, Cambridge and London) kept two members as did 27 larger boroughs with populations of over 50,000.

Results
The Reform Acts of 1867 and 1884 extended the vote to men of the working class. The principle that property brought with it a sense of responsibility and so the right to vote was overturned. In its place was the idea that all men were entitled to some say in the government of the country through the possession of the vote. This principle was further enforced through the 1885 Redistribution Act by which the size of an area's population dictated how many M.Ps. it would have.

In political terms, the two major parties, had to respond to the challenge of a new electorate. This was done through the offer of policies of social reform (see p. 113) and the creation and development of election organization. Both the Conservatives and Liberals possessed local and national party associations whose duties included the distribution of party propaganda and the registering of voters.

The 1867 and 1884 Acts changed the composition of the House of Commons. Since 1832 most M.P.s continued to come from a landed background but by the 1884 Act there were signs that more and more M.Ps. from commercial backgrounds were entering the House. This had been made possible by the abolition of various property qualifications for M.Ps. during the 1850s. By

27

the last decade of the nineteenth century the balance had swung in favour of men with business interests. The middle class electorate created in 1832 preferred to vote for men with landed interests, the working class electorate created in 1867 and 1884 voted for middle class M.Ps.

Representation of the People Acts, 1918 and 1928

Votes for Women
The nineteenth century Reform Acts had each been concerned with extending the vote to men. Votes for women had been suggested by J. S. Mill in 1866 and the matter was discussed when the 1884 bill was being drawn up. For most politicians and men the matter was something of a joke. A cartoon drawn at the turn of the century clearly shows the male attitude to votes for women, by showing pictures of women in military uniform, as judges and conducting business whilst opposite, uncomfortable men are washing dishes, changing nappies and darning socks. The moral was clear, there were certain areas, all of them domestic which belong solely to women and there were other areas, including politics, which were reserved for men only. Such was the attitude which was widespread in the nineteenth and early twentieth centuries. The isolated women and their adherents who asked for the vote were regarded as slightly comic and cranky. Queen Victoria, spoke for many when she condemned 'this mad, wicked folly of "Women's Rights" with all its attendant horrors, on which her poor sex is bent, forgetting every sense of womanly feeling and propriety'. In spite of these and many allied views of distaste for women's rights, the barriers between what was regarded as a man's world and a woman's were slowly being broken down. In the last part of the nineteenth century, more and more women were entering employment. There were women doctors, women graduates from Universities and many more women who worked in offices and factories. Women played tennis and rode bicycles, both activities which might have been regarded as outrageous by their mothers or grandmothers forty years before. One woman who held what could be called a man's job, was a lawyer's widow, **Mrs. Emmeline Pankhurst,** a Registrar of Births, Deaths and Marriages. Through her work she was deeply aware of the degradation of working women in the poorer areas of London. Like many others distressed by social evils, she asked the question what could be done and for her the answer was votes for women. If women had the vote, then they could seek for remedies through Parliament. In a sense her arguments followed directly from those

28

already put forward by supporters of Parliamentary reform. If men were given the vote on the grounds that they had the right to be represented in Parliament since Parliament's actions affected their lives, then why not women?

To press for votes for women, **Mrs. Pankhurst founded the Women's Social and Political Union in 1903**. With the motto 'Words not Deeds', she and her followers wrote pamphlets, made speeches and held processions. They became known as **'suffragettes'** but remained throughout the eleven years before the war, a minority. Their arguments were simple and persuasive. One poster showed a woman university graduate and a male lunatic and asked why should one have the vote and the other not. On the same lines another drawing showed a woman mayoress, a nurse, a mother, a doctor and a factory girl, all without votes, contrasted to a convict, lunatic, drunkard and white slaver all of whom had the vote. These arguments and others like them made little headway; a Parliamentary bill to give women the vote failed miserably in 1905.

The Liberal government was lukewarm towards giving the women the vote but in 1910 a bill was put forward to give the vote to about a million woman. It made little progress and aroused no enthusiasm from M.Ps. The failure of this bill marked a new and alarming stage in the suffragettes' struggle, the appearance of the **militant suffragettes.** Their campaign was noisy, disruptive and destructive. Ministers were assaulted, windows broken, letter boxes and houses burnt, paintings slashed, and in 1913 a mentally unbalanced suffragette threw herself to her death under the King's racehorse at the Derby. The authorities were angered and embarrassed. Suffragettes were arrested, tried and imprisoned for their outrages. When in prison they refused to eat and therefore had to endure the agonies of forced feeding. To avoid scandal and possible deaths, the government passed the **'Cat and Mouse Act' in 1912** which allowed sick prisoners to be released for as long as it took them to recover their health. Even then discharged hunger strikers continued to break the law. The outbreak of war in 1914 ended the suffragettes' campaign and they turned their energies towards the war effort. Their campaigns had goaded the government beyond endurance and the Prime Minister, Asquith, was considering an Act to give some women the vote when the war broke out.

Representation of the People Acts, 1918 and 1928
Lloyd George at the end of the war in 1918 introduced an Act which gave votes to women. In the first place **he had no wish to**

see a revival of suffragette agitation and in the second the **part played by women during the war had** done much to destroy the prejudices which hitherto stood in the way of women's suffrage. The terms of the Act gave the vote to women of 30 and over who were householders or the wives of householders. At the same time all men over 21 were given the vote and polling was limited to one day. Eight million voters were added to the electorate. **The 1928 Act** gave the vote to all women of 21 and over on the same terms of men and added a further 7 million voters.

These two reform acts made little noticeable political impact. Whilst women now had the right to stand for Parliament, few chose to do so. The new voters gave their support to the old parties and their policies.

Conclusion

Between 1832 and 1928 Britain had become a democratic country in that its population was gradually given political responsibility through possession of the vote. Parliament changed more slowly and even by 1928 its members were largely middle class with a number of working men on the Labour and Liberal benches. The most important consequence of these changes was that Parliament came to represent the ideas and opinions of all sections of the community, regardless of their economic power. The landed interest gave way to that of industry which in turn came to share its power with the working classes.

Chapter 3
Domestic Affairs, 1833—46

Whig Ministries, 1833—41

The Whigs were in power for eight years after the passing of the Reform Act, save for Peel's short Conservative government of 1834-5. Earl Grey, who had been Prime Minister since 1830 resigned in 1834, and was replaced by Viscount Melbourne. The general election of 1833 had given the Whigs 320 seats, the Conservatives 150 and the Radicals and Irish 190. Although the Radicals and Irish were not an organized group in Parliament, they had a loose alliance with the Whigs and helped to keep them in power.

The **1832 Reform Act** had created a **new electorate** in which the **middle classes dominated,** and it was the aim of the Whigs to introduce laws which they hoped would appeal to the new voters. Much of the Whig legislation was shaped under the influence of the philosopher **Jeremy Bentham** and his followers. Bentham had argued that laws should be formed with an overriding regard for their usefulness or 'utility'. The value of any law should be judged by asking whether it contributed towards 'the greatest happiness of the greatest number'. If this was so, then the law was a good one. The Whigs also saw themselves as the party of good sense, preserving the liberty of the individual and the rule of law. They believed in reform when it was necessary and could be justified in terms of usefulness and the interests of the community. There were however disagreements among the Whigs as to how far government could go in making changes. The influential contemporary doctrine of *laissez faire* suggested that the government had no right whatever to intervene in many areas of life. Many matters, especially in the running of business, should be left entirely to the individuals concerned. Government interference in such matters was unwelcome trespassing on private liberty. Throughout the nineteenth century this doctrine was slowly overturned, but in the 1830s many men still argued that whilst the government could take measures for the improvement of the community there were some areas where private conscience and duty alone operated.

To make reforms the government needed to know what ought to

be done. Only with full and detailed knowledge of a problem could the government discover the extent of the problem and frame measures to deal with it. In pursuit of knowledge, the Whig government and its successors set up a number of Royal Commissions. These Commissions were made up of men who had been instructed to enquire into a problem, write a report on it and recommend to the government what it should do by way of remedy. Many of the reforms of this period followed the reports of various Commissions.

Whig Reforms, 1833–41

The **Abolition of Slavery** within the British Empire (1833) was the result of over fifty years of agitation and persuasion by a determined group of men. The anti-slavery movement and its leader, Wilberforce, had argued that slavery was cruel, immoral and un-Christian. In 1807 it had persuaded the government to abolish the Slave Trade and for many years after had urged governments to maintain an anti-slave trade squadron off West Africa, where British warships hunted down slave ships. In 1833 all slavery ceased throughout the British Empire and the sum of £20 million was set aside to be distributed among the slave owners as compensation for the value of their slaves. This money was not distributed in South Africa and contributed to the growth of hostility between the British and Boers (see p. 105). In the sugar islands of the West Indies, the end of slavery marked the beginning of economic decline for without the free labour of the slaves, the costs of sugar production went up.

The **Factory Act (1833)** was partly the result of the efforts of the Earl of Shaftesbury, who dedicated his whole life to improving the conditions of children employed in factories. The act concerned only the textile industries, but was an important breakthrough since it established the right of the government to intervene in the day-to-day running of industry, much against the wishes of believers in *laissez faire*. By the terms of the act, the government appointed **factory inspectors** with powers to visit factories and enforce the law. It was made **illegal to employ children under the age of nine** and those between **nine and eleven could only work for 48 hours a week** and they were to receive at least two hours a day of **schooling.** To improve further the education of these children a government grant was made available to pay for schools. Young persons between 13 and 18 were to work a 69 hour week.

The most controversial and far-reaching of the Whig Reforms was the **Poor Law Amendment Act (1834)**. This was the result of the **suggestions made by the Poor Law Commission,** which had recently examined the workings of poor relief in Britain. Before this time poor law had been run along lines known as the **Speenhamland System,** first created in 1795. Under the supervision of local magistrates, the poor would receive weekly payments calculated according to their wages and the cost of bread. This was known as 'outdoor relief' and the money was raised by poor rates collected from property owners in the parish. This was an **expensive** system; it was costing the country £8 million in 1818, and it had contributed to the labourers' riots in southern England in 1830.

A new system was created by the Poor Law Amendment Act. First, the poor were divided into two classes, the infirm and aged poor and the able-bodied poor. The infirm and aged poor were allowed to continue receiving outdoor relief but the able-bodied poor were to be taken into workhouses where they would receive indoor relief. Once inside the workhouse the able-bodied poor would receive the bare necessities of life and be expected to work, usually at such unpleasant tasks as grinding bones for fertilizer or unpicking ropes. Poor children were to be given some schooling. Conditions in the workhouses were tough and disciplined – until 1842 all meals were taken in silence – and the overall effect of these institutions was to discourage any but the most desperate from seeking to enter them.

The administration of the new system was in the hands of the Unions which comprised groups of parishes. Each Union would levy poor rates and the ratepayers would elect a Board of Guardians who would administer poor relief. The central administration of the system was in the hands of the Poor Law Commission in London. In the eyes of the government the new system had two advantages. One was its **cheapness** and the second was that it **discouraged poverty,** which at the time was often seen as the result of laziness. In the **countryside there was widespread resentment,** and in the North riots against workhouses or 'Bastilles' as they were called. Over the years and largely as a consequence of the exposure of scandalous inhumanities, the **harshness** of the system was softened. Still, in its early years and under the narrow and unimaginative direction of Chadwick, the Poor Law Commissioner, the new system caused great distress and unhappiness.

The 1852 Reform Act had reformed Parliament but left local government unaltered. The **Municipal Corporations Act (1835)** was designed to reform and rationalize the administration of local government. Before 1835 local government was in a muddle. There were a great number of incorporated boroughs with their own councils and mayors, some elected by local people, others corruptly chosen from small cliques. Some large towns like Birmingham had no local authorities whilst others, which had once been thriving communities, had a mayor and corporation but only a handful of inhabitants (like Dunwich on the Suffolk coast where most of the township had vanished into the sea). Often the local corporation had very limited responsibilities and the creation of such amenities as paved streets or a fire brigade was left to local Improvement Committees, set up by Act of Parliament.

The Municipal Corporations Act had four main provisions. The first was that all borough councils were to be elected by the adult male rate-payers and that councillors would serve for three years. The councillors would elect a mayor and aldermen, these would make up a quarter of the council and serve for six years. Many of the smaller corporations were swept away and the remaining boroughs were given power to take over the responsibilities of the Improvement Committees. The results of the act were not immediate. Birmingham and Manchester gained the status of boroughs in 1838 and 1839, but in many areas the local authorities were slow to take on themselves the duty of providing local amenities. Later in the century, Parliament would pass a number of Acts which ordered local authorities to take on certain responsibilities, such as Public Health.

The last major reform during this period was the work of **Rowland Hill,** secretary to the Postmaster General, who introduced the **Penny Post** in 1840. Before that date there were no uniform postal rates and payment for a letter had to be made by the recipient. Hill proposed a basic rate of 1d ($\frac{1}{2}$p) for a letter which was to be paid by the sender. Payment was indicated by an adhesive label or as it became known a stamp, the first being the famous Penny Black showing Queen Victoria's head.

The results of the Whig Reforms were far-reaching. The 1833 Factory Act was the first step towards full government control over conditions of work and an important undermining of the ideas of *laissez faire*. The 1834 Poor Law Amendment provided the framework for poor relief over the next seventy years. The

Municipal Corporation Act placed local government on a secure footing and gave local authorities powers to act as agents of reform in the towns and cities. The Penny Post together with the use of the rapidly growing railway system provided cheap and efficient communication for all classes.

Popular Movements, 1833–48

Causes

Once the 1832 Reform Bill had been passed, there were strong feelings of discontent and dissatisfaction from those who had hoped for the vote but had been denied it. **Disillusion with the Reform Act spurred working men to press for the vote.** It was believed that if working men could gain the vote, they could obtain from Parliament laws which would improve their conditions of work and life. At the same time workmen sought ways to obtain easier conditions and higher wages through Trade Unions. The intensity of working class agitation varied throughout this period, being strongest when trade was slack and unemployment high.

Trade Unions

Largely through the efforts of Robert Owen, an enlightened factory owner, the Grand National Trade Union was formed in 1834. It aimed to bring together working men for the purpose of improving wages and hours of work and it quickly obtained nearly half a million members. Its organisers also aimed at political power for, as one leader expressed it, 'the working class aspire to be at the top instead of the bottom of society'. The Union did not survive long. It was not well organized and was stoutly resisted by the employers and local authorities. The government was prepared to enforce the law against would-be trade unionists as shown by the case of the **Tolpuddle Martyrs (1834).** A group of Dorset farm labourers who had gathered together to form a union was prosecuted for taking an illegal oath. They were given sentences of transportation to the Australian colonies but after two years of popular agitation their sentences were remitted and they returned to England.

Chartism

The origins of Chartism lay in working class disappointment with the Reform Act. The movement began with the London Working Men's Association which was founded in 1836. Two years later its secretary, **William Lovett** and the Birmingham radical, Thomas

Attwood introduced the **Charter. This six point programme contained the basic objectives of all Chartists. They wanted the vote to be given to all adult males, a secret ballot, annual Parliaments, the ending of the property qualification for M.Ps, payment for M.Ps and equal sized constituencies.** In all, the Chartist programme was designed to secure a **House of Commons where the interests of the working classes would be represented.**

To gain the acceptance of their programme, the Chartists held meetings and processions in towns and cities throughout the country during 1838 and 1839. The culmination of this agitation was the presentation of the **Chartist petition to Parliament,** backed by a 'National Holiday', which was the Chartist phrase for a general strike. The Chartist petition was overwhelmingly rejected by Parliament and the strike was a poorly organized failure.

The Chartists suffered from many weaknesses. They were divided between the moral force Chartists led by Lovett, who believed that peaceful persuasion and reasoned argument would gain the acceptance of the Charter, and the physical force Chartists who put their faith in armed force. Added to disagreements over methods, the Chartists were split by regional differences. For instance in Ipswich, a Chartist leader who was also a Non-Conformist preacher called upon his followers to 'act with prudence, and carry forward their principles by argument and moral energy'. Meanwhile in Trowbridge in Wiltshire, rowdy Chartists broke church windows and one, who was a druggist, placed bullets in his shop window with the label 'Pills for Tories'. In Birmingham Chartists called for 'the glory and blessedness of a peaceful triumph' but further north a Chartist proclaimed 'There is no argument like the sword – and the musket is unanswerable'.

The **physical force Chartists** met with little success. A mob of several thousand was scattered by a volley fired by troops at Newport (Monmouthshire) in 1839 and elsewhere troops and police were able to contain the disorders. The Newport rising and the rejection of the Charter dampened the Chartists' hopes and the movement declined. There was a **revival in 1842** when a further petition with over 3 million signatures was laid before the Commons but was again turned down. This was a period of a trade slump and the Chartists drew strength from the unrest among the unemployed. Strikes in Lancashire (the Plug Plot) in 1842 broke into riots which were firmly handled by the authorities.

In spite of the setbacks in 1839 and 1842, the Chartist movement continued a flickering existence largely under the direction of **Feargus O'Connor,** the leader of the physical force wing of the movement. Following a trade slump in 1847 and inspired by the revolutions in Europe, the Chartists planned a further petition and a **massed meeting at Kennington,** on the outskirts of London, in 1848. The scheme aroused exaggerated fears in London, where the aged Duke of Wellington was placed in charge of the city's forces of law and order, but the meeting was a flop. (It is interesting than an early photograph of the Kennington rally has been recently discovered; one of the earliest crowd photographs in existence.)

The 1848 petition and meeting were the last gasp of Chartism. Its **lack of success drove away many supporters.** Others were tempted to join other popular movements like the Anti-Corn Law League or the Ten Hours Movement which was agitating for a shorter working day. Local divisions and the split over methods further weakened the movement and the lack of an overall united national organization was an additional hindrance. The movement also lacked continuity, agitation being strongest at times of distress and unemployment and weakest in periods of prosperity.

Peel's Ministry, 1841–6

Introduction

The 1832 Reform Act (see p. 23) had been passed in the teeth of Conservative opposition. Once it had become law, the Conservatives were forced to come to terms with the new electorate and to take notice of its needs. The alternative was to remain in opposition to a Whig-Radical coalition. When Wellington refused to remain as party leader, his place was taken by Sir Robert Peel, who had been a Liberal Tory in the 1820s. It was **Peel's task to adapt his party to the conditions of the 1830s so that it would be able to appeal successfully to the electorate.** The **Tamworth Manifesto,** written by Peel for the electors of the small Warwickshire borough of Tamworth in 1834, was Peel's attempt to make public the changing attitudes of his party. Peel stated that he accepted the Reform Bill and would work according to its spirit. The Conservatives as ever believed in ordered and good government and would, when necessary, introduce change and correct abuses. The Tamworth Manifesto was not a concrete statement of future policy but rather an indication of the path which Peel and his party would follow if elected. From this time the party became known as 'Conservative' rather than Tory, a name which became associated, rather unfairly, with dogged resistance to any change to the existing order. The Conservatives still kept their reverence for tradition, the Crown, the Church of England and the rights of property, but under Peel the party was willing to introduce change and reform when they were obviously needed. In this spirit, Peel accepted the principles of the Municipal Corporations Act of 1835. It must be remembered that the party included men of many different views, not all of which were in line with Peel's. One remarkable Tory of this period, Colonel Sibthorp, M.P. for Lincoln, fiercely opposed every kind of change from railways to the introduction of public libraries, arguing that they all contributed to the total overthrow of ordered society. Splendid in his way, the Colonel was a voice in the wilderness.

The electors responded well to the new pattern of Conservatism and the party increased the number of its M.Ps in the elections of 1834 and 1837. The resignation of Melbourne in 1839 forced Queen Victoria to ask Peel to become Prime Minister. She did so very unwillingly for she was attached to the Whigs and unsympathetic to Peel. She was unwilling to follow the normal procedure and replace Whig members of her Household with Tories. The absurd **'Bedchamber Crisis'** led to the return of Melbourne. He remained in office until **1841 when a general election** resulted in a **Conservative majority of 76.**

Peel's Reforms, 1841–6

The reforms brought about by Peel's ministry were a reflection of the spirit shown in the Tamworth Manifesto and they followed the pattern laid down by the previous Whig ministries. The reports of Royal Commissions into conditions of work in industry resulted in the Mines Act (1842) and the Factory Act (1844). The **enquiry into work in coal mines** had revealed the alarming conditions under which children and women laboured underground. The resulting **Mines Act** banned the employment of all women and children underground and made it illegal to employ any children under 10. Inspectors of Mines were appointed to see that the act was enforced. The **1844 Factory** Act was concerned with conditions of work in potteries, nail-works and other industries. Once again the revelations of the Royal Commission were the basis for the Act. Children between 8 and 13 were limited to a 6½-hour day and all women were to work only for 12 hours a day. Arrangements were made for the fencing off of dangerous machinery so that women's clothing would not get snagged on the moving parts. For the **first time a Factory Act laid down regulations for the employment of adults.** Both acts disappointed supporters of the Ten Hours Movement which wanted ten hours a day maximum for all workers. This was finally achieved in the Factory Act of 1847. For the most part, manufacturers, including such radicals as Bright and Cobden, did all within their power to hinder the passing of these acts, alleging they would bring ruin to industry.

Peel's greatest achievement lay in the field of finance. His financial measures contributed to the increase of trade and did much to recommend his party to the manufacturing classes. The means by which Peel introduced these reforms were his budgets between 1842 and 1845. In each of his budgets, Peel aimed to reduce the amount of duty paid on various commodities, In the **1842 budget** the duties on raw materials were brought down to 5%, on semi-manufactured goods to 12% and on manufactured goods to 20%. Further reductions followed in later budgets. By 1845 many duties had been abolished. The idea behind this policy was known as **Free Trade,** a system by which goods came and left the country without any form of duty. Since Britain was the world's leading manufacturer of goods, low or non-existent duties helped to keep down the prices of raw materials and finished goods. Free Trade, as well as helping manufacturers to produce cheaply, encouraged home consumption. The loss of duties meant that the government lost income and to compensate for this, Peel re-introduced **Income Tax** in 1842 on incomes of £150 a year and over.

The Bank **Charter Act (1844)** was drawn up to encourage stable banking which was necessary for commercial progress. There were many small banks throughout Britain and they issued their own notes for amounts of £5 or more. Often banks issued notes recklessly so that the total value of the notes was greater than the actual money held in the bank. The result was that the banks crashed and became bankrupt. To stop this from occurring, the Bank Charter Act insisted that banks limited their issue of notes to a sum which was no more than the average of notes issued in the twelve weeks before the Act became law. The Bank of England was forbidden to issue notes beyond the value of £14 million without the backing of gold. The act succeeded in its purpose and brought stability to banking.

The Repeal of the Corn Laws

Peel's efforts to reduce duties and encourage Free Trade were applauded by manufacturers. They believed that commercial success lay in ability to buy and sell cheaply – cheapness lay at the heart of competitiveness. **Many manufacturers wanted the government to go further and repeal the Corn Laws which would mean cheap food and incidentally low wages.** Peel shrank from this step because he knew that it would run across the interests of the landowners and farmers. These groups were strongly represented in the Conservative Party and they would have regarded the repeal of the Corn Laws as dangerous and damaging. The **Anti-Corn Law League** had been founded in 1839 and directed by Cobden, a Manchester business man, and John Bright, another factory owner. It aimed to fight a national campaign to repeal the Corn Laws. Through speakers, newspapers and getting supporters elected to the House of Commons, the League waged a determined campaign. **Many Conservatives stood by the Corn Laws, arguing that if they went, British agriculture would be ruined.** Peel gradually came round to the views of the League in spite of his own party. He was convinced that to hold out would lead to a struggle which would damage the landowning classes. The **Irish Potato Famine of 1845** forced his hand and in 1846 he proposed the repeal of the Corn Laws. The measure passed through Parliament, thanks to Whig support. **The Conservative party was split.** Peel was left with his followers whilst the mass of the party led by Disraeli and Lord Bentinck broke away, accusing Peel of betraying the party.

Conclusion

Peel's financial policies and the repeal of the Corn Laws were a victory for the doctrines of Free Trade and perhaps his greatest achievements. A Punch cartoon of 1850 with the title 'The British Lion in 1850 or the effects of Free Trade' gave a popular view of the benefits of Free Trade. The lion, dressed in working man's clothes, is fat and clearly well fed. He smokes contentedly on a cheroot beside a table on which stands a large loaf and a foaming pot of beer. The prosperity which extended to all classes in the mid-nineteenth century was thought to have been based on Free Trade. Free Trade became universally accepted throughout the country and even the Conservatives who had supported the Corn Laws eventually acknowledged the success of Free Trade.

Peel's other achievements were his Factory and Banking Acts. He had, to a large extent, followed the lines set down by the Whigs and ensured the survival of his party. His decision to repeal the Corn Laws divided his party. The remnant of the Conservatives, deserted by the Peelites, remained out of office almost continuously for the next twenty years.

Chapter 4
Foreign Policy, 1815–46

Introduction
A number of basic principles and considerations guided British foreign policy during the nineteenth century. The first was **British naval supremacy.** The Royal Navy ruled the oceans; during the Napoleonic Wars it had destroyed Napoleon's ambitions in Egypt, prevented a French invasion of the British Isles and controlled the seas. In the peace which followed the Navy continued to dominate the seas, watching over the routes which linked Britain to her Empire and protecting British interests throughout the world. One of the most important of these interests was **trade.** By 1815 Britain had established herself as the leading manufacturing and trading nation, and her markets and sources of raw materials were world-wide. The **safety and advancement of British commerce** was a further principle which helped shape British foreign policy.

Relations with the other powers of Europe were guided by a **reluctance to allow any one power to grow too strong and so dominate the continent** in the way which Napoleon had done. Britain saw no need to enter into close alliances with European powers and preferred, as far as it was possible, to be friendly with all her continental neighbours. There were occasions when a friend in Europe was useful, especially when British security was endangered. **Britain's own security** was another major concern in guiding British foreign policy. British governments had no wish to see the coast of Belgium fall into the hands of an unfriendly power since this might threaten British control over the Channel and North Sea and make the English coast vulnerable to invasion. The **security of India** was another factor which influenced British foreign policy, especially towards Russia. **The British were determined to prevent Russia from taking territory from the shaky and enfeebled Turkish Empire,** since Russian gains at Turkish expense could have placed in jeopardy the **overland route to India** which ran across the Middle East. Russian expansion in the Middle East or in south eastern Europe (the Balkans) could also have led to a Russian challenge to British naval power in the Mediterranean. Freedom to buy and sell unhindered across the world, naval supremacy and a Europe in which no one nation was dominant were the main aims of British foreign policy during the first half of the nineteenth century.

A sympathy towards movements for national or political freedom also contributed to the forming of British foreign policy during this era. Britain possessed an elected Parliament and the Britisher enjoyed considerable freedom to think, say and do as he wished. The people of Britain were proud of their system and their liberty; they thought that it was superior to the systems which existed in many European nations. By contrast the people of Russia, Prussia, Austria, the Italian and German states and France (until 1830) had very little freedom and little or no say in how they were governed. Their rulers were absolute monarchs with almost total authority over their subjects and they governed through obedient civil servants, police, spies, and armies. There were liberal movements in these countries which worked for greater personal freedom and elected Parliaments (like that in Britain) and many people in Britain, Whigs, Tories and radicals were warmly sympathetic to these movements. There were also sympathies extended towards the Poles, Italians and Greeks, all of whom wanted freedom from foreign domination.

The **conduct of foreign policy** was in the **hands of the Foreign Secretary,** a member of the cabinet, backed by the Foreign Office staff which numbered only 21 in 1821. During this period three able and important men held the post of Foreign Secretary, **Lord Castlereagh (1815–22), George Canning (1822–27)** and **Viscount Palmerston (1830–34 and 1835–41)**. Each was able to place the stamp of his own character and beliefs on the making of British foreign policy.

Castelreagh, 1815–22

The **Congress of Vienna** followed the defeat of Napoleon in 1814–15. Here the representatives of the victorious powers, Britain, Prussia, Austria and Russia assembled to create a new Europe out of the chaos left by the wars. Each nation wanted territory for itself as a reward for the part it had played in the wars, and all wished to make sure that there would be no resurgence of French power. **Britain's share in the spoils of war reflected her commercial and naval interests** for she got Heligoland (an island in the North Sea off the German coast), Mauritius (in the Indian Ocean), Cape Colony (on the southernmost tip of Africa) and the West Indian sugar islands of St. Lucia, Trinidad and

Tobago. Castlereagh, Britain's spokesman at the Congress, was anxious, like the other diplomats, to promote future peace and stability in Europe. The **Congress system** was Castlereagh's contribution to future European harmony. From time to time the great powers agreed there would be Congresses to which their representatives would come and discuss international problems and settle their differences. If successful the system would have reduced the likelihood of war and created a sense of harmony between the powers. One snag with Castlereagh's scheme was the **Holy Alliance.** the creation of Czar Alexander I of Russia. He, the King of Prussia and the Emperor of Austria formed a personal union and promised to uphold Christian ideas, which for each of them meant resisting any threats to their own absolute power. Britain did not join the Holy Alliance. King George III was insane and confined in Windsor Castle, and in his place, his son, George, ruled as Prince Regent. The Prince Regent liked the idea of the Holy Alliance but Castlereagh forbade him to join. He ruled with the consent of Parliament and could not make personal alliances, and moreover, public opinion was very cool towards leagues of absolute monarchs.

Although not part of the Holy Alliance, Britain played an important role in the European Congresses. At the **Congress of Aix la Chapelle (1818),** Castlereagh supported the evacuation of France by allied soldiers and welcomed the admission of France into the ranks of the Congress powers. This was a sensible and clear-sighted policy which ensured that France would not suffer for ever the humiliation of a conquered nation nor feel excluded from its rightful place as a major power. At the **Congress of Troppau (1820),** relations with Russia, Austria, Prussia and France became strained. The members of the Holy Alliance announced their intention of using their joint power to crush liberal movements wherever they occurred in Europe. Britain would have no part in this; she had no wish to play 'policeman' in Europe, and neither Castlereagh nor the British government was willing to support a cause which would have aroused public anger. Britain's refusal to help the great powers stamp out revolution did not prevent the Austrian army from crushing the liberals of Naples. At the **Congress of Laibach (1821)** Britain made clear that she reserved the right to act independently in the future.

Castlereagh's Congress system played a valuable part in keeping the peace. The British government could not however throw its weight behind the schemes of the Holy Alliance and join the conservative powers in seeking out and putting down liberalism and revolution. It was suspected by some European diplomats that Castlereagh privately sympathized with such plans, but he could not endorse them openly, let alone give them British backing. To have done so would have stirred up opposition in Parliament and in the country.

George Canning, 1822–27

Canning's sympathies were liberal and his unwillingness to co-operate with the major European powers was more noticeable than Castlereagh's. Relations with Russia, Prussia and Austria became chilled during his period at the Foreign Office although he deliberately sought Russian and French co-operation when it suited British interests.

The 1820s saw Britain intervening to help liberal and nationalist movements in Portugal, South America and Greece. Canning's motives for using British influence were a mixture of sympathy and a **keen eye for commercial advantage.**

In **Spain,** there had been a conflict between Ferdinand VII, who wished to reign as an absolute king, and the liberals who wished him to govern through an elected assembly. In 1822 the French army had intervened in support of the King and within a year his opponents were broken, and he was back with all his old powers. France had acted with the blessing of the Holy Alliance and the disapproval of many people in Britain. With Ferdinand in full control of Spain, backed by a French army, the question arose as to what would happen to the old **Spanish colonies.** In the past twenty years the Spanish colonies in South and Central America had rebelled, thrown out their Spanish rulers and set up republics. The new republics had established cordial relations with Britain and British businessmen were quick to exploit new outlets for trade. In 1823 there was a likelihood that **Spain, supported and aided by the Holy Alliance powers, would attempt to regain her lost possessions. Canning was determined to prevent this.** He had one advantage in that **Britain controlled the seas which split Spain from her own Empire** and another in that he was able to obtain the **co-operation of the United States.** In 1824 Britain formally recognised the South American republics of Mexico, Buenos Aires and Colombia. The American President, James Monroe, issued what has become known as the **'Monroe Doctrine'** which warned the European powers that the United

States would regard any attempt to establish colonies in the Americas as an act hostile to the United States. Faced with British sea-power and United States firmness, Spain and her friends had to give up any hope of recovering the lost colonies. Canning, who had brought about Anglo-American co-operation remarked 'the daughter and the mother stand together against the world'. His final triumph in his policy towards South America came in 1825 when he persuaded the King of Portugal to recognise the independence of the Portuguese colony of Brazil.

In **Portugal** itself there was a struggle between two contenders for the throne, Dom Pedro (who favoured a constitution) and his brother, Dom Miguel (who favoured an absolute monarchy) and was backed by Spain. When in 1826 the Spanish threatened to send troops to assist their ally, Canning sent British forces and warships to Lisbon. The liberal party was successful and Portugal kept constitutional government.

Greece presented a larger problem for Canning. In 1821 the **Greeks had risen against their Turkish masters** and their cause quickly found supporters all over Europe. The upper and middle classes of Britain had received a classical education and they regarded Greece as the source of western literature, art and philosophy in particular ideas of liberty. The friends of Greece ('philhellenes') collected money and some, including the famous poet Lord Byron, went to fight alongside the Greeks.

There was naturally popular pressure for Britain to give official help to the rebels, particularly after Lord Byron's death at Missolonghi in 1825. The new Czar of Russia, Nicholas I, also felt impelled to help the Greeks, who were, like him Orthodox Christians. Russian involvement immediately aroused British suspicions and to prevent Russia from acting on her own and to end the troubles in Greece, Canning decided to intervene. He obtained the co-operation of Russia and France through the **Treaty of London (1827)** which called on the Greeks and Turks to cease fighting and sent naval forces to Greece. The Greek war had recently been complicated by the arrival of Ibrahim Pasha with warships and soldiers from Egypt where his father, Mehemet Ali, was viceroy for the Sultan of Turkey. Ibrahim had been promised Morea (in southern Greece) for his services and was unwilling to stop fighting. His and the Turkish fleet were confronted by a French, Russian and British naval force under Admiral Codrington (who was pro-Greek) at **Navarino Bay (1827)**. A misunderstanding led to the allied ships firing on the Turks whose fleet was sunk. This naval engagement ended Turkish attempts to hold down Greece. In **1830, Britain, Russia and France guaranteed the independence of Greece and settled the boundaries of the new state.**

Canning's foreign policy marked a change from that of Castlereagh's. He had given **assistance to liberal movements in Portugal** and **prevented the reconquest of the ex-Spanish colonies in South America,** policies which put him at loggerheads with the Holy Alliance powers. He had not scrupled to use two of these powers, Russia and France, to impose a settlement in Greece. For some his views and actions were distasteful. Wellington was hostile to his friendship for 'modern revolutionists', the same men whom he had fought and beaten at Waterloo.

Palmerston, 1830–34, 1835–41

Viscount Palmerston had been a Tory supporter of Canning who had deserted the Tories in 1830 over the Reform Bill, which he strongly supported. He had held various offices in the government since 1812. During his years at the foreign office, he **built up a reputation for ability and popular following throughout the country which formed the basis for the successes of his later career.** He came to be known as a bold and plainly spoken defender of British interests, and a sympathiser with liberals and nationalists throughout Europe. This side of his beliefs was often exaggerated although it helped him win much radical support. In 1831 when a Polish nationalist asked him for help against Russia, Palmerston made clear his position, 'Now the English nation is able to make war, but it will only do so where its own interests are concerned. We are a simple and practical nation, a commercial nation'.

To a large extent Palmerston's policies followed those of his predecessors. He appreciated the **commercial interests of Britain,** the **need for a balance of power in Europe,** and the necessity of **guarding British and Indian security.** He wished to keep up friendly relations with the European powers, but he especially wished to **establish a harmony with France,** which after the 1830 Revolution had become a constitutional monarchy like Britain.

Russian ambitions in the Near East were one of Palmerston's major problems. For some time the peace and stability of the Turkish empire had been undermined by **Mehemet Ali,** the viceroy of Egypt. Mehemet, a capable, greedy and determined man was virtually an independent ruler, and in 1832 he demanded Syria from his master, the Sultan. The Sultan refused and Mehemet attacked and defeated the Turkish army. Constantinople and the Turkish empire was at Mehemet's feet and the desperate Sultan turned to Russia for assistance, Nicholas I was delighted to be in the position to help the Turks and so place the Sultan in his debt. Russian warships anchored off Constantinople and Russian soldiers appeared in the city. Mehemet Ali stepped down and was granted hereditary rights over Egypt and Syria. The grateful Sultan repaid his Russian saviours by signing the treaty of **Unkiar Skelessi (1833).** By this the Russians promised to give military help to the Turks if they were again threatened and Turkey agreed to close the Straits to all foreign warships save those of Russia. This meant that the Black Sea coast of Russia was protected from attack and her ships had free access to the Mediterranean. In the same year Russia, Prussia and Austria made an agreement for co-operation at Münchengratz.

The **Treaty of Unkiar Skelessi caused anxiety to Britain for it pointed the way to the growth of Russian influence in the Middle East and Mediterranean.** A further source of fear came from **Russian conquests in Central Asia during the 1830s** which brought **the Czar's armies to the borders of Afghanistan, north of India. Palmerston saw the need for curbing Russian influence over Turkey** and at the same time preventing any increase of Russian power in the Mediterranean. His chance came in 1839 when **war again broke out** between **Mehemet Ali and the Sultan of Turkey.** Mehemet Ali defeated Turkish forces and the problem was complicated by the fact that he enjoyed some support from France. Palmerston re-acted by enlisting the co-operation of Russia, which had no wish to see France gain any advantage in the Middle East, Austria and Prussia. At the **London Conference (1840)** these powers imposed terms on Mehemet Ali and forced him to give up control over Syria, Crete and Arabia. In return he was allowed hereditary rule over Egypt. At the same time British and Austrian forces helped to drive Mehemet's troops out of southern Syria. The **Straits Convention (1841)** settled the problem of sea-power in the eastern Mediterranean by banning all foreign warships from the Straits whilst Turkey was at peace. Russia was satisfied as this agreement gave her protection to her Black Sea coastline and Britain no longer feared Russian warships operating in the Mediterranean. Turkey was restored to stability and any ambitions the French may have had in this area were, for the moment, frustrated. Palmerston had acted skilfully in gaining the co-operation of the great powers although the French were dismayed.

Palmerston was also successful in dealing with the problem of **Belgium.** In 1830 the Belgians had rebelled against their ruler, the King of the Netherlands, who had been imposed on them by the Congress of Vienna in 1815. The future of Belgium was discussed by a conference of the great powers in London at the end of 1830 but their decisions pleased neither the Belgians nor the Dutch. There were disagreements over the boundaries of the new state and who would be its ruler. The suggestion of a French prince (the son of the new French king, Louis Philippe) as the new king of Belgium alarmed Palmerston as did French demands for Belgian border fortresses. Finally, after some wrangling, a German prince, Leopold of Saxe-Coburg, was chosen but this provoked a Dutch invasion. The Belgian forces were overcome and they called in French troops. Palmerston was again alarmed but thanks to the support of Prussia and Russia, he was able to ensure that the French withdrew. By 1832 the major difficulties had been smoothed over and the **1839 London Conference** finally settled the problem of the creation of the new state. Belgium was to be neutral and its neutrality was guaranteed by the great powers. Palmerston had again achieved a successful outcome and protected British interests by keeping the French out of Belgium and ensuring that the new state would remain neutral. No threat was posed to British control over the Channel and North Sea.

The furtherance of British commercial interests was central to British foreign policy and Palmerston saw it as his duty to do all that he could to pursue this end. **The Opium War (1840-42)** was the direct consequence of Palmerston's defence of the rights of British traders to do business freely. One-sixth of Britain's overseas trade was with China, and one half of British exports consisted of the drug, opium, grown in India and sold to the Chinese. Relations between the Chinese and Europeans were based upon mutual contempt. The Europeans adopted a high-handed and bullying attitude towards the Chinese who responded with disdain. The Emperor of China refused to accept European ambassadors in Peking and, like his subjects, considered all Europeans as 'barbarians', inferior in every way to the Chinese. British traders were allowed to conduct their business in one port, Canton, and their transactions were closely supervised by the Chinese authorities. Friction became worse after 1836 when the Chinese Imperial Government began to take measures to cut down opium addiction. Imported in great quantities, the drug was widely taken and led to the weakening of the population. In Canton the job of enforcing the new laws against opium was in the hands of Commissioner Lin whose seizure of traders and confiscation of opium soon led to clashes with the British. In 1839 matters came to a head when Chinese war junks were fired on by Royal Navy warships anchored off Canton. Palmerston was determined to impose his will on the Chinese and he demanded an apology, compensation for seized opium and the opening of a further four ports to British merchants. He was prepared to back his words with troops and warships, and when the Chinese government spurned his requests, war broke out. Canton quickly fell to British forces and left the Chinese with little choice but to make peace. The **Treaty of Nanking (1842)** opened Shanghai and four other ports to British trade, paid compensation to British merchants for losses in Canton and handed over to Britain the island of Hong Kong. **The war had been a success and new markets were opened for British goods.** There were critics of the war, which, in the words of the young Tory M.P., Gladstone, was 'unjust and iniquitous' and fought only 'to protect an infamous contraband traffic', that is to say, the opium trade. Yet when moral considerations clashed with British interests, British interests won. When Britain was able to impose her will on smaller and weaker nations, she did not hesitate to do so. That is, as long as the Navy was able to act as the instrument of British policy. The middle class electorate, aware of the importance of British trade, applauded such policies and Lord Palmerston.

In 1841 the Whigs fell from power and **Lord Aberdeen** succeeded Palmerston as Foreign Secretary in Peel's administration. His main concern was the settlement of the boundary between the United States and Canada. Until 1842 the border between the two countries had been ill-defined and there was considerable dispute over the Oregon territory, on the Pacific coast. The **Webster-Ashburton Treaty** of 1842 ended the disagreements and defined the boundaries between the two nations to the satisfaction of both.

There was a brief storm in 1844 when the United States President Polk had claimed large areas of Canada by announcing that the

54th parallel of latitude should be the border. The British government stuck by the 49th parallel and the Americans withdrew their claim. Aberdeen also built up a closer understanding with France, who had been annoyed by Palmerston's policy towards Turkey which had ignored French interests.

Conclusion

The foreign policy followed by Britain between 1815 and 1846 had been designed to advance and protect British interests throughout the world. Castlereagh had encouraged the Congress System as a means to foster co-operation between the great powers of Europe but he had stood back from openly backing the repressive policies of Russia, Prussia and Austria. His successor Canning had shown favour to nationalist and liberal movements in Greece, Portugal and South America. Palmerston had demonstrated skill to uphold a favourable balance of power in the Middle East, secured an independent Belgium which would not threaten Britain and had employed force to promote British commercial interests in China. As a champion of Britain, especially in 1840–2, he had earned himself widespread popularity which would serve him well later in his career. His reputation as a Foreign Secretary proved to be the basis of his future standing as the most popular and influential figure in British politics.

Chapter 5
The Age of Palmerston, 1846-65

Introduction

The **political life of Britain between 1846 and 1865 was dominated by one party, the Whigs, and one man, Lord Palmerston.** He was Foreign Secretary from 1846 to 1851, Home Secretary in Lord Aberdeen's coalition of Whigs and Peelites from 1852 to 1855, Prime Minister from 1855 to 1858, and after a brief Tory ministry, from 1859 to his death in 1865. Behind Palmerston's political success lay his **widespread popularity** with the middle class electorate. He appeared to embody all the true British virtues, commonsense, manliness, cheerful good humour and a contempt for 'humbug' – a word he used often. It was typical of Palmerston that he turned a blind eye to an illegal open-air prize fight and happily subscribed a guinea to a fund for one of the boxers. Even his private scandals were turned to his advantage. When, at the age of 79, he seduced a married woman less than half his age, the Tory leader, Disraeli, sourly commented that he had done it to increase his popularity just before a General Election.

The public views and policies of the man *Punch* called 'our Champion' were also in tune with the ideas of his countrymen. **The 1850s and 1860s were years of commercial success and prosperity** and the fruits of expansion began to spread to all classes. Wages rose and the prices of many commodities fell. The years of distress, upheaval and Chartism had passed and in their place was a period of economic and social stability. The national mood was marked by a sense of pride and satisfaction with achievement, and this was well reflected in the **Great Exhibition of 1851.** Here in the novel structure of iron and glass were displayed the many wonders of technology and industry. The whole world had contributed to the show but it was only fitting that the exhibition was held in London, the capital of the nation which proudly called itself 'the workshop of the world'. It was equally fitting that the people of Britain, rich and poor, should mingle freely together as they walked around and admired the exhibits. Not only did the British lead the world as makers of goods, but they taught the world a lesson in social harmony. Palmerston spoke for many when he voiced his views on the ideal nature of British society:

'We have shown the example of a nation in which every class accepts with cheerfulness the lot which Providence has assigned to it; while at the same time each individual of each class is constantly trying to raise himself in the social scale, not by violence and illegality – but by persevering good conduct and by the steady and energetic exertion of the moral and intellectual faculties with which his creator has endowed him.'

Palmerston was describing a society, which in his view, worked well and efficiently. He saw no reason to tamper with the social system since it was running smoothly and effectively. He **did not, therefore, see any need for policies of far-reaching reform and he had no wish to alter the electoral system which had been created by the 1832 Reform Act.** He hindered the efforts of his fellow Whig, Lord John Russell, to introduce a new Reform Act, designed to extend the vote to the more prosperous members of the working class. Electoral reform was effectively held back until after Palmerston's death in 1865.

New laws were introduced with Palmerston's blessing where they were shown to be absolutely necessary and useful. The **Truck Act (1853)** banned employers from paying their workmen in goods rather than cash and from forcing employees from spending their wages at company owned shops. The **Factory Act of 1853** made night-work by juveniles illegal and removed loopholes left by previous acts. The **1857 Matrimonial Causes Act** (or Divorce Act) was more far reaching since for the first time it gave men and women the right to seek divorce from a law court. By the terms of this act, divorce could be obtained on the grounds of adultery, desertion or cruelty. A husband could divorce his wife by proving only one of these misdemeanours, a wife all three. Palmerston faced unyielding opposition from churchmen led by Gladstone when he introduced this act, and it was only his determination and a willingness to keep Parliament in session during the month of August which led to the act getting through.

Foreign policy was Palmerston's main interest and it was in this area that he made and maintained his reputation. **His lines of policy followed closely those laid down earlier but it was Palmerston's personality which gave them vigour and force.** His bluffness and forthright expression of his views also earned him enemies, in particular Queen Victoria and her husband,

Albert, the Prince Consort. In many European countries, Palmerston was seen as a troublemaker, the friend of revolutionaries and hectoring champion of British self-righteousness. An incensed Austrian frontier official saw Palmerston's signature on a passport, struck it out with his pen and added the insult 'It is a hateful name'. Such an incident would have boosted Palmerston's popularity at home as most Britishers would have regarded the ill-mannered hostility of a minor official of a despotic Empire as a token that Palmerston was doing his job. Palmerston did in fact cock a well-deserved snook at powers which denied freedom to their own subjects but he never allowed such sentiments to stand in the way of Britain's interests. Like the majority of his countrymen he despised the autocratic governments which denied political liberty on the British pattern, but he was careful not to involve Britain too deeply in civil strife in Europe. He gave plentiful advice to the European powers on liberty and **he showed open sympathy with reformers and revolutionaries but he did not go further and actually offer these men physical assistance. The fundamental demands of security, the protection and furtherance of trade and the need for a balance of power in Europe dictated Palmerston's actions and he never allowed himself to lose sight of these goals.**

Foreign Secretary, 1846–51

The **Spanish Marriages** were the first problem which faced Palmerston at the Foreign Office in 1846. For a few years Britain and France had built up a friendly and co-operative relationship but this was endangered by the French King, Louis Phillipe, meddling in the affairs of his southern neighbour, Spain. He had planned to marry his son, the Duke of Montpensier, to the sister of the Queen of Spain. Britain was suspicious of a move which advanced French interests in Spain and before and after the wedding, Palmerston vigorously protested. Relations with France were soured, but the fall of Louis Phillipe in 1848 ended any fears of French domination in Spain.

The **revolutions of 1848** were an upsurge of liberal nationalism across the whole of the Continent. The French monarchy fell, the rulers of the German and Italian states were forced to grant political reforms and Hungarian nationalists broke from the rule of Austria. Public opinion in Britain was heartily pleased and there was much noisy sympathy with the champions of liberty in Europe. Such views were shared by many British politicians and ministers but the internal problems of friendly foreign powers was of no direct concern to Britain. Palmerston lectured the Queen of Spain on the virtues of giving way to demands for Parliamentary government and elsewhere he counselled caution and compromise. By 1849 the old régimes were back in the saddle and the revolutionaries in retreat. Only in France did the republic survive under the presidency of Louis Napoleon.

One consequence of the revolutions which proved a nuisance to Palmerston was the visit to England in 1850 of the Austrian **General Haynau,** a commander who had taken a prominent part in the suppression of the Italian and Hungarian uprisings. He was little loved by the English; *Punch* described him as 'branded with deeds of the basest atrocity – the merciless hanging of brave men and the dastardly flogging of noble women'. On visiting a London brewery, Haynau was recognised, greeted with shouts of 'Down with the Austrian butcher', and was then pelted and buffeted by the draymen. Palmerston naturally apologized to the Austrian government for Haynau's rough treatment, but added that he had been ill-advised in visiting Britain. **The affair of Don Pacifico,** also in 1850, was a triumph for Palmerston and demonstrated as clearly as possible, his determination to defend not only the wider interests of Britain but the interests of individual British subjects. Pacifico, a Portuguese Jewish money-lender, possessed a British passport, as he had been born in Gibraltar. His Athens house had been looted by a Greek mob with little or no hindrance from the Greek police and Pacifico later claimed £27,000 in damages from the Greek government. They refused and Palmerston, already irritated by other clashes with the Greeks, ordered the Mediterranean fleet to blockade Piraeus (the port for Athens). This was Palmerston's way of showing that Britain would stand by the rights of her subjects, but to many members of Parliament it looked like high-handed bullying of an obviously weaker nation. A vote of censure was proposed in the House of Commons but Palmerston was able to defend himself and he obtained a comfortable majority in his favour. The gist of his argument was that it was the automatic duty of the British government to champion the interests of its subjects throughout the world. He compared the Britisher to the Roman who could claim, when threatened, *'Civis Romanus Sum' – 'I am a Roman citizen'*. Such a statement gave him immediate legal rights. Palmerston followed with the argument, 'so also a British subject, in whatever land he may be, shall feel confident that the watchful eye and the strong arm of England will protect him against injustice and wrong'.

This was true as long as the offending nation was unable to resist 'the strong arm' of Britain, in other words, her navy. It could not and did not help a negro, who was a British subject, arrested and imprisoned in Charleston in the United States in 1850 for it would have been foolhardy to have sent warships to challenge the United States government. Nevertheless **the principle was popular in Britain** and Palmerston earned himself much approval by its application over Don Pacifico.

Palmerston's tendency to act independently, ignoring his cabinet colleagues and his clashes with the Queen and Prince consort had been a cause of ill-feeling since he had taken office in 1846. Queen Victoria had insisted on the right to read over foreign office despatches before they were sent and, when she thought necessary, alter them. Both she and her husband, Albert, felt that they had the right to make changes, but Palmerston was unco-operative. She had been indignant at Palmerston's despatch to the Austrians over Haynau and she had personally cancelled it, sending another more conciliatory note. She was further annoyed when Palmerston showed signs of wishing to meet the Hungarian rebel and popular hero, Louis Kossuth, and she forbade Palmerston to have any contact with him. She was also highly critical of Palmerston's policies in general, in particular his private views in favour of liberal and nationalist movements. A major clash between the Queen, the cabinet and Palmerston came at the end of 1851 when Louis Napoleon declared himself 'Emperor of France'. The Queen and many ministers were suspicious of a Bonaparte again in charge of France, but Palmerston, who admired the Emperor's 'pluck, firmness and prudence', congratulated him on taking power. **The Queen insisted that the Prime Minister, Russell, demand Palmerston's resignation. Palmerston had no choice and resigned.** Palmerston's revenge was quickly achieved. In February 1852 he voted against the government and swayed enough of his followers within the House of Commons to join him. Out-voted, Russell's government fell and Palmerston boasted that he had got his 'tit for tat'. He was not out of office for long as he joined Lord Aberdeen's coalition of Whig and Peelites as Home Secretary at the end of 1852, after the fall of a short Tory ministry. For the next three years, he had little to do with the conduct of foreign affairs. As a result of a re-opening of the Eastern Question, this was a **period of international tension which led to Britain's declaration of war on Russia in 1854.**

Origins of the Crimean War

Britain had always followed a policy which **defended the Turkish empire** against the interference of other powers, in particular Russia. In 1844 **Czar Nicholas I** had visited Britain and in his conversations suggested that Turkey and her empire were fast falling apart. Further, he argued that it would be useful if Britain and Russia prepared for the day of final collapse by making plans to split up Turkey and her possessions. That day, the Czar thought, was very near at hand. The British government noted his views but did not take them seriously. The Czar continued to plan for Turkey's collapse and to consider what might fall to Russia when 'the sick man', as he called the Turkish empire, fell in ruins. **Constantinople** was often in his mind and he once remarked, 'If the English, French or other forces wish to seize Constantinople, I shall chase them away . . . I shall be on the spot before either of their forces. Once in Constantinople, I shall not withdraw'. The new **French Emperor, Napoleon III,** was also interested in the Turkish empire. He had negotiated with the Turks for French catholic monks to have the keeping of the **Holy Places** of Palestine. To back up his demands, he sent a steam battleship to Constantinople. The Turks granted his request and the French monks replaced Orthodox monks in the churches at Jerusalem, Bethlehem and Nazareth.

Russia, which had regarded itself as having a special relationship with Turkey was offended and determined to show her power to the Turks. The Czar revived his schemes for dividing up the Turkish empire which he confided to the British ambassador in St Petersburg (the capital of Imperial Russia). A **Russian embassy was sent to Constantinople** and **demanded that the Holy Places be returned to Orthodox control,** which was granted by the Turks. The **Russians then went further** and asked that **the Czar be made protector of all the Christians under Turkish rule.** The **Sultan** of Turkey refused this request which he saw as a **gross attempt to interfere with his own rights.** If the Russians were given such power, it would open the way for them to meddle directly in the affairs of Turkey. Until the Russians made this demand, the British ambassador in Turkey, Lord Stratford de Redcliffe, had advised the Turks to accept the Russian requests. On the matter of the Czar as Protector of the Turkish Christians, he urged the Sultan to stand firm. **Britain would not stand by and let the Russians obtain such influence in the Turkish empire.** Britain was now alarmed. To show that she was prepared to help the Turks to resist Russian bullying, **Britain, backed by France, sent a fleet of warships to the entrance of the Straits in 1853. Russia,** believing that she had the support of Austria and Prussia, **applied force** to make the Turks give way. **Russian troops invaded the Turkish provinces of Moldavia and Wallachia,** and in **October 1853 Turkey declared war on Russia,** confident of Anglo-French support. Soon after, the Turkish fleet was attacked by the Russians and destroyed at **Sinope.**

Britain and France had shown themselves the friends of Turkey, willing to stand beside the Turks in the face of Russian bullying. **Public opinion** in **Britain** was becoming more and more **anti-Russian** and calling for a strong line from the government. The Czar was popularly regarded as a tyrant and the radicals had not forgotten how his army had crushed the Hungarian revolt in 1849. **After Sinope, the Russians controlled the Black Sea** and accordingly **British and French naval forces entered the Straits.** Both the **British and the French governments demanded that the Russians withdrew** their forces from the Turkish provinces they had occupied. **The Russians refused and at the end of March 1854, Britain and France declared** war. The declaration of war was widely welcomed in Britain with patriotic outbursts and the expression of firm hopes of quick and glorious victories.

Britain's motive for going to war was simple. **It was the protection of the Turkish empire from Russian intimidation and influence.** Britain hoped moreover to restore the balance of sea power in the Black Sea. The first motive was soon removed as the Russians quickly withdrew from the Turkish provinces they had lately invaded. Russia had found herself isolated in Europe. Britain and France had declared war, Prussia was neutral and Austria, frightened that the Russians might be able to control the mouth of the Danube, a major route for Austrian trade, was hostile. There remained **Russian naval power** and **Britain and France decided to launch an attack on Sebastopol, destroy it and so remove Russia's major naval base in the area.**

The Crimean War, 1854–56
The great **Russian base at Sebastopol on the Crimean penin-sula** was the **objective of the Anglo-French navies and armies** in 1854. The joint plan was to land forces, take the fortress city, demolish the defences and withdraw. This simple plan proved difficult to carry out and what had been anticipated as a short war,

lasted for two years. The British public which had dreamt of victories was soon bitterly disturbed by tales of mistakes, incompetence and suffering.

The **British army** which sailed for the Black Sea in the spring of 1854 was described by *The Times* 'as the finest army that has ever left our shores'. The 30,000 men were under the command of **Lord Raglan,** a veteran of the Napoleonic Wars, a man of courage but limited experience of command. The same inexperience was noticeable in other officers. Lord Lucan, commander-in-chief of the cavalry, and his subordinate officers, Lord Cardigan and General Scarlett, had never heard a shot fired in anger. Elsewhere the quality of leadership was often poor; Sir George Brown, a senior general, was described by a junior officer as an 'old wretch who is more hated than any man was. He blusters and bullies everybody he dares and damns and swears at everything an inch high'. The wind of reform which had changed and rationalized other areas of British life had not blown through the army. Officers obtained their commissions by purchase (a colonel of a cavalry regiment could pay up to £70,000 for his position) and were drawn for the most part from the upper classes. What they lacked in training, they made up for in bravery. **The organisation of clothing, food and other essential supplies was haphazardly managed.** High command was shared out between the incompetent, inexperienced and bloody minded. One officer prophetically remarked, 'This Army is a shambles'. In September 1854, the Anglo-French army, finally landed in the Crimea and disembarked at Calamita Bay. After leaving their ships, the troops moved across country towards Sebastopol. At the **River Alma,** Russian troops occupying high ground beyond the river, barred the allied advance. Raglan ordered a frontal assault and after suffering heavy casualties, the British took the heights and the Russians were driven off. The way to Sebastopol was open and the city, lightly defended was ready for capture. The chance was missed and allied delays gave the Russians time to strengthen the defences. When the siege began, **Sebastopol was stoutly defended** with earthworks and artillery which made quick capture unlikely. Late in October, the Russians sallied out of Sebastopol and attempted to cut the British off from their coastal base, Balaklava. The **battle of Balaklava** saw three remarkable and famous actions by British forces, the incident of the 'Thin Red Line' when the 93rd (Highland) regiment held off masses of Russian cavalry, and the charge of the Heavy Brigade, in which outnumbered British cavalry charged uphill and routed a large detachment of Russian horse. Most famous of all was the **Charge of the Light Brigade.** As a result of an ambiguous order sent by Lord Raglan, Lord Cardigan and over 600 men of the Light Cavalry regiments (Lancers, Hussars and Light Dragoons) charged a Russian artillery position. Fired on from three sides the British cavalry took the guns and returned, under fire and pursuit from Russian cossacks. Over two thirds were killed or wounded and the French and the Russians were astonished. Prince Liprandi, the Russian commander, asked captured survivors whether they had been given brandy or whisky before charging. He was told that thanks to the British supply system, none of the troopers had been given any food that day. He gave them vodka.

The Charge of the Light Brigade thrilled and angered the British public. It threw into **sharp contrast the courage of the soldiers and the slipshod, dull-wittedness of their commanders.** Further evidence of mismanagement came to light as the British forces settled down to endure the harshness of the Russian winter. The miseries of the soldiers and the problems they faced were summed up in a letter of Colonel Hodge of the 4th Dragoon Guards:

> 'We have no huts or stabling. Our men are employed from morning to night carrying provisions to the front and returning with sick men. The road is a ploughed field all the way for seven miles. Last week 121 horses died from overwork and exposure.'

Men too died in **great numbers** from the **cold conditions, lack of adequate clothing and food.** The fate of the wounded was even worse. They were carried by ship across the Black Sea to a hospital at **Scutari,** where they languished without medicines, chloroform or clean dressings for their wounds. The medical and supply sections of the army could not cope and the soldiers suffered. Remembering the patriotic noises which had begun the campaign, Colonel Hodge grimly remarked, on the last day of the year 1854, 'As to honour & glory, they are empty bubbles'. **The bungling, lack of supplies and wretchedness of the men were known in Britain. W. H. Russell,** *The Times*'s war correspondent sent back report after report, filled with details of the mishaps and shortcomings which marked the progress of the campaign. The public, which had hoped for glorious victories, was enraged. In the press and in the House of Commons, the government was under attack. A motion of censure was put down in January 1855 and **Lord Aberdeen resigned.** The **public**

call was for Palmerston who succeeded him as Prime Minister.

1855 saw improvements. Efforts were made to overcome the problems of supply, a railway linked Balaklava harbour with the front line and suitable accommodation was provided for the troops. Florence Nightingale, with Lord Palmerston's blessing, led a party of 30 nurses to Scutari and began a sweeping and thorough reform of the conditions there. The death-rate amongst the wounded fell dramatically. A by-product of the government's concern was the sending of a photographer to the Crimea, Roger Fenton. His pictures were the first which showed modern warfare and are a remarkable record of the campaign.

The fighting continued through 1855 with the main brunt of the action being taken by the French. Russia, whose armies suffered leadership which was worse than that of the allies, was anxious to end the war. Sebastopol had fallen in September 1855 and Russian military weaknesses had been exposed.

The Treaty of Paris (1856) ended the war. Russia surrendered territory which gave her control over the Danube, the Black Sea was declared a neutral area, the provinces of Wallachia and Moldavia became independent (they became the basis of Rumania) and the Turkish government promised to reform their administration.

The results of the war for Britain were limited. The Russian threat had been temporarily removed from Turkey and Russian naval and military power in the area had been destroyed. In Britain the mood of excitement which had marked the beginning of the campaign had changed to one of astonishment and anger. The war had exposed weaknesses in the British army and administration which upset the confidence of the British people. The power of the press had been shown through the articles of Russell, which had set in motion an agitation which brought down the government. For the bravest of the returning soldiers there was a new medal, the Victoria Cross, and thanks to the work of Florence Nightingale, a movement for the modernisation of hospitals, civilian and military, had begun. In the long term there would be reforms of the administration and army, undertaken by Gladstone in the 1870s. For the moment Palmerston would not agree to any changes in the recruitment of officers or civil servants; he kept his faith in what was called 'the aristocratic principle'. In a speech to the Commons in 1855 he pointed out that the courage of Lord Cardigan at the head of the Light Brigade was a fine example of the principle which gave leadership and command to members of the upper classes.

Prime Minster, 1855–65

Shortly after the end of the Crimean War, Palmerston was faced with a crisis which involved British relations with **China**. For a long time relations between British merchants and the Chinese authorities at Canton had been strained and there had been a series of clashes between them. In 1856 a pirate vessel, the **Arrow,** had been arrested by the Canton authorities, an incident which led to war between the British and Chinese governments. The Arrow had been registered in Hong Kong and had been flying the British flag although her registration had lapsed. In spite of this the **governor of Hong Kong, Sir James Bowring,** demanded an apology. When one was not offered, **he ordered navy ships to shell Canton.** The Chinese retaliated by attacks on British traders and their property. When news of this incident reached London, **Palmerston gave his approval of the governor's motives and his actions.** He was criticized in Parliament by M.Ps from all parties who represented the business as arrogant bullying. Palmerston lost the vote (1857) and called a **General Election.** For the first time in British politics, he drew up and issued an election address which he intended to be read by electors throughout the country. He put his case simply, 'An insolent barbarian wielding authority in Canton has violated the British flag'. Were the electors going to let this go unpunished? This appeal to patriotism won Palmerston the election and he and his supporters returned to power with an increased majority. The **1857 election showed that the British voters approved of such forceful dealings with foreign powers.** The war against China continued until 1858 when the Chinese were forced to concede the British demands. They quickly went back on their word and an Anglo-French force was sent to Peking (1860). The allied troops took the city and burnt down the Emperor's summer palace. Palmerston was 'heartily glad' that the palace lay in ashes, and the helpless Chinese were left with no choice but to give all that the 'foreign devils' required. Fresh opportunities were opened up for British trade and the Chinese were forced to afford greater accommodation to British merchants.

Having gained public support for a strong line with China, Palmerston found himself just as quickly thrown out of office for showing consideration to France. In 1858 an Italian terrorist, **Orsini,** had tried to assassinate Napoleon III with a bomb. Orsini and his fellow conspirators had found much support from radical circles in England and the French were justifiably enraged. Palmerston responded to their protests with the **Conspiracy to Murder Bill (1858)** which intended to make it a crime to conspire to commit murder in a foreign country. Feeling against France was running high, especially as it was known in Britain that some French officers had boasted that they would burn London down in revenge for the attempt on the Emperor's life. In parliament, **many M.Ps thought that Palmerston was truckling to the French and so they voted against him.** The result was a defeat for Palmerston and a Tory ministry, under Lord Derby, took over the government.

Derby's ministry relied for its survival on a group of renegade Whigs, who in 1859 returned to their old allegiance, and Palmerston returned as Prime Minister. He was immediately faced with the **problem of Italy.** The Prime Minister of the north Italian kingdom of Piedmont, Cavour, had enlisted French military help for a war to drive the Austrians from northern Italy. Many people in Britain, including Palmerston, were sympathetic to the cause of Italian unity. The presence of the French created a problem as Britain did not want the new Italian state to be in the pocket of France. Napoleon backed out after heavy losses against the Austrians, but in 1860 he approached the British for joint action against the revolutionary nationalist Garibaldi. **Garibaldi** had led a successful uprising in Sicily and was planning to cross to the mainland and carry the rebellion to Naples and southern Italy. The British did not wish to hinder his progress and later Palmerston made it openly clear to the powers of Europe that **Britain gave warmest sympathy and encouragement to the people of Italy,** 'building up the edifice of their liberties, and consolidating the work of their independence'. With some dry humour, the Austrians informed the British government that they hoped that British support for people seeking freedom might also extend to Ireland and India!

The United States Civil War (1860–5) provided some serious problems for Palmerston and brought Britain to the verge of war. Upper-class sympathies in Britain were for the Confederate (southern) states against the democratic Union (northern states) which was supported by many of the middle and lower classes.

The British government was neutral but was nearly drawn into the war by the incident of the steamship **Trent** (1861). The Trent was a British ship sailing from Havana (Cuba) with two Confederate diplomats, Slidell and Mason, as passengers. Their intention had been to cross to Europe where they hoped to raise support for the Confederate cause. Forewarned of their plans, a Union cruiser stopped the Trent at sea and removed Slidell and Mason. This was a violation of British rights and against the law of the sea and with this in mind, the Foreign Secretary, Lord Russell, demanded an apology and the return of the two men. Messages between Russell and President Lincoln were sharp, but the heat was taken out of the quarrel by the Prince Consort, who toned down the draft of one despatch. The Americans too stepped down (Lincoln remarked to his Secretary of State, 'One war at a time, Mr. Seward') and Slidell and Mason were released.

Another ship, **the Alabama**. strained relations. It was an armoured cruiser and had been ordered by the Confederate government from a shipyard in Birkenhead. The Union ambassador was aware of this and protested to Russell, but the government was dilatory. The result was that in 1863 the Alabama sailed and in the following year sank many Union vessels. The Union government was outraged at what they regarded as British connivance at the building and launching of an enemy warship. The Americans demanded damages but Palmerston refused; the affair was later settled by Gladstone (see p. 126).

Palmerston's final problem of foreign policy demonstrated the weakness of Britain's position with regard to other European powers. The duchies of **Schleswig and Holstein** lay in the south of Denmark, on its border with Germany. By the London treaty of 1852, they had been placed under the rule of the King of Denmark. In 1863 the Danish crown made clear its intention to bring them into the Danish kingdom and the German speaking inhabitants protested. These protests were directed towards Prussia and Austria. Both were willing to assist Schleswig and Holstein. Palmerston stood by the Danes, but he was unable to stand up to the combined strength of Prussia and Austria. Russia was friendly with Prussia and had no wish to co-operate with Britain, the country which had fought her in the Crimea. France was tied down by a war in Mexico. **Britain stood alone during the crisis (1863), unable to act.** Contemplating the possibility that the British might send an army to north Germany, the Prussian chancellor Bismarck, drily remarked, 'I shall send a policeman to arrest it'. A great sea-power, Britain could not face up alone to the combined armies of Prussia and Austria. Palmerston was powerless without friends. In 1864 the Austro-Prussian forces invaded Schleswig and Holstein and quickly defeated the Danes. Palmerston's bluff had been called and his efforts on behalf of the Danes were described as 'meddle and muddle' by Lord Derby.

Conclusion

Palmerston's career ended in a humiliation for Britain. The flaw in British foreign policy had been revealed over the question of Schleswig and Holstein. Britain could not act alone against the powers of Europe with their strong armies. Sea-power on its own did not make Britain capable of imposing its will in Europe. In the past British power had been exerted over smaller, weaker nations such as Greece or else had been helped by France, as in the Crimea. Palmerston nevertheless had enjoyed many successes in the furtherance of what he regarded as British interests. At the height of his career he had made Britain respected as a world power and won himself the warm regard of his countrymen.

Chapter 6
Gladstone and Disraeli, 1868-1886

Between the passing of the Second Reform Act and 1886, **the political life of Britain was dominated by Gladstone, the Liberal leader and Prime Minister from 1868 to 1874 and 1880 to 1885, and Disraeli, the Conservative leader and Prime Minister from 1874 to 1880.** Both were men of extensive abilities and each stamped his own personality and ideas on his party.

The 1867 Reform Act had transformed British political life. A new electorate had been created, largely made up of working men. The two political parties had to adapt their ideas and methods to meet the demands of the new voters. A larger electorate meant that more care had to be taken over party organisation so that the party's policies could be effectively publicized at elections. To this end the National Union of Conservative and Constitutional Associations was formed in 1867 and in 1877 the National Liberal Foundation was founded. Each national organisation directed the work of the local party organizations. The **new electorate also demanded new policies.** In preparing their policies both parties had to keep in mind the needs and wishes of the voters, especially the working classes. **Liberals and Conservatives both offered and carried through programmes of social reform** which were designed to assist working men and raise their standard of living. Yet both parties took care not to lose sight of the national interests and attempted to shape their policies with the needs of the community as a whole in mind. Lastly the increase in size of the electorate encouraged the party leaders to appeal directly to the voters. Both Gladstone and Disraeli travelled the country making speeches in order to give their beliefs the widest possible audience. Both were strong and persuasive speakers (men would walk miles to hear Gladstone) and in the popular mind, they became the embodiment of their parties.

Gladstone's First Ministry 1868–1874

Gladstone's early career
Gladstone had entered Parliament as a Tory in 1833. He first held office as Secretary of the Board of Trade (1841–46) under

Peel. There he **enthusiastically supported Peel's Free Trade policies** and in **1846 he sided with Peel over the Repeal of the Corn Laws**. As a Peelite he joined Lord Aberdeen's coalition in **1852 as Chancellor of the Exchequer.** He planned to **reduce government spending as much as was possible** and hoped to **abolish income tax by 1860** (a plan which was upset by the Crimean War in 1854). By **1859 he was firmly in the Liberal camp** and he held the office of Chancellor of the Exchequer under Palmerston. His major achievements were the **Cobden Chevalier Trade Treaty** (1860) which established Free Trade between Britain and France and the **steady reduction of income tax and duties.** His work at the Exchequer made Britain a completely Free Trade nation. His **Post Office Savings Bank (1863)** was designed to promote saving among the working classes. Gladstone was **a deeply religous man, whose political ideas and actions were dictated by his strong moral sense.** He hoped that by encouraging Free Trade he would reduce the cost of living and promote the prosperity of all classes. If people were prosperous they would improve morally. Behind all of Gladstone's actions was a desire to see a godly, virtuous and free Britain. The achievement of this end was his and the Liberal party's duty, a duty which in his case, had been placed on him by God. **In terms of politics, he saw issues in terms of right and wrong and his great campaigns were therefore moral crusades.**

His **election campaign in 1868** was a moral crusade on behalf of Ireland and the disestablishment of the Irish church (see p. 80). The new electorate responded to this campaign and his party won by 379 seats to the Conservatives' 279.

Gladstone's Reforms

Gladstone regarded his first ministry as the one in which he accomplished his greatest and most important reforms. The measures taken by his government concerned the country's administration, education, political life and the Trade Unions. To take first the administration of the country, Gladstone was convinced that a rational and well-run administration was necessary for the well-being of the country. A start was made in 1870 when **competitive exams were made compulsory for entry to the civil service** (this did not apply to the Foreign Office). Previously civil servants had been recruited by patronage, that is through the influence of an entrant's family or friends. Under the new examination system, Gladstone had hoped to attract the most talented men from the Universities for the highest posts. In 1873 the **Judicature Act** re-organized the Law courts and created a new Court of Appeal.

The misfortunes of British forces in the Crimea had illustrated the need for **Army Reform** and the amazing successes of the Prussian army in France in 1870 further highlighted the backwardness of Britain's army. The reforms were undertaken by **Cardwell**, the Secretary for War. First the **purchase of commissions was abolished**, opening the way for promotion by ability. Next the **condition of service for rank and file soldiers was changed. Flogging was abolished** as a punishment in peace-time, but kept for active service. It was last used during the Afghan campaign in 1879–80. **Enlistment was limited to six years,** followed by six years in the reserves. The **old regiments** had been known by their numbers (e.g. the 39th, 40th and 41st Regiments of Foot) but **as a result of Cardwell's reforms they were known after the counties from which they drew most of their recruits.** Britain was split into 69 districts each with its regimental depot. Thus the 39th Regiment became the Dorset Regiment with its main depot at Dorchester. Each of the new regiments had two battalions, one always available for duty abroad whilst the second would remain in Britain. New equipment was introduced including the **Martini-Henry** breech loading rifle which greatly increased the fire power of the infantry. The fruits of these reforms were the highly successful campaigns in 1874 against the Ashantis (in Ghana) and in 1882 in Egypt. Britain had been given a well organized, well equipped modern army.

The weakness of Britain's educational system had caused anxiety for some time and the creation in 1867 of a working class electorate drew attention to **the need for mass literacy.** The new technology which was being adopted by industry required an educated workforce and there was a growing fear that Britain was lagging behind such countries as Prussia in providing education for the masses. The **1870 Education Act,** named after **W. E. Forster, was drawn up to provide a system by which all children received some basic learning,** particularly in what were called the 'Three R's, reading, 'riting and 'rithmetic'. The Act continued grants made to Voluntary schools, founded and run by religious denominations. Where no such schools existed, new schools, called Board Schools, were to be set up. These would be run by locally elected Schools Boards, which had the power to raise money from local rates. There was one problem, that of religious teaching, which naturally concerned Anglicans and Non-conformists. It was solved by the Board Schools having religious instruction which was non-denominational and designed not to offend any group. Forster's act provided basic education for all children up to the age of 13 although it was not compulsory until 1876. The basis had been laid for education for all children throughout the country.

The **University Test Act (1871)** abolished all prohibitions on Non-Conformists, Jews and Catholics at Oxford and Cambridge, whereas before they could not gain scholarships or hold teaching posts.

The **Ballot Act (1872)** introduced the secret ballot and replaced the old open voting system. This had encouraged corruption, in particular bribery. One consequence of this act was that the Irish were free to vote for candidates of their choice rather than do as their landlords bade. The Home Rule party was therefore able to pick up 57 Irish seats in the 1874 election and dominate Irish politics for the next forty years. The Trade Union movement was assisted by one of Gladstone's Reforms. **The Trade Union Act (1871)** gave Unions rights before the law. They could possess their own property and be protected by the courts if their funds were stolen. This had not been so before as one Union found to its cost after an official ran off with the members' subscriptions. The Unions' gain was offset by the **Criminal Law Amendment Act (1871)** which denied Unions the right to picket during a strike. Picketing, by which strikers approached and persuaded non-strikers to join them, was essential to Trade Unionism.

A large section of Liberal support came from non-conformists and supporters of Temperance, who believed that 'Drink was the enemy of the Working Classes'. There was some truth in this and the working classes were certainly well-provided with places where they could drink. The **1871 Licensing Act** was designed to close down some public beer houses and to limit drinking by imposing drinking hours. For some, the basic freedoms of British men and women were at stake, or as a Conservative bishop expressed it, 'England free rather than sober'.

Conclusion

Gladstone's remaining reforms dealt with the Irish problem (see p. 80). He had, between 1870 and 1873, altered many aspects of British life, and at the same time, upset many people. Public opinion had been turned against him and the Liberal party had lost a number of by-elections. In the beginning of 1874 he called a general election with the intention of campaigning for the abolition of income tax.

1874 General Election

Gladstone had mistaken the mood of the public and the Liberals were defeated. The Conservatives had 350 seats in the House of Commons, the Liberals 245 and the Irish Home Rulers 57. **The reasons for the Liberal defeat stemmed largely from Gladstone's reform programme,** although his foreign policy earned him much criticism (see p. 126). The upper classes were displeased with the civil service reforms and the Church of England by Irish Disestablishment (see p. 80) and the University Test Acts. The non-conformists were dissatisfied with the religious sections of the Education Act. Trade Unionists were angry that peaceful picketing had been made illegal and the consumers and producers of drink were incensed at the prohibitions placed on their activities. It was the hostility of the drinking public and the providers of drink which provoked Gladstone to remark that he and his party had 'been borne down in a torrent of gin and beer'. Such a remark was typical of a man who saw political issues in terms of moral right and wrong. Shortly after his party's defeat Gladstone retired to study and write on religious subjects.

Disraeli's Ministry, 1874–80

Disraeli's early career

Disraeli had been born in 1804, the son of a well-to-do writer and country gentleman, Isaac Disraeli. His family was Jewish and Benjamin Disraeli lacked nearly all the qualifications for a political career in the Conservative party. After many setbacks, he entered Parliament in 1837 where his first speech was greeted with hoots and jeering. What told against him was his colourful dress which matched his exaggerated manner of speaking. These shortcomings were overcome and by the 1840s he had established a reputation as a witty and impressive speaker which lasted throughout his life. At this stage in his career he was the leader of a small group of M.Ps known as the **Young England** party. All Conservatives, they believed in an alliance of the nobility with the working classes to work together for social reform. Social problems concerned Disraeli and they formed important themes in two of his political novels, *Sybil* and *Coningsby*.

Disraeli, in spite of considerable efforts on his own behalf, did not get a place in Peel's cabinet. His chance to advance himself in the Conservative Party came in **1846 when he took charge of the Conservative opposition to the repeal of the Corn Laws.** By challenging Peel, he split his own party which for the next twenty years was only in office twice. Disraeli was Chancellor of the Exchequer in the 1852 ministry and again in 1858-59. His chance finally came in 1866 when he was **instrumental in passing the Second Reform Bill** (see p. 25). The resignation of the Conservative leader, Lord Derby, gave up the party leadership and briefly, in 1868, he was Prime Minister. In 1874 he led the party to an election, the first it had had since 1841.

Throughout his career, Disraeli had endured criticism and the most persistent charge against him was that he was an 'adventurer'. In spite of his flirtation with social reform in the Young England days, **Disraeli's great interest lay in the conduct of foreign policy** (see p. 126). Nevertheless during his ministry, a number of important measures of social reform were passed.

Disraeli's Social Reforms, 1874–80

The **reforms of this ministry followed the tradition of the Liberals,** although most were concerned with **practical matters such as Public Health and Housing** rather than administration. Their success owed much to the Home Secretary, **Sir Richard Cross.**

The **Artisans' Dwelling Act (1875)** was intended to reduce slums and establish better quality housing for working people. Under its terms, local authorities had power to demolish foul and poorly built housing and build new housing estates, where working people could rent houses. This measure provided Joseph Chamberlain, the Mayor of Birmingham, with the means to undertake slum clearance and rebuilding in that city. The **Public Health Act (1875)** brought together all earlier Health Acts under one heading and provided the framework for local authorities to appoint Medical Officers of Health. These officials had powers to investigate threats to health and take the appropriate action. One area in which they were given authority to act in the public interest was that of the adulteration of food. The **Food and Drugs Act (1876)** banned the adding of harmful substances to food – in the past red lead and arsenic had been added to certain foods to improve their colour or flavour! Under the new law local authorities could prosecute those responsible for such dangerous practices.

The Trade Unions benefited from two acts. The **Conspiracy and Protection of Property Act (1875)** made peaceful picketing legal (and so reversed Gladstone's Act) and protected strikers from prosecution under the conspiracy laws. The **Employers and Workmen Act (1875)** gave working men another form of protection, this time from prosecution for breach of a contract with an employer. The **Ten Hour Act (1874)** limited hours of factory work to 56 a week, ten each weekday and six on Saturdays. A further benefit to working men was the **Merchant Shipping Act (1876).** This had been introduced through the determination and effort of **Samuel Plimsoll,** an M.P. who was deeply concerned with the conditions of merchant seamen. He exposed the trick by which some shipowners sent to sea unworthy and overloaded vessels. When these sank, as they inevitably did, the owners would claim and get the insurance. Through Plimsoll's endeavours, the Merchant Shipping Act gave the Board of Trade powers to stop the sailing of overloaded ships and introduced the practice of putting a line on the waterline of the ship's hull. The Plimsoll Line, as it became known, was a means by which it could be seen whether a ship was overloaded.

The pattern of Conservative legislation between 1874-80 showed that the party was now in the forefront of social reform and was a fulfilment of some of Disraeli's early ideas. As Prime Minister he was only slightly involved with this legislation for **he gave most of his attention and energies to foreign policy, in particular the Eastern Question** (see pp. 126-8).

The 1880 Election
Disraeli's conduct of the Eastern Question and the Bulgarian atrocities had brought Gladstone out of retirement in 1876. With pamphlets and speeches he had led a **moral crusade on behalf of the suffering inhabitants of Bulgaria and** the wickedness of Disraeli's pre-Turkish policy. This was a fore-runner for his **1880 election campaign to which he devoted all the moral fervour he could summon up.** He was determined to overthrow what he called 'Beaconsfieldism' (Disraeli had been made Earl of Beaconsfield in 1876) by which he meant the immoral and adventurous Imperial policies adopted by Disraeli. The wars in Zululand (with the disaster of Isandlwana) and Afghanistan (with the murder of the British envoy at Kabul) (see pp. 106 and 101) were for Gladstone reckless and wasteful adventures.

The background to Gladstone's campaign was an unfortunate

one. Agriculture was suffering from the massive imports of foreign corn from American and Canadian prairies and in 1879 there had been a disastrous harvest. In Ireland terrorism was spreading. The election went badly for the Conservatives. The Liberals returned 353 M.Ps, the Conservatives 238 and the Irish Home Rulers 61. In the following year Disraeli died.

Disraeli's achievements

Between 1846 and 1874 no Conservative government had been elected and when in power the Conservative party enjoyed short ministries, relying on Whig support. In the twenty five years after Disraeli's death, the Conservatives won three general elections (1886, 1895 and 1900) and were in power for seventeen years. The revival of the Conservative party was certainly one of Disraeli's lasting achievements. **He identified the party with patriotism and Imperialism** (see p. 92), both popular causes capable of rousing the enthusiasm of voters. **He also placed it on a level with the Liberals as a party of reform,** dedicated to raising the living standards and conditions of work of the working classes. From a party which had been labelled 'the stupid party' and had represented a narrow section of landowners and their dependents, **the Conservative party had become a widely based party with strong popular support.** This was sometimes described as **'Tory Democracy'** and it owed its birth and existence to Disraeli.

Gladstone's Third Ministry 1880–5

Problems

Gladstone had returned to politics from retirement in 1876 as the champion of the Bulgarians and in 1880 he had led his party to victory in the election. **His campaign had been fought as a crusade against the Conservatives.** Throughout the election Gladstone had emphasized his opposition to what the Conservatives had done and made no offers to the electorate of reform. **When he achieved power in 1880 he had no plans for future reforms.** He believed that his earlier ministry (1868-74) had been his great reforming ministry.

Two problems quickly emerged to occupy Mr. Gladstone. The first was **Ireland** (see p. 80) and the second was **Egypt and the Sudan** (see p. 102).

Added to these difficulties was the **division within his own party.** On one side was the Whig section, led by Lord Hartington, which was conservative in attitude, and on the other were the radicals. The **radical spokesman was Joseph Chamberlain**, the ex-mayor of Birmingham, who wanted to see the Liberal party turn to a programme of social reform. Only Gladstone as leader was able to impose unity on his party and he was far from sympathetic to Chamberlain's radicalism.

A further problem was that of **Charles Bradlaugh**, the Liberal M.P. for Northampton, who was atheist. When asked to take the customary oath as an M.P. in 1880, Bradlaugh refused on the grounds that the oath was a religious one and that he did not believe in God. There was a way round this problem but the young Conservative M.P., **Lord Randolph Churchill**, was quick to exploit the embarrassment of the government. The upshot was that Bradlaugh was expelled from the Commons, re-elected three times and only allowed to take his seat in 1886. Throughout the ministry the Bradlaugh affair was an irritation to Gladstone and his government. Lord Randolph Churchill, a wayward but capable M.P., kept up the pressure on Gladstone in the House of Commons to the Prime Minister's extreme annoyance. It was said that Churchill used Gladstone like a telescope – he pulled him out, saw through him and then shut him up.

For Gladstone his **main objective came to be the pacification** of **Ireland** (see p. 80) and this he believed was the first duty of the Liberal party. His obsession with Ireland made Chamberlain and the radicals impatient. Chamberlain was, however, able to obtain the **Reform and Redistribution Acts of 1884–5** (see p. 85) which gave the vote to working men in the country areas. Chamberlain wished to go much further and force the Liberal party to introduce sweeping reforms for the benefit of the poorer classes. His **unauthorised programme** in the 1885 election campaign was Chamberlain's direct appeal to the people, made in a series of speeches up and down the country. He called for the redistribution of land by allowing local bodies to buy land and parcel it out in small-holdings. Every farm labourer would have his 'three acres and a cow', a prospect which did not appeal much to the landowners but did attract the votes of the newly enfranchized farm workers. Chamberlain called for heavy taxes on the rich to finance free schools and social reform.

Chamberlain believed that his programme won the Liberal party many votes although it frightened many of the property-owning classes. **Gladstone did not take up the points of the prog-**

74

ramme but instead, at the end of 1885, turned his party towards the goal of obtaining Irish Home Rule.

Conclusion

The greatest achievement of Gladstone's Third Ministry was the 1884 Reform Act. Otherwise it fulfilled the description **'the Ministry of Sorrows'. Gladstone had been forced to follow an Imperialist policy in Egypt which led to disaster in the Sudan** (see p. 103) **and he was constantly distracted by the problems of Irish unrest** (see p. 80). **His own party was divided and the division became split in 1886 when he introduced his Home Rule Bill.**

Chapter 7
Ireland, 1815–1939

Introduction

From 1815 until 1939 successive British governments found themselves faced with what was called **'The Irish Problem'** or **'The Irish Question'**. This was a complicated and often troublesome issue which can be divided into three parts, **political, economic and religious** although often the three areas became merged together.

The **political side of the Irish Problem** was the product of the **Act of Union (1800)** which had abolished the Irish Parliament in Dublin. In place of their own Parliament the Irish were allowed to elect just over 100 M.Ps. to the United Kingdom Parliament at Westminster, where Irish affairs were debated. The administration of Ireland was controlled by the government in London which ruled through a Viceroy in Dublin Castle who headed a staff of officials who were mainly British. Throughout the nineteenth century, there was widespread resentment of this system and a wish by Irishmen for direct control of their own affairs. After 1870 this strong desire for self-government was expressed through the Home Rule Party.

Nearly all Irishmen made their living by growing food. The natural resources of Ireland were few and, unlike the rest of the British Isles, Ireland did not experience an Industrial Revolution. As a result, **the population had to support itself through agriculture** which was, for the most part, backward and seldom able to produce enough food to feed the population adequately. The **farmers of Ireland were,** almost to a man, **tenants** who paid rents to landlords, many of whom lived in England and ran their estates through agents. The farms were small and usually produced just enough to support the farmer's family with little or nothing over to pay the rent. Unable to pay his rent, the Irish farmer lived under the threat of eviction, that is being put off his farm by the landlord who would find another man to take over in the hope that he would be able to pay the rent. To make this problem worse, the population of Ireland grew rapidly in the first part of the nineteenth century; by 1841 there were 8 million people living in Ireland. The total Irish population dropped after the famines of 1845–7 but this fall did not relieve the pressure on the land. **The pattern of farmers, unable to pay their rents, being evicted and replaced continued until the end of the century.** This problem increased bitterness and led to terrorism.

The **religious problem of Ireland** was a consequence of the religious wars of the seventeenth century. The majority of the Irish were Roman Catholics. At the beginning of the nineteenth century they were effectively banned from holding offices in government and being elected as M.Ps for Parliament. Irish farmers paid land taxes (tithes) for the support of the Protestant Church of Ireland, a further source of resentment. Later, in the 1880s, a further problem emerged, that of the Ulster Protestants. The four northern Irish counties of Antrim, Armagh, Derry and Down were predominantly Protestant and their inhabitants grew increasingly hostile towards Home Rule, preferring instead to remain under the rule of Westminster.

During this period, the Irish problem passed through three phases. The first, from 1815 to 1868, was dominated by the struggle for Catholic Emancipation, the Potato Famine of 1845–7 and the growth of movements for self-government. The second, from 1868 to 1922 was a period of struggle for Home Rule and the third, from 1922 to 1939 was concerned with relations between the Irish Free State and the British Government.

1815–70

O'Connell and Home Rule movements
During the first half of the nineteenth century, Irish affairs were dominated by **Daniel O'Connell (1775–1845)** whom the Irish came to call 'The Liberator'. O'Connell was a Catholic lawyer whose determination and passionate oratory won him a widespread following within Ireland. His **political objective** was the **re-introduction of an Irish Parliament,** elected by Irishmen and running the affairs of Ireland. The first stage towards this end was the gaining of **Catholic Emancipation** which meant the repeal of those laws which banned Catholics from sitting in Parliament and holding public offices. Beyond this O'Connell wished to see the end of the powers and privileges of the Protestant church in Ireland and then the Irish people, free from religious restrictions, ordering their own country.

The **campaign for Catholic Emancipation** was carried on in the teeth of opposition from a powerful group, including Church of England bishops, in the House of Lords. In 1812, 1819 and 1821 bills for Catholic Emancipation had failed to get through Parliament in spite of the support of Castlereagh. O'Connell's answer was the formation of the **Catholic Association** in 1823, a mass movement in Ireland devoted to the cause of Emancipation. The size of the movement alarmed the authorities who ordered its suppression in 1825. In the same year the House of Commons passed Emancipation but the bill was thrown out by the Lords. In 1828 O'Connell defied the law and stood for Parliament and was elected. This and the dread of violence in Ireland persuaded the Prime Minister, the Duke of Wellington, to put his weight behind Emancipation. **In 1829 the restrictions on Catholics were abolished** and Catholics were free to hold public offices in Ireland and sit as M.Ps in Parliament.

Emancipation was O'Connell's greatest success. His other dreams were less easy to fulfil because both the **Whig and Tory Parties were determined not to overthrow the Irish church nor repeal the Act of Union.** Neither party was insensitive to the needs of Ireland and measures were taken to improve conditions there. In **1835 the Municipal Corporations Act was extended to Ireland as was the 1834 Poor Law Act.** Thomas Drummond, who was Under-Secretary for Ireland from 1835 to 1840 did much to encourage Catholic participation in local government and ensure that Catholics were fairly treated by the law. The government grant to **Maynooth College** (where Catholic priests were trained) was increased from £9,000 a year to £26,000 in 1845 by Sir Robert Peel. At the same time **Peel discouraged O'Connell's campaigns** and in 1843 O'Connell was arrested. The government was unable to secure his imprisonment as the charges were dismissed by Irish judges. Nevertheless, by the movement of troops to Ireland, Peel showed his determination to resist pressure for the repeal of the Act of Union.

Irish nationalism had been aroused by O'Connell's movement but its lack of success bred anger and frustration. O'Connell, in spite of his often fiery language, had faith in peaceful methods but his successors were more inclined to violence as the only means by which the Irish cause could be advanced. The **Young Ireland** movement which grew up in the 1840s imitated similar movements in Italy and preached a doctrine of intense nationalism. Like its European counterparts, the Young Ireland movement appealed to young people, encouraged national culture and the

Irish language and thrived on hostility to all that was English. In 1848 leaders of the movement were stirred by the Revolutions in Europe and attempted their own uprising in Tipperary. The rebellion was a farce and the local authorities had little trouble in putting it down. The ring-leaders were arrested, tried and transported to Australia. One of them, James Stephens, was pardoned in 1856 and returned to Ireland where he threw himself into the work of a new nationalist group, the Fenian brotherhood.

The Fenians had been started in 1858 in the United States where there were plenty of Irish immigrants willing to join a movement which was anti-British. The **aims of the Fenians were revolutionary,** they hoped to foment, arm and lead the Irish peasantry in a rebellion against British rule. The Fenians made little headway in Ireland and by 1867 they had found little sympathy there. In England they caused a number of alarms. During 1866–7 there was the threat of a massed gathering at Chester and two rescues of prisoners, one at Manchester and the other at Clerkenwell. These caused loss of life, a policeman shot at Manchester and a dozen killed by an explosive device at Clerkenwell, and several Fenians were executed for murder including Michael Barrett, the last man publicly hanged in the United Kingdom. The American Fenians, by far the largest body, made two armed raids into Canada in 1866–7 but were beaten back without difficulty.

In spite of the grievances of the Irish peasantry, **the Fenians had been unable to create a mass revolutionary movement.** Their efforts were anticipated by the government which had penetrated the movement with an undercover agent. For the next forty years Irishmen seeking self-government were to revert to peaceful methods.

The Potato Famine, 1845–7

The potato was the main crop of the Irish tenant farmers. In 1845 the potatoes were affected by a blight and the amount harvested was seriously reduced. **The crops of 1846 and 1847 were totally ruined,** leaving great numbers without any food. The Whig government under Lord John Russell, which had come to power in 1846 offered a programme of public works which would provide work and when this proved ineffective, widespread outdoor relief of money and food was authorised. The machinery of the Poor Law and the efforts of the government were unable to prevent deaths from starvation. Faced with famine, Irishmen and their families turned their backs on Ireland and **emigrated to the United States.** Over a million went to America, many losing their lives on the unseaworthy 'coffin ships'. A further million left between 1852 and 1861. They carried with them a bitter hatred of England and they and their descendants would encourage Irish nationalists with words and money.

For Ireland **the famine meant a fall in population of over two and a half million.** Pressure on the land was not relieved and the old pattern of tenant farmers growing subsistence crops under the constant threat of eviction continued. Many landlords had been ruined by the Potato Famine and they had been forced to sell their estates to newcomers. The new landlords, sometimes called 'gombeen men', were successful businessmen and townspeople who proved just as demanding as their predecessors. So the 1850s and 1860s saw continual and often violent conflict between landlords and tenants.

Home Rule, 1868–1922

Gladstone and Ireland
In December 1868, shortly before he formed his ministry, Gladstone announced, 'My mission is to pacify Ireland'. **From then until the defeat of his second Home Rule Bill in 1893, Gladstone was to devote much energy and passion on the solution of the Irish problem.** To start with he concentrated on two aspects of Irish affairs, the church and land. His efforts here and elsewhere were sincere and well-intentioned but within Ireland a powerful movement for Home Rule was growing up. By 1885 Gladstone was convinced that self-government would be the only satisfactory solution to the Irish problem; unfortunately neither his party nor the British electorate was in agreement. The **Disestablishment of the Irish Church (1869)** was Gladstone's first measure to remove Irish discontent. The Protestant Church of Ireland ceased to be the established church, it lost some of its property and the right to collect tithes (taxes on land) from the Irish people. A long-standing grievance was removed and money was obtained by the government from the church which was spent on Irish education, sea fisheries and various public works. The **Land Act (1870)** was drawn up by Gladstone and was a very complex piece of legislation. Gladstone had designed it as a means to protect Irish tenants from unfair eviction and give them some compensation for improvements which they had made to their farms. The Bill was not well received by the House of Lords which

made several alterations including one which substituted 'exorbitant rent' for 'excessive rent'. No law court could say exactly what an exorbitant rent was so the Act was unworkable. The evictions continued.

The **agricultural depression** which began in 1875 caused further distress in Ireland and the number of farmers evicted from their farms rose to over 2,000 in 1880. **Terrorism** spread and attacks were made on farms, hay ricks burnt and cattle maimed. Alongside the violent activities of the 'moonlighters', as the terrorists were called, was the growth of the **Home Rule** movement. The Home Rule Party had been formed in 1870 by Isaac Butt. Its influence grew and thanks to the Secret Ballot Act of 1872 Irish voters were able to elect Home Rule M.Ps without fear of their landlords' pressure. By the **1880 election over 80 Home Rule** M.Ps were elected for Irish seats under the leadership of **Charles Stewart Parnell.**

Parnell had become leader of the Home Rule Party in 1880. He was a country landowner who wished to merge the efforts of the Irish M.Ps with the movement for land reform in Ireland. To this end he attached himself to the **Land League** of Michael Davitt, a body which had been formed to protect the Irish tenant farmers. In the long term the Land League hoped to obtain ownership of the land for Irish farmers but its immediate task was the struggle against evictions. Parnell threw himself behind the League and in 1880 became its President, so leading both the Home Rule Party and the movement for land reform. Speaking to the Land Leaguers, Parnell had called on them to take action against the men who took over the farms from which the previous tenants had been evicted. Such men, claimed Parnell should be 'isolated from his kind as if he was a leper of old'. The most famous victim of this Land League policy was **Captain Boycott,** a landlord and land agent in west Ireland. In an area where landlords had been shot, Boycott found that local tradesmen would not deal with him and no one would harvest his crops. He was cut off and shunned, in other words 'boycotted' for his name gave a word to the English language.

Gladstone and Home Rule, 1880–1914
When **Gladstone was re-elected** in **1880** and began his second ministry, **Ireland was in turmoil.** Evictions increased daily and there was violence and disorder everywhere. In Parliament there was a solid body of Home Rule M.Ps, who, under the direction of

Parnell, were prepared to obstruct and hinder the business of the House of Commons.

Gladstone's first reaction was a **Coercion Act (1881)** which gave the Irish authorities power to arrest and imprison without trial anyone suspected of criminal activities. The **second Land Act (1881)** followed in the hope that it would remove the grievances which lay behind the violence. Irish tenant farmers were given the **'three F's'**. These were Fair Rents (fixed by tribunals), Fixity of Tenure for those who paid their rents and Free Sale of tenancies. Together these changes gave the Irish farmer greater security than he had ever had. The Land Act did not end the guerrilla activities of the Land League and in October 1881 Parnell was arrested and imprisoned under suspicion of having encouraged violence.

The disturbances continued and in 1882 Gladstone went to speak to Parnell in **Kilmainham Gaol** in Dublin. At what was called the Kilmainham Treaty, Gladstone promised an extension of the Land Act and in return, Parnell agreed to co-operate with the Liberal party in the House of Commons and do what he could to reduce violence. The **Phoenix Park murders** of 1882 upset this harmony. Lord Frederick Cavendish and another senior official of the Irish administration were stabbed in a Dublin park by a gang of terrorist assassins. The murderers were caught and executed but the anger felt in Britain led to a further and tougher Coercion Act.

Parnell had gained some co-operation from the Liberal party and after the **1885 election** he found himself at the head of 86 Home Rule M.Ps in the House of Commons. This number was the exact difference between the Liberal and Conservative M.Ps and so the **Home Rule Party had the balance of power.** At the end of the year, it was widely known that **Gladstone had become converted to Home Rule** and would introduce a Home Rule Bill in the first session of the new Parliament.

Gladstone's **first Home Rule Bill (1886)** proposed than an Irish Parliament should be set up in Dublin with control over all aspects of Irish life save foreign policy, defence and customs. There would be no Irish members in the London Parliament. This **bill dismayed many Liberals, including Joseph Chamberlain the radical and Lord Hartington, who led the more conservative Whig section of the party.** The opponents of Home Rule claimed that the measure would lead to the break up of the United

Kingdom and the violence of the Irish over the previous years had angered many Englishmen. Feeling against the bill was so deep that **93 Liberal M.Ps, led by Chamberlain, voted against it and it was defeated.** A third of the Liberal party had changed sides and Gladstone, his party divided over Home Rule, called a general election. The result of the 1886 election was a majority for the Conservatives under Lord Salisbury. **Home Rule for Ireland found little support from the British electorate.**

Gladstone's second Home Rule Bill (1893) was introduced after the Liberal election victory. It was similar to the first but with the added provision that Irish M.Ps were to be returned to Westminster where they could take part in debates and vote on Imperial and Irish business. This bill was passed by the House of Commons but **rejected by the House of Lords.** Gladstone wished to fight the Lords and call for a general election, but his cabinet colleagues suggested otherwise. They realised that the country was not wholeheartedly in favour of Irish Home Rule and that the Liberals could well be defeated as they had been in 1886. Gladstone had not solved the Irish problem although he had showed more shrewdness and imagination in dealing with it than any other English politician of his period. He had removed the problem of the church and, in his Land Act of 1881, done something to lessen the miseries of the tenant farmers. Yet together these measures were not enough as Gladstone realised. Ireland was a nation and would only have been satisfied with some form of self-government. Gladstone realised this and devoted the closing years of his political career to securing Home Rule. He had allied his party, the Liberals, to Home Rule, but he had also, in 1886, split his party.

The **Conservative Party,** which was in power from 1886 to 1892, was determined to follow **a policy of firmness towards Ireland** which was carried out by the Chief Secretary, Arthur Balfour. Whilst dealing with unrest, the Conservatives were also prepared to meet the grievances of the Irish farmers. In 1903 **Wyndham's Land Purchase Act** enabled Irish farmers to buy their farms with loans from the government. These loans were charged at $2\frac{3}{4}$% and were to be paid back over sixty-eight and a half years. At last the Irish farmers were satisfied, they were the owners of the land they long believed to be their own by right.

The **Irish Home Rule Party,** after the disappointment of 1886, soon faced difficulties. Its leader **Parnell,** 'the uncrowned king of

Ireland', faced charges of involvement in terrorism, made in a series of articles in *The Times* during 1887. He successfully defended himself against the smears but in 1890 he was named as a co-respondent in a divorce case brought by a Captain O'Shea. Parnell's adultery with Mrs O'Shea was proved and this shocked both non-conformist liberals and Catholic Irish. Parnell ignored demands for his resignation and the Home Rule Party was split between Parnellites and his critics. He died in 1891 leaving his party divided.

In 1900 the Home Rule Party was reunited under the leadership of John Redmond. He realised, following the policy which had been begun with Parnell, that Irish Home Rule could only be achieved with the **co-operation of the Liberal Party**. After the first election of 1910 the Liberals found that they needed the votes of the 70 Home Rule M.Ps to ensure that Lloyd George's Peoples Budget would pass through the Commons. As in 1886 the Liberals needed the Irish to remain in power. This situation was repeated after the second (December) election in **1910** and **the Liberals required the Irish votes for the Parliamentary Bill.** Irish support for the Liberals was obtained in return for the promise of a Home Rule Bill. This was now certain of success, since the Parliament Act of 1911 made it no longer possible for the Lords to veto Home Rule. All the Lords could do was to postpone the measure for two years.

The third Home Rule Bill was introduced in **1912.** Ireland would have its own Parliament with control over Irish affairs and a reduced number of Irish M.Ps would be returned to Westminster which would have supreme power. The bill was passed by the Commons and **delayed by the Lords so that it became law in the summer of 1914.**

There was, however, bitter and **determined opposition to Home Rule from the people of Ulster.** Ulster, the northern area of Ireland, was predominantly Protestant and in 1885–6 many of its inhabitants had shown hostility to Home Rule on the grounds that they might become dominated by the Catholic majority in the south of Ireland. At that time the slogan 'Home Rule, Rome Rule' had been shouted. In 1912 these feelings were revived with fresh intensity and a new slogan was created 'Ulster will fight and Ulster will be right'. In England, the **Conservative party leader, Bonar Law joined forces with the Ulster Unionist leader, Sir Edward Carson,** and called for 'resistance' in a number of dangerous and inflammatory speeches. Actions followed words and the **Ulster Volunteer Force** was formed, armed with smuggled rifles and machine guns. By the end of 1913 it appeared that the Protestants of Ulster would fight and that they would be encouraged by the Conservatives and Unionists within the British Parliament. Redmond and the Home Rule Party refused any suggestion that Ulster should be separated from the rest of Ireland and this view was upheld by Asquith and the Liberal party. Seldom in British political life was there ever such violence of language and sentiments expressed by the leaders of both sides. Churchill believed that the Ulstermen's actions were those of rebels and traitors, and early in 1914, planned to send warships to the chief city of Ulster, Belfast. More trouble followed when officers of the British army, serving at the **Curragh** base in southern Ireland, stated that they would resign rather than fight the Ulstermen. The Curragh Mutiny, as this threat was called, added further to the likelihood of a civil war in Ireland once Home Rule became law later in the year.

During the early summer of 1914, the future of Ireland was in the balance. The Prime Minister, Asquith, and King George V urged that Ulster should be excluded from Home Rule but Redmond and his supporters disagreed. **The discussions on Ulster were interrupted by the outbreak of war in August.** With Britain at war, all parties agreed that **the Home Rule Act would not become law until the end of hostilities.** So the question of Ireland's future government was put off, although it seemed likely that when Home Rule came about, Ulster would not be included with the rest of Ireland.

During the years of bitter debate about Home Rule, **new political groups had emerged inside Ireland.** Of these the **Irish Republican Brotherhood** was the most important. A secret society, it had as its objective an Irish republic with no ties with Britain. The Brotherhood gave support and leadership to the **Irish Volunteers,** formed in 1913 to answer the challenge of the Ulster Volunteers and fight for Home Rule. To the supporters of an independent republic, the First World War seemed an opportunity to strike at Britain. Attempts were made to gain German help and arms for an uprising and to this end, an ex-British diplomat, Sir Roger Casement visited Germany and returned to Ireland with some arms. He was arrested in 1916, tried for treason in London and executed. In the same year a group of Irish Volunteers and the Irish Citizen Army seized several parts of Dublin and held them for four days against British forces. The **Easter Rising (1916)** changed Irish politics. The rebels had declared an Irish republic but, at first, they had received a poor response from the Irish people. After the rebellion the British authorities were determined to make examples of the ringleaders who were tried by court martial and shot. Fifteen, including James Connolly, Tom Clarke and Padraic Pearse met their deaths and soon they became 'martyrs', warriors who had died for Ireland's freedom.

The Rising strengthened the Republican cause. Republicanism now seemed the only answer to Ireland's problems and more and more Irishmen rallied to this cause. The **Sinn Fein** ('ourselves alone') movement which had been a group for Irish cultural and economic revival became, by 1917, the main republican party. Its leader was Eamonn de Valera, a veteran of the 1916 Easter Rising.

Sinn Fein showed its strength in the General Election of December 1918 when it gained 73 M.Ps. They refused to go to Westminster and instead set up their own Parliament, called the **Dail Eireann,** in Dublin in January 1919. **The first act of the Dail was to declare Irish independence,** claim for itself the right to make laws for Ireland and demand the withdrawal of British troops from Ireland.

Sinn Fein had become the party which spoke for Ireland and the old Home Rule party was all but dead. The British government faced with the claims of the Sinn Fein party and the declaration of independence by the Dail, reacted in two ways. The first was to pass the **Government of Ireland Act (1920)** which set up a separate Parliament for the six counties of Ulster and admitted the right of the Dail to govern southern Ireland. The second was to enforce partition against the overwhelming will of the republicans. From 1919 to 1921 there was a civil war in Ireland, fought between the guerrilla forces of the Irish Volunteers and the forces of the British government. This period was known as 'the Troubles' and saw terrorism and counter-terrorism, murder and reprisal by each side. In 1919 the Royal Irish Constabulary was supplemented by recruits from England, known after their green and khaki uniforms as **'Black and Tans'** and they in turn were augmented by other police auxiliaries.

In July 1920 negotiations began between the British government, under Lloyd George and the Irish Dail, represented by Arthur

Griffith and Michael Collins, the Director of Intelligence for the Irish forces. There had been widespread horror in Britain at the methods of the government forces and the government was under pressure to end the fighting and the Irish insurgents were being hard pressed. The talks lasted for six months until the signing of **Anglo-Irish Treaty of December 1921.** By this agreement British troops withdrew from southern Ireland, which was to have dominion status, that is its own Parliament but owing allegiance to the British crown. Much to the dismay of many Irish republicans, Ulster remained separated from the rest of Ireland with its own Parliament.

The Treaty had not achieved a united Ireland and although southern Ireland had virtual independence, dominion status was less satisfactory than a republic. The Treaty was approved by the Dail but its opponents were determined to fight. From 1922 to the middle of 1923 there was a second civil war in Ireland, between the supporters of the Treaty ('Free-Staters') and its opponents. Military victory went to the Treaty's adherents.

Independent Ireland, 1922–39

Eamonn de Valera, who had been hostile to the 1921 Treaty, and his Fianna Fail ('soldiers of destiny') party won the Irish general election of 1932. His objective was to transform the Irish Free State into a republic, free of any links with Britain. He revoked the provisions of the Anglo-Irish Treaty which insisted upon dominion status and led Ireland along a policy of neutrality during the 1930s. In 1938 he negotiated a revision of the treaty which gave Ireland full control over her ports – previously the British, for reasons of naval security, had reserved the right to commandeer ports in western Ireland in the event of war. Full republican status came for Ireland in 1949.

Conclusion

The southern Irish received self-government in 1922 but this did not end the Irish problem. The six counties of Ulster, Protestant but with a sizeable Catholic minority, remained separate with their own government. Dreams of a united Ireland with one government were not fulfilled and even though the opponents of the Anglo-Irish treaty were beaten in 1923, there has remained a widespread feeling in southern Ireland that Ulster should be part of one Ireland. The problems created by partition are still with us and show no sign of being solved to the satisfaction of all involved.

The long struggle for Irish self-rule was marked by much violence which created bitter memories. These too remain.

For Britain the Irish problem had special significance. The Potato Famine of 1845–7 forced the Prime Minister, Sir Robert Peel, to repeal the Corn Laws and so divide his party. A further consequence was the exclusion from power of the Conservative party for the next twenty years. Gladstone, more determined to solve the Irish problem than any other British politician, allied his party to the cause of Home Rule in 1885. The consequence was the division of the Liberal Party. When, in 1912, the Liberals introduced the Third and last Home Rule Bill, they did so not because of any burning belief that it was right but in thanks for the support which Irish Home Rule M.Ps had given for Lloyd George's budget and the Parliament Act of 1911. The result of this bill was the alliance between the Ulster Unionists and the Conservative Party and the threat of a civil war in Ireland. The final act in the struggle, the fight between British government forces and supporters of the Irish Republic, also influenced British politics. Lloyd George was discredited by the brutality of the Black and Tans and criticized for 'shaking hands with murder' when he negotiated with the Irish. The Irish problem was, to some extent, the graveyard of British politicians. That this was so was largely their own fault for action, whether on Home Rule, the Irish Church or the Land problem had always come too late. It was this slowness to act which made many Irishmen finally lose faith in Britain and turn to their own form of direct action.

Chapter 8
British Empire, 1815–1939

Introduction

In 1815 Britain's overseas territories were few and scattered. Save for India, the British Empire was made up of trading posts, naval bases and small settlements like those on the Australian coast. By 1939 Britain was at the head of an Empire which covered 13 million square miles and contained a population of over 450 millions, of which two-thirds lived in India.

Why did this remarkable expansion occur? The major reasons had been **trade, settlement by British emigrants** and **political and military necessity.** Parallel with the growth of the Empire went the spread of **Imperialism,** a collection of ideas about the Empire which became widely fashionable towards the end of the nineteenth century. At the heart of Imperial thinking was the conviction that it was Britain's destiny and duty to acquire and govern an empire. The British were marked out by their honesty, inventiveness and a strong sense of justice and fair play. These qualities enabled them to fulfil the responsibilities which were an essential part of Imperialism, for it was believed that Britain had a moral duty to bring order and civilization to every corner of the world. Alongside such elevated ideals were more down to earth arguments for Imperial expansion. **Britain's growing Empire added to her international standing** among the great powers of Europe. Some politicians, like Joseph Chamberlain regarded the Empire as a potential source of economic power at a time when Britain's share of world trade was dropping.

Background, before 1870

Trade was significant as a cause of Imperial expansion before and after 1815. The Industrial Revolution had put Britain far ahead of her commercial rivals in 1815 and her trade was world-wide. In order to maintain her position as well as to open up new markets, **Britain needed to acquire ports.** In 1824 Singapore was annexed and in 1842 the Chinese government was forced to surrender Hong Kong, both valuable bases for trade and shipping in the Far East. British international trade and shipping needed security which was provided by the Royal Navy. The Navy required bases, especially after 1850 when coal burning steam-ships came into use. Naval requirements therefore ensured the occupation of Malta and the Falkland Islands. These commercial and naval considerations did not however lead to widespread occupation of territory during this period.

The settled colonies such as Australia and Canada were still under-populated and were not therefore good markets for British goods. The doctrines of Free Trade, which dominated political and business thinking between 1840 and 1860, saw the whole world as Britain's market. Businessmen and investors preferred foreign countries, especially the United States, as a source of expansion and investment. **Free Trade legislation** of this period **ended any special commercial relationship between Britain and her colonies.** In 1854 West Indian sugar no longer enjoyed special advantages in the British market (as a result the West Indian islands faced bankruptcy and collapse) and during the 1860s Sweden replaced Canada as Britain's source of timber.

Emigration. Whilst the colonies brought Britain no commercial advantages, they were regarded as a potential home for surplus population. Britain's population rose from 10 million in 1801 to 16 million in 1831, a rise which many economists feared would lead to overpopulation and the resulting miseries of unemployment and poverty. To meet this threat, a group of radical thinkers, including J. S. Mill and **Gibbon Wakefield** and called the **Colonial Reformers** urged organised emigration. Wakefield proposed that the government should sell the lands it held in colonies such as Australia to emigrants from Britain. The money raised, he suggested, would create a fund to pay the fares of more emigrants. Wakefield favoured the emigration of families for family men would be more willing to work hard, and the presence of families would bring stability to the growing colonies. His ideas were adopted by the Australian state of New South Wales in 1831 and were very influential in other colonies. Propaganda for emigration naturally emphasized the attractiveness of the colonies and the opportunities for advancement which existed there. A drawing of the 1830s showed a pauper family, bare footed and ragged on a British street alongside the same family plump and about to tuck into a large meal, on a colonial farm. Poverty and the hopes of a new and better life encouraged great numbers of emigrants during the 1840s and 1850s and thanks to the persuasion of the Colonial Reformers, lands were available for them. During the 1840s Australia was receiving annually about 14,000 emigrants and the number increased, not surprisingly, after the discovery of gold there in 1851. Between 1815 and 1914 Canada received 4 million emigrants and Australia and New Zealand 1½ million. By far **the greatest number of British emigrants, 13 million,** ignored the colonies and **made their way to the United States,** a land where the opportunities and rewards always seemed greater.

Emigration meant that the populations of Canada, Australia and New Zealand grew and with this growth came **the problem of their political future and their relations with Britain.** Some radicals such as Cobden argued that these colonies should tread the path already followed by the United States and eventually become independent. Yet the settlers had no wish to break the ties with Britain. The Durham Report of 1839, compiled by Lord Durham, one of the Colonial Reformers, argued that the colonists of Canada should be given 'responsible government' with each province free to manage its own affairs through an elected assembly. Certain matters, such as foreign policy and defence, were to be left to Britain and Durham observed, there was no wish to be separate from the British crown. The results of this report were considerable. The Canadian provinces were given responsible government in 1855, the Australian states between 1855 and 1890, Cape Colony in 1872 and New Zealand in 1876. With populations of British stock, running their own affairs, these colonies remained strongly loyal to Britain and willing to uphold the Imperial link.

Background, after 1870

Trade
After 1870, Britain's domination of world trade was challenged by growing competition from Germany and the United States. By 1880 Germany had already become the world's second largest exporter of manufactured goods whilst **Britain's share in world trade fell from 38% in 1881–5 to 27% in 1913.** Britain's new rivals rejected Free Trade doctrines and placed duties on imported manufactured goods. Trade with the British Empire increased, especially the settled colonies, and by 1913 the Empire was taking 50% of British exports. The struggle for world markets persuaded some politicians that Britain ought to abandon Free Trade and replace it by an Imperial Free Trade area with duties imposed on foreign goods. At the same time it was suggested that closer links could be forged with the Empire which could lead to an Imperial Federation, headed by Britain.

The British public was not impressed with such schemes and before 1914 the electorate showed a clear preference for the continuing Free Trade.

The commercial opportunities of Imperial expansion were taken advantage of during this period by **Chartered Companies,** licensed by the government with powers to develop areas in Africa for their own profit.

The completion of the **Suez Canal** in 1869 was of immense commercial and Imperial significance as it was **vital to Britain's interests in India and Far Eastern trade.** The defence of these interests led to British occupation of Egypt and the Sudan. Imperial communication and the protection of trade also contributed to the expansion of the navy from the 1880s onwards.

Political

During this period **Britain's Imperial expansion was concentrated on Africa.** The continent had been opened up by explorers like David Livingstone, some of whom had brought back tempting descriptions of its **potential wealth.** The weapons of industrial technology, such as repeating rifles and machine guns, made conquest easy and improvements in medical knowledge made it possible for Europeans to survive the climate and diseases. From 1870 to 1900 the great European powers, Britain, France, Germany and Belgium took part in the **'scramble for Africa'** in which the continent was occupied and divided. There were **economic arguments** for this division but perhaps more important were matters of **prestige.** Territorial acquisition was a measure of power. Britain was therefore anxious not to be left behind, and through the efforts of forceful individuals such as Cecil Rhodes was able to acquire considerable territory especially in southern and central Africa. The **partition of Africa led to war** – with natives, such as the Zulu War of 1879, and more expensively, with the Boers in 1880–1 and 1899–1902. There was also **international tension,** as in 1898, when Britain and France clashed over the ownership of the southern Sudan. Another Imperial activity, the expansion of economic and political power in an area by negotiation with local rulers (known as 'spheres of influence') also created tension, as in China in the 1890s and 1900s.

Imperialism

Imperial expansion enlarged and fed national pride. It also encouraged ideas, popularized by politicians and newspapers, of

Imperial duty and destiny. For over a hundred years missionaries had been sent from Britain with the purpose of bringing Christianity to native peoples. Reports from men such as Livingstone, of the wretchedness and barbarism of some of these people, as well as tales of the horrors of slavery had aroused widespread anger. Did the civilized nations not have a duty to bring order and peace to such people? Not only the blessings of religion but those of law, education and technology were needed. Britain was well suited to bring such benefits. Such arguments were put forward by the Imperial poet Rudyard Kipling in the poem significantly entitled 'The White Man's Burden':

> Take up the White Man's Burden –
> Send forth the best ye breed –
> Go bind your sons to exile
> To serve your captives' need;
> To wait in heavy harness
> On fluttered folk and wild –
> Your new-caught, sullen peoples,
> Half devil and half child

Imperialism stirred patriotic emotions. The popular press of the late nineteenth century extensively reported the progress of imperial armies and their conquests, stories which aroused excitement, imagination and pride. Looking back on her girlhood in the 1880s, Flora Thompson remembered:

'. . . the day of the bayonet and the Gatling gun, of horse drawn gun carriages and balloon observation, of soldiers fighting in tight-necked scarlet tunics. The most gallant among them knelt before a gentle, white haired woman to be decorated. Some had spoken of her as Victoria the Good . . .'

Queen Victoria had become a symbol of Empire, the Queen Empress who ruled over and united the separate peoples of her Empire. Her Golden Jubilee in 1887 and Diamond of 1897 were celebrations not only of her reign and her people's progress but of the Empire. Themes of crown and Imperial conquest mingle in A. E. Houseman's '1887':

> It dawns in Asia, tombstones show
> And Shropshire names are read;
> And the Nile spills his overflow
> Beside the Severn's dead.

> We pledge in peace by farm and town
> The Queen they served in war,

And fire the beacons up and down
The land they perished for.

Imperial ideas formed popular political rallying cries. Disraeli and the Conservative party became **identified with Imperialism** in the 1870s and later, but rather reluctantly, many Liberals jumped on the bandwagon. Soldiers and administrators aboard, the men on the spot, often led the way with aggressive Imperial policies (sometimes called **'forward policies'**) in the knowledge that their actions would win popular approval. 'Empire builders', men like Cecil Rhodes, became heroes.

India, 1815–1939

Introduction

In 1815 the British were undisputed masters of India. In the two hundred years since the East India Company had begun trading in the sub-continent, British influence had grown and its rivals had been eliminated. The French and the Dutch had been defeated and expelled, many native princes had submitted to British overlordship and large areas of land had passed directly into British hands. The process of expansion continued after 1815; in 1824 the coastal area of Burma came under British rule, in 1843 Sind was annexed and in 1849, after two wars, the Sikh province of the Punjab was conquered.

The acquisition of land in India brought with it problems and responsibilities. Until 1783 the government of British territories had been in the hands of the East India Company whose chief interests had been the making of profits. The India Act of 1783 began the process of making India the responsibility of the government in London. A Board of Control, whose members were appointed by the government, supervised and directed the East India Company. The Company remained in charge of the day-to-day administration of India but its senior officials, including the Governor General, had to be appointed with the approval of the government in London. This system was altered by a further **India Act of 1833** which insisted that the East India Company ceased to concern itself with trade and instead devoted its energies to ruling in the interests of its subjects. The greatest importance of this Act was its claim that the governing of India should be conducted in the interests of the Indian people and that a new code of law proposed for the country should be based upon local customs rather than English traditions.

It was not surprising that the **ideals of reform** which guided so many British politicians and thinkers at this time also **extended to India.** The British government had found itself in charge of large territories and great numbers of people and, inspired by the humanitarian ideals of the time, felt that it had a duty to assist these people in every possible way. Such sentiments were also shared by the men who ruled India. In 1824 one British official observed, 'We must look upon India not as a temporary possession but as one which is to be maintained permanently, until the natives shall have abandoned most of their prejudices, and become sufficiently enlightened to frame a regular government for themselves, and to conduct and preserve it'. In this spirit, two governors-general, Lord Bentinck (who ruled from 1828 to 1836) and Lord Dalhousie (1848-56) began a series of reforms which brought about widespread changes and also aroused bitter hostility from the native population.

The governors-general and officials who introduced these reforms were humane men, who sincerely believed that by bringing European ideas and skills to India they would help its people. First among these blessings was Christianity. There had been few missionaries during the eighteenth century but after the 1833 Act which allowed Europeans freedom of access to all parts of India, their numbers and influence grew. One important feature of their activities was the provision of **schooling.** The government was also keenly concerned with spreading education and gave money to help new schools. Thanks to the arguments of Lord Macaulay, one of Bentinck's advisors, this money was, after 1835, solely devoted to schools which taught in English and **spread western ideas.** One consequence of this decision was that English became the language of learning in India but the insistence on western values offended both Hindus and Moslems, who regarded the spread of European and Christian teaching as a threat to traditional religious customs. The **Hindu religion was directly threatened** by Bentinck's **suppression of suttee,** a custom by which Hindu widows threw themselves on the burning funeral pyres of their husbands. This was made illegal in 1829 and together with a new law which permitted Hindu widows to remarry aroused deep suspicions. Bentinck also put down the custom of **Thugee,** murder and robbery carried out by Thugs, followers of Kali, the Hindu goddess of destruction. The Thugs were gradually eliminated after 1829 and although their disappearance saved many lives, it appeared that the British were tampering with traditional religious beliefs.

Under **Lord Dalhousie** further far reaching changes were begun. New trunk roads were built, telegraph lines were set up and railway tracks laid. Efforts were undertaken to develop India's natural resources, both industrial and agricultural. All these innovations, introduced for the highest motives, aroused deep misgivings. The new railway carriages forced Hindus of different castes to mix, something which was deeply offensive for the caste system was an integral part of Hindu religious and social life. Loss of caste caused deep distress to the Hindu and the railway system together with the introduction of communal feeding in gaols appeared to many Indians as indications that the British wished to destroy the caste system and with it the Hindu religion.

Many native rulers still existed in India, their authority guaranteed by treaties made with the British. In several states the quality of government did not meet with British approval and the government sought ways to bring them under direct control. To this end Dalhousie had introduced the **doctrine of 'lapse'** by which the British took over the lands of a native ruler when he lacked an heir. This scheme disregarded the old Indian custom by which a childless ruler could adopt an heir. The doctrine of lapse was applied in 1856 to the state of Oudh and provoked widespread resentment there.

Causes of the Mutiny
The policies adopted by successive governors-general before 1856 had been designed to improve conditions of life for the people of India. In many areas they provoked anger and resentment for they seemed to be **undermining traditional, social, political and religious life.** The Hindus saw their customs of suttee and thugee put down and what appeared to be an assault on the caste system. Moslems, especially in populous Oudh, resented the removal of a Moslem ruler. Both Hindus and Moslems feared the spread of western education and suspected a conspiracy to impose Christianity on India. Lord Roberts, then a young officer in the Indian army, summed up the mood of the Indians in 1857, 'By a great many acts and measures we made them feel how completely our ideas differed from theirs. They preferred their own and strongly resented our increasing efforts to impose ours upon them'.

Simmering discontent, the reaction to sudden changes, came to a head in 1857 among native soldiers (sepoys) of the Indian army. At that time there were 257,000 sepoys in India and

45,000 European troops. The fighting reputation of British troops had been tarnished by that defeat in 1842 in the Afghan wars and rumours circulated which claimed that one hundred years after the battle of Plassey (1757) the British would be driven from India. Many sepoys were troubled by tales that the British were deliberately grinding cow and pig bones into the flour issued to native soldiers – the pig was unclean for Moslems and the cow sacred to Hindus. This rumour was followed by another which finally sparked off the Mutiny. This alleged that the new **Enfield Rifle,** shortly to be issued to the sepoys, had cartridges which had to be bitten and that these had been greased with cow and pig fat. This revelation confirmed the rumour that the British planned to

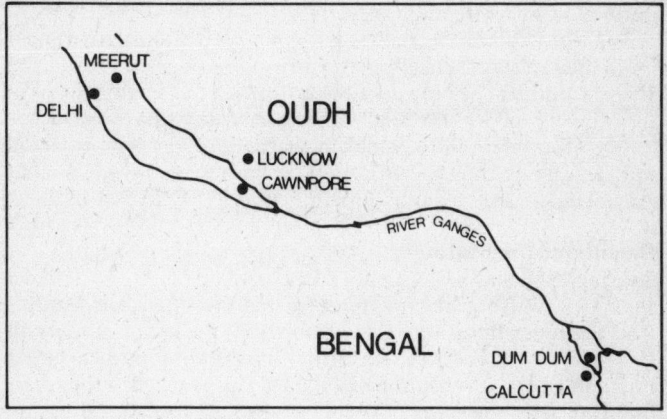

Figure 1. Indian Mutiny, 1857

destroy the religion of the Hindus and the Moslems, by destroying the caste system of one and defiling the other. To make matters worse many European officers attempted to convert their sepoys to Christianity, a manoeuvre which added more fuel to the fires of unrest. **The alarms of the sepoys were added to the long term resentment aroused by innovations and prepared the way for the Mutiny.**

The Mutiny

The Mutiny broke out in May 1857. Sepoys at **Meerut,** who had been imprisoned after refusing to handle the greased cartridges, broke from gaol and murdered their British officers, their wives and children. Then the mutineers marched on Delhi, seized the

97

city and declared a descendant of the old Mogul rulers, Emperor. **From its start the Mutiny was a revolt of soldiers.** Few civilians joined the rebels and they came for the most part from the discontented state of Oudh although the mutineers received aid and encouragement from some discontented native rulers like Nana Sahib, the dispossessed ruler of Peshwa. **The spread of the rising was soon halted by the prompt and efficient action of the military authorities, often forewarned by telegraph.** Columns of troops were quickly mustered, drawn from British regiments, Sikhs, Ghurkas and other loyal troops and were moved to the troubled areas. Often outnumbered by as many as five to one, the government troops were able to re-take Delhi by September and at the same time detachments under General Havelock occupied Cawnpore and relieved Lucknow. Here and elsewhere the mutineers and their allies had murdered European women and children with gross brutality. These outrages incensed the British commanders and their troops and led to a terrible retribution in which guilty and innocent were executed without discrimination. Massacre and counter-massacre turned northern India into a slaughterhouse and left bitter memories which soured Anglo-Indian relations for generations.

Results of the Mutiny

By May 1858 Sir Colin Campbell had subdued Oudh and within a short time outlying areas of unrest had been pacified. The **Mutiny had been confined to parts of northern India and nearly all those in arms against the British had been sepoys.** Great numbers of Indians had remained loyal and done all within their power to assist the suppression of the uprising. In spite of this, the Mutiny and the tales of horror associated with it deeply affected the people of Britain and contributed towards a change of attitude to the coloured races of the Empire. Feelings which had inspired earlier reformers, missionaries and the enemies of slavery and had led to efforts to 'improve' and 'convert' were undermined by a sense of betrayal. Some began to argue that Imperial government needed to be stern and that native peoples required to be treated as untrustworthy children. **There were several direct consequences of the Mutiny.** The number of native troops was reduced and that of British increased. **The India Act (1858)** abolished the East India Company and brought India under the direct supervision of the Secretary of State for India, a member of the Cabinet, who would be assisted by a council. Local administration remained much as it had been, with the Viceroy in Delhi directing an administration, dominated by Europeans, which controlled every aspect of Indian life. Since 1853 the Indian Civil Service had been recruited by competitive examination in Britain and its members were a dedicated élite which ran the legal system, police, taxation and railways. The raj (as British rule was called) relied on these men backed by vast numbers of locally recruited minor officials – there were three million in 1910. Each high court had one Indian judge but elsewhere only a handful of senior government posts was filled by Indians. In essence this system remained unchanged until 1939.

The movement for self-government

One of the most important features of British rule before and after the Mutiny was the **growth of education.** Three universities had been founded in 1857, the number of schools increased and many Indians completed their education in Britain. Through learning many Indians became aware of the British system of government and political ideas, especially political freedom. Contact with and study of British ideas aroused a strong wish for self-government, along the lines established in Canada and Australia. In **1885 the Indian Congress was founded with the objective of obtaining for Indians the right to govern themselves.** From then until the granting of independence in 1947, the Congress dominated Indian efforts to obtain political responsibility and the end of British rule. Pressure mounted and by the beginning of the twentieth century there was violent agitation – in 1912 the Viceroy, Lord Hardinge, was severely wounded by an assassin.

British officials in India were reluctant to accept that the Congress spoke for all Indians, claiming that it represented a small but noisy educated minority. Some believed that the Indians were not ready for political responsibility. There was one obvious stumbling block, the Moslem minority which feared that in a self-governing India with a Parliamentary democracy, it would be swamped by the Hindu majority. In 1906 a Moslem League had been founded and thereafter Congress tended to be dominated by Hindus. In Britain there was much sympathy for the Congress movement, especially from members of the Liberal and Labour parties, many of whom had never been happy with Imperial ideas and who found it easy to represent the British raj as overbearing and even tyrannical. On the other hand the beliefs in political liberty expressed by Congress seemed in accord with traditions dear to the Liberals. In 1909 the **Morley-Minto reforms,** designed by the Liberal Secretary of State for India, John Morley, and the Viceroy, Lord Minto, were introduced with the intention of allowing the Indians limited participation in the lower areas of government. All literate Indians were permitted to vote for members of the provincial councils. These elected members would be in the majority on the councils but their powers were limited and they had no means of controlling the executive. Small numbers of Indians were allowed to join the Viceroy and Secretary of State's council. This cautious reform did not satisfy the Congress and agitation continued.

The attitude of the British government was changed by the First World War. Alarmed by the continuing agitation and impressed by India's loyal response with men and money, **the British government in 1917 promised dominion status for India.** This pledge was renewed by Lord Irwin, the Viceroy, in 1929 but the actions of the government remained cautious. Unappeased by promises, Congress and its supporters kept up the struggle and in 1919 there were widespread riots and bloodshed. The Congress had come to be dominated by **Mahatma Gandhi** (1869–1948), a British educated lawyer, who advocated passive resistence as the means to put pressure on the British. He combined large demonstrations against the authorities with a campaign for the betterment of the 'untouchables', those without caste and, in every sense, the underdogs of Indian society. Faced with unrest and defiance, the British reacted in two ways. In India disorder was met with force and in Britain politicians looked for a political solution. A commission, led by Sir John Simon advocated, in its report of 1929, that Indians should have full control of the provincial councils, a form of local self-government with national affairs still controlled by the Viceroy in Delhi. This formed the basis for discussions at three Round Table Conferences in 1930, 1931 (attended by Gandhi) and 1932 but none reached a satisfactory conclusion. In **1934 the Government of India Act** gave responsible elective government to the provinces (along the lines suggested by Simon) with a complicated electoral system to protect Moslem rights. This was a step towards full self-government but it did not quieten agitation for full self-determination.

The question of India's future now concerned politicians in Britain and whilst **Ramsay MacDonald and Stanley Baldwin both favoured eventual dominion status, there was much opposition from some quarters, led by Winston Churchill.** A young officer in India in the 1890s, he had seen the raj at the height of its power and magnificence at a time when it seemed that Britain would rule the sub-continent for ever. Yet the British had brought with them not only soldiers and administrators but ideas and these, adopted by the Indians, had shaken the security of the raj and prepared the way for its eventual end in 1947.

Afghanistan and the North West Frontier

One recurring problem which had dogged the rulers of India and their masters in Britain was the security of India's North West Frontier. This mountainous region was the border with Afghanistan and through this country ran the **Khyber Pass,** the major routeway to northern India. To the north of Afghanistan lay an area of Central Asia which, during the nineteenth century, was being conquered by Russia. **British politicians** watched this development with alarm and became **obsessed with a fear of a Russia invasion of India from the north.** The attack never came nor was it likely that Russia could ever have mounted it. Nevertheless the fears of a Russian army in the Khyber troubled British and Indian officials and twice led to British armies entering Afghanistan. Fear of Russian agents in Kabul, the Afghan capital, led to the First **Afghan War (1842–3)** after a British force installed a puppet ruler in 1841. This army was isolated, British agents were murdered and the troops were forced to retire, harried almost to extinction by Afghan tribesmen. After this catastrophe, the Indian government sent a punitive force to Kabul which ended the First Afghan War. The **Second Afghan War (1878–80)** followed closely the pattern of the first. The refusal of the ruler of Afghanistan to receive a British envoy and rumours of his friendship for the Russians provoked the Viceroy, Lord Lytton, to send a force there with a British envoy. His murder was followed by a successful and arduous campaign by Anglo-Indian forces under Lord Roberts. The return to power in 1880 of Gladstone ended the war, for the new Prime Minister regarded such adventures as aggressive, wasteful and immoral. A subsequent scare about Russian infiltration **(the Pendjeh Incident, 1885)** came to nothing and was settled by negotiation. **The Anglo-Russian entente of 1907 ended disputes and alarms over this region.**

The Frontier itself was a lawless area and the scene of what Kipling called the 'Great Game', a struggle of skirmishes, wars and intrigues between British soldiers and agents and the fierce, warlike and reckless tribesman of the Himalayan foothills. The 'Great Game' was played throughout this period and contributed much to romantic notions of the Indian Empire set down in newspaper reports of campaigns and the stirring tales of such as G. A. Henty's *With Roberts to Kandahar*.

The Middle East

Egypt and the Sudan

Stable and benevolent regimes in the Middle East were important for the security of British trade in the area and the protection of routes to India and the Far East. The opening of the Suez Canal in 1869 increased British interest in the area; three-quarters of the ships which passed through the Canal were British owned.

Egypt

Britain's involvement in Egypt began in **1875** when **Disraeli purchased shares in the Suez Canal on behalf of the British government for 4 million pounds.** The ruler of Egypt, thanks to self indulgence and over-spending, was bankrupt and Disraeli used the opportunity to advance Britain's interest in the canal which was so vital to shipping and communication. In order to straighten out chaotic Egyptian finances and protect European investment Britain and France imposed **dual control** on the Egyptian treasury in 1876.

Foreign infiltration, growing British and French control over the government and mismanagement provoked unrest in Egypt and in 1879 an army colonel, **Arabi Pasha** led a **nationalist revolt**. Europeans were killed in the riots that followed and in 1882 Gladstone reluctantly sent a squadron of warships to **Alexandria** in order to protect British lives and property. **Admiral Seymour's warships shelled the harbour forts** and landed marines to put down the rioting and looting. The French showed no further interest in Egypt and Gladstone and the cabinet decided that the only solution to the Egyptian problem would be for Britain to take over the government. In 1882 an expeditionary force under Sir Garnet Wolesey was sent to Egypt and defeated the Egyptian army at **Tel-el-Kebir.** A garrison was installed to protect the Suez Canal and the Egyptian government was placed under British supervision. It was **Gladstone's purpose to give Egypt firm, efficient and just rule** through the British Consul General in Cairo, **Sir Evelyn Baring** (later Lord Cromer). Under Baring's guidance social reforms, public works and financial re-organization were carried out.

Egypt possessed an elected Assembly and there gradually emerged a wish to remove British supervision. The growth of anti-British feeling led to rioting and in **1922 the British protec-**

torate over Egypt was ended by the agreement of both sides. British influence remained as did British forces guarding the Suez Canal.

Sudan

When the British took over the government of Egypt, the Sudan was an Egyptian province. The territory had been misruled and was in the middle of violent upheavals caused by the **Mahdi.** A Moslem mystic and prophet, the Mahdi and his fanatical followers had swept aside Egyptian troops. In 1883 he defeated an Egyptian army under a British commander, Colonel Hicks, at El Obeid and threatened the Sudanese capital, Khartoum. The British government under Gladstone rejected sending a British army against the Mahdi, a course of action which was regarded as costly and unnecessary. Gladstone decided to abandon the desert province to the Mahdists but mindful of duty to the Europeans and Egyptians in Khartoum sent **General Gordon** to the city with instructions to evacuate these people. Gordon, a popular hero who had earlier played a vigorous part in the suppression of slavery in the Sudan, found the task of withdrawing from Khartoum distasteful to his principles. He stayed on, organized the city's defence and faced a siege by the Mahdi. His stubbornness won much approval in Britain where he was portrayed as a champion, defending the Sudan against barbarism. Angered by Gordon's disobedience, Gladstone succumbed to popular pressure and ordered a British force to march south through the Sudan and save Gordon. This force was too late; in January 1885 Khartoum fell and Gordon was slain. The British army withdrew to the Egyptian border and the wrath of the British people fell upon Gladstone who was held responsible for the *debâcle*.

The Mahdi died shortly after Khartoum fell and under his successor, the Khalifa, the Sudan was plunged into war and famine. British concern over the area was aroused again in 1896 after the disastrous defeat of an Italian army in Ethiopia. Such a setback to European arms could not go unavenged and Lord Salisbury's government sanctioned an Anglo-Egyptian expedition to conquer the Sudan. This army, under **Lord Kitchener,** advanced parallel to the Nile and in 1898 totally defeated the Khalifa's forces at **Omdurman.** The Sudan passed into Anglo-Egyptian control.

Palestine

The end of the First World War in 1918 saw large areas of the Middle East in the hands of Britain and her allies against the

Turks. The problem of the future of these ex-Turkish territories was an awkward one but by 1922 **Britain was granted a mandate for the Arab kingdoms of Jordan and Iraq**. Both were Arab states with Arab rulers and after assistance from Britain were able to establish their own governments. **Palestine was a more difficult problem since its population was mixed**. In the two decades before 1918, Jewish settlers had arrived in Palestine, inspired by Zionist ideals. In 1917 before the Turks had been driven from Palestine, the British government had issued the **Balfour Declaration** which recognised and encouraged the Jews to regard Palestine as 'a national homeland'. In 1922 one-ninth of the population was Jewish and as a result of immigration this proportion had risen to one-fifth by 1936. The effects of Nazi persecution in the 1930s added to the number of Jews who wished to settle in Palestine. The **Arab inhabitants became increasingly hostile to** this influx. The General Moslem League, formed in 1922, demanded Arab self-government along the lines which had been promised to Iraq and neighbouring Jordan. **Friction between Arabs and Jewish settlers grew stronger, flared into occasional violence and, in 1936, led to a full-scale Arab revolt.**

Britain by international agreement, had been given the mandate for Palestine in 1923 and was responsible for its government and political future. Various schemes were proposed for the political settlement of Palestine but none met the approval of both sides. A Royal Commission Report of 1937 suggested that the state should be divided into self-governing Arab and Jewish territories but Arab opinion was hostile. The Arabs argued that earlier treaties, made during the war, guaranteed the area as Arab and that provision for a Jewish homeland did not mean the establishment of a Jewish state. **Unrest and tension continued until 1939 when no solution had been found.**

South Africa, 1815–1939

Introduction

In **1815** and in accordance with the terms of the Congress of Vienna, **the British government took control of Cape Colony**. British occupation had been intended to secure the naval base of Cape Town, which safeguarded the sea-routes to India. The arrival of the British in this area began a three-cornered and often violent conflict of ambitions between them, the Boers and the Black Africans which has not yet been finally resolved.

British and Boers, 1815–1881

The Boers of the Cape Colony were the descendants of Dutch emigrants who had arrived in the seventeenth century. They were an independent people, believers in a stern Calvinist religion which taught them that they were a 'Chosen People' like the Israelites of the Old Testament. Their way of life was farming. Their idea was one in which the farmer, his family, servants and slaves lived in semi-isolation on a farm of at least 6,000 acres.

The Boers had little use or love for governments and they soon learned to loathe the British. They regarded Africans as a subject people, fit for slavery like the 'hewers of wood and drawers of water' of the Bible. The British administrators' humanitarian ideas then common in Britain had claimed equality before the law, actually hanging Boers for the killing of Africans. **Friction between Boers and British came to a climax when slavery was abolished within the British Empire in 1833.** The Boers saw no reason whatsoever for this move and were further incensed when they received little or none of the compensation which had been promised. The ending of slavery was the final blow and the Boers concluded that they must leave British ruled land in order to preserve their way of life. The **Great Trek** as the mass migration was called began in 1836 and Boers, their families and servants moved eastwards in great convoys of ox driven wagons.

At first the **British had no wish to give up control over the Boers and in 1842 annexed Natal,** the eastern coastal area where the Boers had settled. **This provoked the Boers to move again, this time northwards to the inland plain – the Veldt – and the lands which became known as the Orange Free State** (nominally annexed by the British in 1848) and the **Transvaal.** Whilst the authorities in Cape Colony were anxious to keep power over the Boers, the political mood of the Whig administrations in Britain regarded annexation and occupation of land in southern Africa as unnecessary and wasteful. If the Boers wished to go, then they should not be hindered. This thinking meant that the British gave up responsibility for them. In 1852 the **Sand River Convention** agreed that the Boers had control over vaguely defined lands in the South African hinterland and in 1854 the British surrendered sovereignty over the Orange Free State at the **Bloemfontein Convention.**

The Boers were left with their own self-governing republics, the Orange Free State and the Transvaal. Their migrations had, however disturbed the balance of native peoples and in the 1870s relations between Transvaalers and their neighbours the Zulus deteriorated to a stage when war seemed likely.

The Zulu and First Boer Wars

The **Transvaal** was **vulnerable to a Zulu invasion** from the north east and its ramshackle government was incapable of meeting the threat. This situation worried British officials in Natal and in 1877 **Theophilus Shepstone,** with a handful of police, formally **annexed the Transvaal** as an emergency measure. The problem of Zulu aggressiveness remained (the Boers had raided Zulu lands for slaves). It was the tradition of the **Zulus,** a brave and warlike race which was well organised in peace and war, that young warriors 'washed their spears' in blood before marriage. Aware of this and the likelihood that the washing might take place in the Transvaal, the British tried to impose terms on the Zulu king, Cetewayo. He refused and war began in 1879. The **Zulu War** opened disastrously for the British. A column of over 900 Imperial troops was all but annihilated at **Isandlwana** where Zulus with assegais and spears beat rifle armed forces. Nearby at **Rorke's Drift** over a hundred men of the 24th Regiment broke a force of several thousand Zulus in a heroic defence which led to the award of eleven Victoria Crosses. The war was soon over with an overwhelming **British victory at Ulundi and Zululand was brought under British rule.**

The emergency which had led to the annexation of the Transvaal had ended and the **Boers, suspicious of annexation, began to demand independence.** Fighting broke out in 1880 and a British force was defeated at Majuba Hill. Gladstone's newly elected Liberal government, deeply opposed to Imperial adventures, conceded Boer demands, The **Pretoria Convention** of 1881 gave the Transvaal independence although the British were granted 'suzerainty', a vague word which suggested overlordship.

Origins of the Second Boer War

From 1881 to the outbreak of the second Boer war in 1899, South Africa was dominated by the ambitions of two men, Cecil Rhodes, politician and businessman, and **Paul Kruger, President of the Transvaal.**

Rhodes, the son of an English clergyman, had emigrated to South Africa in 1871 and for several years he worked on the diamond fields of Natal. In this time he founded a business empire which grew steadily until 1880 when he established the De Beers Corporation. By 1888 Rhodes was one of the richest men in the world. He was an Imperialist and intended to **devote his wealth to the expansion of British power.** In 1877 he stated that he wished his money to be employed for 'the occupation by British settlers of the entire Continent of Africa'. Four years later he entered the Cape Colony Parliament and began the fulfilment of his dreams. First of these was a railway, which would run from Cape Town north to Cairo, never leaving British territory. In pursuit of this Cape to Cairo railway, Rhodes was instrumental in the **annexation of Bechuanaland** (now Botswana) in 1884–5, and in **1889 he founded the British South Africa Company,** which was chartered by the British government for the purposes of European settlement and development in the lands to the north of Bechuanaland. In 1890 the settlers moved north into these lands and Rhodes made treaties with Lobengula, the chief of the dominant Matabele tribe. The land which the settlers entered would soon be called **Rhodesia,** after Rhodes.

The occupation of Bechuanaland and Rhodesia extended British influence to the north of the Transvaal and Orange Free State, and therefore prevented Boer expansion. By the early 1890s the two Boer republics were cut off from the sea, and all but surrounded by land controlled by Britain and Rhodes' company.

Kruger and the Uitlanders
Whilst British power spread in southern Africa, the social, economic and political life of the Transvaal had been changed after the **discovery of gold in 1886.** The gold mines of the Witwatersrand drew in thousands of fortune seekers and miners; so many that in a few years the native Boers were outnumbered by over three to one. The newcomers or **Uitlanders,** as the Boers called them were, for the greater part, a vulgar roistering crew and were regarded with disdain by the simple, godly Boers. Paul Kruger, while sharing his people's loathing for the Uitlanders, welcomed the profits which came from the mining. With this money, Kruger purchased arms from Germany and strengthened the Transvaal. It now seemed that the **Boers were capable of challenging Britain's supremacy in South Africa.**

The Uitlanders of the Transvaal had no vote and Kruger had no intention of letting them have it. If they voted, the Uitlanders would easily have swamped the Boers and possibly supported some union with Britain. In 1895 the Johannesburg Uitlanders laid a plot, conspiring with Cecil Rhodes to cause an uprising to topple Kruger. The rebels would be supported by troops raised from British South Africa Company employees in Bechuanaland and led by Dr. Jameson, an employee of Rhodes. The **Jameson Raid** of 1896 was a dismal failure; the Uitlanders did not rise and Jameson's men surrendered. Kruger was now certain of Britain's hostility and he was congratulated by Kaiser Wilhelm of Germany **(the Kaiser's Telegram).** Rhodes was discredited and there were suspicions that Chamberlain, the Colonial Secretary, was party to the conspiracy. From 1896 to 1899 relations between Britain and Boers worsened.

Chamberlain, having survived the Jameson scandal, was **anxious to halt the growth of Boer power** and with the willing help of **Lord Milner,** governor of Cape Colony and High Commissioner in South Africa, **took up the Uitlander's cause.** Milner pressed Kruger to give political power to the Uitlanders but discussions broke down; Kruger observed to Milner, 'It is our country that you want'. **Determined to fight for their independence and anticipate the British, the Transvaal and Orange Free State declared war in October 1899.**

The Boer War, 1899–1902
The Boers were sturdy fighters and excellent marksmen with their Mauser rifles. Their fighting forces or Kommandos moved swiftly on horseback and knew the countryside well. In 1899 several Kommandos invaded Natal and Cape Colony and laid siege to **Ladysmith** and **Mafeking,** hoping that Boers in these areas would join them. In 'Black Week' (December 1899) three British armies were defeated at the **Tugela River, Magersfontein** and **Colenso,** much to the horror and astonishment of Britain. **Reinforcements** from Britain and the Dominions of Canada, New Zealand and Australia **poured into South Africa** and the increased forces, commanded by Field Marshall **Roberts** and General **Kitchener** soon got the upper hand. In 1900 the Boer General Cronje surrendered at **Paardeburg** and the Boer capitals of Pretoria and Bloemfontein were taken. **The Orange Free State and Transvaal were annexed. Boer resistance persisted.** Using their knowledge of the open countryside, Boer Kommandos fought a guerilla war for the next two years. To overcome this dogged resistance, **the British were forced to take stern measures.** Blockhouses were scattered over the open Veldt, miles of barbed wire fences parcelled up the countryside

and the farms of men who fought were burnt down. Women and families were moved to camps where diseases spread rapidly, killing one in six of the inmates. Such methods aroused harsh criticism from Liberals at home and newspapers and politicians in Europe.

Peace and Results
In March 1902 peace was signed at Vereeniging. All Boers surrendered and swore allegiance to Edward VII. To rebuild and

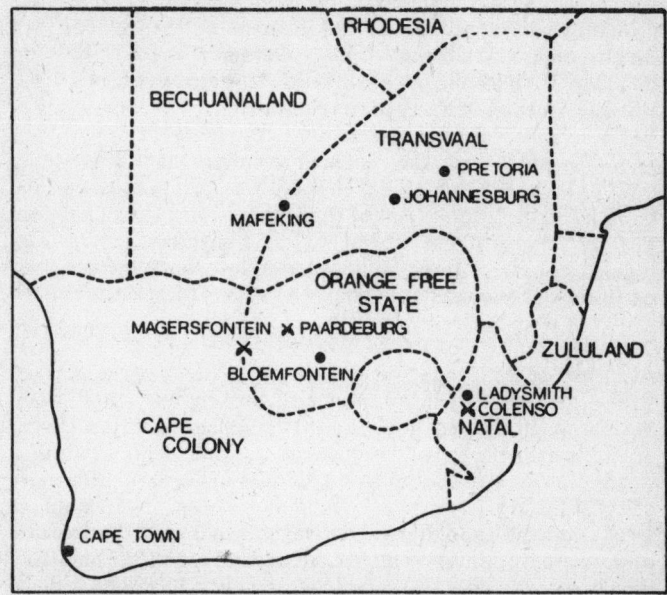

Figure 2. South Africa, 1899–1902

restock farms, the British government advanced £3 million and the **Boers were promised eventual self-government under the British crown.** This came sooner than expected in 1906, after the Liberal party's election victory. The Orange Free State and Transvaal were given self-government, and in **1910** joined with the Natal and Cape Colony to form the **Union of South Africa.** In 1902 and later, when self-government was discussed, the question was raised as to whether the black South Africans should be able to vote. This the Boers never wanted and the British prevaricated; the question has never been solved.

The Dominions; Canada, Australia and New Zealand

By 1900, when they rallied round and sent troops to fight in the Imperial army in South Africa, these three nations, settled by British people in the past century, were all self-governing dominions under the crown. They had reached this position as a result of a number of peaceful changes which reflected the wishes of their own people and the British government.

Canada was the first colonial territory to become a self-governing dominion. In 1815 Canada had been split into Upper and Lower Canada, each with its own elected government. Quarrels between the two areas and a breakdown in government led to rioting and disorder in 1836 and in 1838 **Lord Durham** was sent by the British government to report on the situation. His report (see p. 91) formed the basis for Canada's future. The old provinces were abolished and in their place smaller provincial assemblies were set up for Ontario, Nova Scotia, New Brunswick and Quebec. The **British North America Act of 1867** established a Confederation. The British crown was represented by a governor general who ruled through a cabinet of ministers drawn from the majority party in the Canadian Parliament. This system formed the pattern for other dominion governments.

Australia in 1815 was still regarded as a dumping ground for British convicts. Convicts continued to be sent until 1868, when the British government finally ended the system, largely as a result of Australian pressure. Throughout the nineteenth century a steady flow of British immigrants settled in Australia drawn by **sheep-farming** (there were 16 million sheep in Australia in 1850) and the **gold fields. Representative and democratic government followed settlement** and between 1855 and 1859 the settled provinces were granted assemblies. In **1901 a federal government** was established at Canberra to handle, as in the Canadian model, affairs of national importance.

New Zealand had come **under British sovereignty in 1840.** The British annexation was followed by the arrival of settlers which provoked a series of intermittent **Maori Wars** with the natives, which ended in 1872. A constitutional Act of 1852 established representative government with provincial councils. In 1875 the provincial councils were replaced by county councils, concerned with local affairs whilst the elected central government in Auckland handled national business. By 1890 the New Zealand government had anticipated the British and introduced welfare legislation which provided for medical services, Old Age Pensions and national insurance. Not only was British democracy extended to lands settled by the British, but the settlers were able to lead the way in reforms.

Conclusions

The expansion of the Empire was one of the major features of the nineteenth century. Britain had passed from being a major trading power in 1815 to the world's greatest Imperial power in 1914. Trade, political and military necessity, prestige and settlement had all played their part in bringing this about. In areas settled by British people, British political systems of representative government had followed and, by 1939, there were signs that India too would be granted responsible government.

Chapter 9
Conservatives and Liberals, 1886–1914

Introduction

The end of the nineteenth and beginning of the twentieth centuries was a period of crisis and insecurity in Britain. Political life was troubled with problems which seemed beyond the power of men to solve and which often led to violence. **Ireland haunted British politicians and added bitterness to political life** (see pps. 84–85) and **Trade Unions,** defending and advancing the interests of the working classes, **found themselves in conflict with both employers and government.** The **reforming measures of the Liberal government in 1909 contributed further turmoil and led to a struggle between the House of Commons and the Lords. Abroad the security of the growing Empire was not great enough to prevent Britain from seeking the friendship of France and re-building her navy to meet the threat from Germany** (see pps. 131 and 133).

The **root cause of Britain's political problems** in this period was **economic. British industry was not growing** and British businessmen were **losing foreign markets to competitors** such as Germany and the United States. From 1873 to 1898 there was a long depression, which was followed by a recovery and, from 1910 to 1914, a brief boom. The apparent recovery of British industry at the beginning of the century could not obscure or remove long-term trends. Britain was less competitive than she had been and her industry was less able than her rivals to adapt to new technology and methods. The modernization of industry required money and this was not available. For some time British investors had preferred to invest money abroad in foreign industries which often offered a better return on money. The Trade Unions were often hostile to innovations, which they regarded as threats to their members' jobs. Comparing British industrial expansion with that in the United States and Germany, a French historian remarked 'Neither Carnegie nor Krupp had to deal with trade unions'. At the same time British management did not show the ingenuity or willingness to take risks which characterized such men as the American industrialist, Carnegie. The working classes suffered from industrial stagnation. Up to 1900 prices had fallen and so the value of wages went up, if only slightly. The following recovery boom did not see wages rise and the conditions of the workers did not improve. It was only natural that the workers pressed their claim to share in industrial prosperity. Stagnation created unemployment. In the 1850s this had been less than 5% but during the years of depression it had risen to over 7%. One answer was emigration and between 1880 and 1914 over 7 million, mostly aged between 18 and 30, left Britain. **A stagnant industry, a declining workforce and a working class anxious to improve its wages were the underlying features of British life at the beginning of the century.**

Social Reform

A by-product of industrial depression was poverty. During the 1890s a number of carefully conducted surveys of working class life were made and reports produced. In 1899 **Charles Booth** produced *Life and Labour of the People in London* and in 1901 **Seebohm Rowntree** published *Poverty: A study in Town Life* which was the result of his enquiries in York. Rowntree concluded that over 40% of the working class were living in conditions of poverty, that is were unable to pay for the bare necessities of life from their wages. Alongside poor or inadequate diet, many working people suffered from living in wretched and unhealthy housing. These disturbing findings were confirmed by the statistics produced by the Army in 1903 which revealed that just over a third of recruits for military service were medically unfit.

Politicians and Social Reform

The extent of the problem (sometimes known as 'the condition of the people') was known, but the question remained as to what was to be done. The electoral reforms of 1885 had given the vote to nearly all working men, who were now in a position to make their influence felt upon political life. Some politicians had quickly realized the need for widespread social reform. The most important of these was **Joseph Chamberlain** who hoped that social reform would be carried out by the Liberal party. After he broke with the Liberals in 1886 when he refused to support Irish Home Rule (see pp. 82–3), **Chamberlain and his 'Unionists' joined the Conservatives.** Inside the Conservative Party his schemes met with suspicion, and in 1895 he chose to channel his energies into Imperialism when he became **Colonial Secretary.** The Liberals under Gladstone remained fixed in their purpose of giving Home Rule to Ireland, which Gladstone argued was necessary before turning to domestic reform. Between Gladstone's resignation in 1894 and the Liberal election victory of 1906, the party was divided. The Liberal Ministry of 1906–14 was able to face and

113

tackle social reform in a drastic manner. By this time a new force, the Labour Party, had emerged, and from 1903 it was in alliance with the Liberals. The **Labour Party** promised far-reaching reforms which would directly benefit working people. It aimed at the redistribution of wealth which would both stimulate the home market for manufactured goods by putting more money in the pockets of the working class and alleviate poverty (see pps. 156–162). When arguing for social reform Chamberlain had warned of the dangers of 'class politics', which he thought would lead to bitter divisions in society and a government which acted for one class rather than the whole country. This had come about at the beginning of the century.

The problems of British economic and social conditions not only played a part in the creation of a new political party, they contributed to the break-up of an old one, the Conservatives. **In 1903 Chamberlain had proposed an end to Free Trade.** In its place would be taxes on foreign imports and Imperial Preference, which meant, in effect, that goods from the Empire would pay no import duties. This, said Chamberlain, would speed economic recovery and provide cash for social reform. Chamberlain's ideas were a bombshell. They split the Conservatives and helped unite the Liberals round their old slogan 'Free Trade'. In conclusion the background of political life between 1886 and 1914 was one of uncertainty and upheaval. In Ireland unrest continued and the demand for Home Rule was as strong as ever (see p. 85), in Europe there was an arms race and uneasy peace between the great powers (see pps. 133–4) and in Britain there were the consequences of economic recession and a falling share of world trade.

Salisbury's first Ministry, 1886–92

Lord Salisbury was mainly interested in and concerned with foreign and Imperial policy (see pps. 130–32). He did not care for reform, except when it was unavoidable and necessary. **The resignation in 1886 of Lord Randolph Churchill meant the loss of one Conservative politician with a passionate interest in social reform.** The domestic achievements of the Conservatives were therefore limited. The **Local Government Act (1888)** introduced 62 county councils into England and Wales. 61 boroughs with over 50,000 inhabitants became county boroughs with their own councils, and a separate council, the London County Council, looked after London and much of the surrounding suburbs. The new authorities were given the power to collect rates for various aspects of local administration and were controlled by councillors elected for three years. In **1891 fees for elementary school children were abolished** and the employment of children under 11 was made illegal.

Gladstone's Fourth Ministry, 1892–5

In 1891 the Liberals had produced the **Newcastle Programme** in which they promised the electorate a series of reforms which appealed to non-conformists, the working class and Trade Unionists. First and foremost in this programme was Home Rule for Ireland, which Gladstone introduced in 1893 (see p. 83) but which was rejected by the House of Lords. Shortly after Gladstone resigned (over the issue of increased naval expenditure) and his place was taken by Lord Rosebery. In 1894 **Sir William Harcourt**, the Chancellor of the Exchequer, introduced **Death Duties,** taxes on inherited wealth. They were not seen as a means of redistributing wealth but as a measure to raise funds for new warships.

The Liberal party's promised reforms did not appear, largely because of opposition from the almost entirely Conservative House of Lords. The Liberal party was divided between those who wanted sweeping reforms and those who were more cautious. Some Liberals were hostile to Imperialism (see p. 94), others like Rosebery favoured Imperial expansion. A divided party, which had not fulfilled its promises, was defeated in the 1895 General Election.

Salisbury's Second Ministry, 1895–1902

The Conservatives received an overwhelming victory in the 1895 election. They received 340 seats in the House of Commons and the support of 71 Unionists, followers of Chamberlain against 177 Liberals and 82 Irish. **The Conservatives benefited from their association with Imperialism and patriotism and their alliance with Chamberlain.** The radical Chamberlain had always enjoyed a widespread popularity with the working class and his supporters hoped that his influence would force the Conservatives to follow policies of social reform. They were largely unsatisfied for Chamberlain took the office of Colonial Secretary and concentrated on Imperial policies. Chamberlain had always been an outsider in politics; he was a non-conformist in a Church

115

of England party and a businessman in a party dominated by country gentlemen and aristocrats. The **Workman's Compensation Act (1897)** was one result of Chamberlain's influence. By its terms workmen were to be given cash compensation for injuries they received whilst working.

The **government's energies** during this ministry were **largely directed towards South Africa and the Boer War** (see pps. 105–9). In 1900 they were re-elected with a handsome majority in what was called **'the Khaki election'** in which the Conservatives presented themselves as the patriotic, Imperial party. The Liberals were disunited, some favouring the war, others, like Lloyd George, condemning the war. The election victory of 1900 suggested that the Conservatives were set to remain in power for many years to come, at least as long as their opponents were divided over policy. In **1902 Salisbury resigned** and his place as Prime Minister was taken by his nephew, **Arthur Balfour.**

Balfour's Ministry and Tariff Reform, 1902–5

Arthur Balfour, a highly intelligent bachelor, had been Secretary for Ireland in the 1886–92 Ministry and was a shrewd and able politician. His ministry was one of misfortunes for his party and paved the way for the sweeping Liberal victory of 1906.

The scientific and technical advances made by Britain's commercial rivals had increasingly become a cause of concern in Britain. One product of this concern was the **Education Act of 1902** which had as its objective the improvement of standards within British schools. The Act abolished all the old school boards and placed control of education in the hands of county or borough councils. These authorities had power to establish secondary and technical schools, to be paid for from the rates and from a government grant. The voluntary religious schools were also placed under public control and were to receive grants from the rates. This last measure raised a storm of anger from the non-conformists who protested that rate-payers' money would be used to pay for Church of England schools. Since most of these schools were Church of England schools, the non-conformists had a case and several went to prison rather than pay rates.

Tariff Reform
In 1902–3 **Chamberlain** had visited South Africa and he returned enthusiastic for a new cause, **Tariff Reform.** His Birmingham

Speech (1903) which outlined his new ideas was intended to challenge the old faith in Free Trade and prepare the way for a new commercial policy which would boost Britain's ailing industry. Chamberlain proposed duties (tariffs) on foreign goods entering Britain. This would protect British industry from competition from the United States and Germany and stop the 'dumping' of cheaply produced foreign manufactures in Britain. There would be no tariffs on goods or raw materials from the Empire (Imperial Preference) and so Britain would create a Free Trade Area between herself and her Empire. This, Chamberlain argued, would lead to closer ties between the Empire and Britain and so help to create an 'Imperial Federation'. The money raised by duties on foreign goods would provide funds for a vast programme of social reform, including old-age pensions and medical care. To further this programme, Chamberlain founded the **Tariff Reform League.**

The immediate challenge to Chamberlain came from the **Liberals,** shocked at the assault on Free Trade, who **claimed that duties on foreign goods would mean a tax on food.** This too was feared by Balfour and many Conservatives. Chamberlain admitted that he would tax foreign food and his critics accused him of wishing to raise the cost of food. The **Conservatives were divided.** Some like Balfour, favoured limited duties on foreign goods but not on food, others followed Chamberlain and others, like Winston Churchill, stood by Free Trade and joined the Liberals. Chamberlain's campaign for tariff reform had led to the break-up of the Conservative party.

General Election, 1906

In December 1905 **Balfour resigned, unable to govern with a party divided against itself.** The Conservatives were unable to resist the propaganda of the Liberals. **For the first time in years the Liberals had become a united party.** The non-conformists were angry about the Education Act and temperance groups were opposed to a Licensing Act of 1904 which they thought favoured the brewers. There was widespread indignation over the use of Chinese coolies in South Africa which was turned into a crusade against the Conservatives. After the end of the Boer War in 1902 (see p. 109), great numbers of Chinese labourers had been brought into South Africa to help reconstruct the mines. The government's methods and tales of flogging led many to believe that the coolies were little more than slaves. Working men in

117

Britain wondered if the importing of cheap labour in Africa might be tried in Britain, and many felt angry that Chinese labourers had been given jobs which might easily have gone to emigrants from Britain.

The debate over Tariff Reform overshadowed all other issues. The Liberals loudly and frequently proclaimed that Tariff Reform would mean higher food prices; the Tories would tax the poor man's bread. To punch home this simple but effective point the Liberals produced a persuasive poster. On one side was a fat, large loaf with the label 'Free Trade Loaf' and on the other was a mean, thin loaf with the label 'Tariff Reform Loaf'. In reply, the Conservatives produced a poster in which a poor workman and his wife stared at a window full of cheap, imported foreign goods. The woman drew attention to their cheapness but the husband remarked that they had no money to buy them; in the background the unemployed march by and a queue waits outside the emigration office.

The Big Loaf won. **The Liberals swept back into power with their Labour allies.** The Tories were left with 157 seats, less than half those which they had had in the previous Parliament. Chamberlain had split his party and caused its defeat, but he had also converted it to Tariff Reform for most of the remaining Conservatives in Parliament were supporters of his ideas. After the election Chamberlain suffered a stroke and remained an invalid until his death in 1914. His beliefs in social reform had helped the Conservatives in 1895 and 1900 but in 1906 these ideas coupled with Tariff Reform had broken the party.

The Liberal Government, 1906–14

Introduction

The Liberal government which came to power after the landslide election victory of 1906 remained in power, thanks to Irish and Labour help, until the outbreak of war. In this time it helped prepare the armed forces for the forthcoming war, laid the foundations of the Welfare State, secured Irish Home Rule and reduced for ever the powers of the House of Lords. Few other governments have made so many sweeping changes in national life. Two successive **Prime Ministers, Sir Henry Campbell-Bannerman** (who resigned through poor health in 1908) and **H. H. Asquith** (who remained in power until 1916) led the Liberal Party and they were well-served by a number of talented ministers. Of these

118

the most outstanding was the Welshman, **David Lloyd George,** who was Secretary of the Board of Trade from 1906 to 1908 and afterwards Chancellor of the Exchequer. **Winston Churchill** also served in the Liberal cabinet at the Board of Trade and Admiralty. Foreign policy was in the hands of a Northumberland country gentleman, **Sir Edward Grey,** who cemented Britain's friendship with France and achieved a conciliation with Russia (see p. 132).

Reforms, 1906–9

The reforms of the Liberal government were almost entirely devoted towards the alleviation of suffering caused by poverty. In making these reforms, the Liberals encountered fierce opposition from the Conservatives, who were determined to use their majority in the House of Lords to frustrate some, but not all, of the Liberal schemes.

In **1906** the Liberals introduced **free school meals for the needy** (to be paid for from local rates) and **extended the Workman's Compensation Act to all industries.** In return for the co-operation of the Labour Party, the Liberals introduced the **Trades Dispute Act (1906).** This measure assisted the Trade Union movement which had suffered a considerable setback as a result of the **Taff Vale case** of 1901. Following a strike by members of the Amalgamated Union of Railway Servants, the Taff Vale Railway Company had sued the Union and claimed damages for the loss of trade. The courts held that the Union was responsible for damages caused by the strike and ordered it to pay £42,000 to the railway company. This judgement alarmed the Trade Union movement which now realised that each Union would have to pay for losses which resulted from a strike. Trade Unionist and Labour supporters demanded a change in the law but the Conservatives had refused. The Liberal **Trades Dispute Act meant that the Unions would not have to pay for losses which resulted from strikes by their members.** The **1908 Budget** introduced **Old Age Pensions** which were payable to those over 70 whose income was less than 8 shillings (40p) a week. A single person received 5 shillings (25p) weekly and a married couple 7 shillings and 6d (37.5p). Within a year over a million people were claiming these pensions. Old Age Pensions were the work of Lloyd George, and Flora Thompson remembers old people in north Oxfordshire, collecting their pensions from the village Post Office. They blessed 'Lord George' for they argued only a Lord could be so generous! Lloyd George's colleague,

Churchill, introduced the **Trade Boards Act (1909)** to control the wages of 'sweated' workers (those who worked long hours for short pay in such trades as clothing manufacture) and **Labour Exchanges** where the unemployed could register for work.

In spite of the old people of Oxfordshire blessing 'Lord George', the **House of Lords** was less than happy with the Liberal government and its measures. There were 602 hereditary peers (titled noblemen) in the Lords and more than half were Conservatives or Unionists. In **1893** they had **rejected Irish Home Rule** and in 1893-5 opposed other Liberal measures. In **1906 the Lords** had **destroyed a Liberal Education Bill** designed to satisfy the non-conformists. **A Licensing Bill and a Plural Voting Bill** (to prevent voters from having two votes) **were also turned down by the Lords.** The Lords frustrated the Liberals and did so with the encouragement and blessing of the Conservative leader, Balfour. (The attitude of the House of Lords earned it the title 'Mr. Balfour's poodle', a creature which obeyed its master).

Lloyd George's Budget, 1909

Lloyd George's Budget of 1909 was the cause of the major clash between the Liberals and the House of Lords and led the way to the Parliament Act (1910) which limited the power of the Lords. In 1909 Lloyd George had to find an extra £16,000,000 in taxes in order to pay for the building of more battleships, the reorganization of the Army and Old Age Pensions. To get this additional money, **Lloyd George increased existing taxes and created new ones.** It was Lloyd George's plan that the weight of **the new and extra taxes would fall upon the rich.** Income tax on money from shares and rents went up, and Death Duties were raised. A new form of income tax, called 'Supertax', was imposed on incomes of over £3,000 a year. The owners of land were made to pay other new taxes. Where landowners received income from coal, iron or other minerals found on their land, this revenue (or royalties) would be taxed. When the value of land worth over £5,000 increased and the land was sold at a profit, 20% of that profit would be paid to the government. There were also new taxes on cars and petrol which were designed to pay for the costs of road improvement. The Liberals greeted these new taxes with delight and described Lloyd George's Budget as the 'People's Budget'.

The Conservatives were less happy and called the Budget a socialist measure and 'theft'. **By tradition the House of Lords always passed the Budget** and Balfour advised his supporters there to let Lloyd George's Budget through. They did not and by 300 votes to 75 **the Budget was rejected.** The battle lines were now drawn for the struggle between the Liberals and the House of Lords. **For Lloyd George it was a battle between the people and the peers, a fight between the rich and the poor.** Speaking at Limehouse in 1909, he told his audience of London East-enders of his recent visit to a coal mine. He described the horrors underground and of how in a mine close to the one he had inspected, over a hundred miners had died in an explosion. He turned, in fury, to the House of Lords.

'And yet when the Prime Minister and I knock at the door of these great landlords and say to them – "Here, you know these poor fellows who have been digging up royalties at the risk of their lives, some of them are old, they have survived the perils of their trade, they are broken, they can earn no more. Won't you give them something towards keeping them out of the workhouse?" – they scowl at us and we say – "Only a ha'penny, just a copper." They say, "You thieves!" And they turn their dogs on to us, and you can hear them bark every morning.'

Parliament Act, 1911

The Lords' refusal to pass the Budget forced Asquith to call a **General Election so that the opinion of the country could be known. The January 1910 election** gave the Liberals 275 seats, Labour 40, Irish 82 and Conservatives 273. With Irish and Labour help, the Liberals were still in a majority. With the backing of Labour and Irish M.Ps, the Liberals introduced a **Parliament bill.** The Lords would no longer be able to turn down the Budget but would have to pass all Finance Bills. If a bill had passed the House of Commons three times, then the Lords could only delay it for two years, after which it would become law. Parliaments would last for five years instead of seven. **The Lords,** after the General Election, **had passed Lloyd George's Budget, but they were unwilling to pass the Parliament Bill.** King Edward VII (who died in May 1910) and his son, George V, tried skilfully to get the leaders on both sides to compromise. They would not. The 'diehard' Lords led by Lord Curzon (an ex-viceroy of India) and Lord Wylloughby de Broke refused to give way. Asquith asked King George to create 250 Liberal peers to make certain that the bill was passed.

At the King's suggestion a **General Election was held in December 1910.** The result of this second election was that **the Liberals and their allies had a 42 seat majority.** Threatened by the creation of a mass of new lords, the 'diehards' in the Lords reluctantly gave way. **The Parliament Act became law in 1911.**

The result of the struggle between the Liberals and the Lords was the reduction and limitation of the powers of the House of Lords. **The Liberals had to pay the price of Irish support,** without which they would not have won, and introduce a Home Rule Bill in the following year (see p. 84).

Liberal Reforms, 1911–14

The victory over the Lords meant that the Liberals were free to press ahead with their reform programme. The **1911 National Insurance Act,** devised in imitation of a scheme which had been followed in Germany for thirty years, aimed to help the poor and unemployed. It was the work of Lloyd George and offered free medical treatment and medicines as well as weekly pay whilst absent from work to working men (but not their families). To pay for this a workman paid 4d (2p) a week, his employer 3d (1.5p) and the government 2d (1p). Workers in engineering, shipbuilding and building were given unemployment pay if and when they were laid off work. The administration of this scheme was in the hands of insurance companies and friendly societies. This Act, together with Old Age Pensions, began the Welfare State. By tackling poverty in old age and the fears of sickness and unemployment (the poor could not afford to be ill), a start had been made, if a small one, to remove some of the miseries of the poor.

The Liberals also gave assistance to their allies, the Labour Party. This had suffered as a result of the **Osborne Judgement (1910)** in which the senior judges (the Law Lords) had claimed that it was unlawful for Union funds to be used to help the Labour Party. Since the Labour Party leaned heavily on money from friendly Trade Unions, they were going to be short of money. The **payment of M.Ps was introduced in 1911** and gave M.Ps a salary of £200 a year, which helped make it possible for working men to remain in the House of Commons. The **Trade Union Act of 1913** permitted Unions to use their funds for political purposes although individual Trade Unionists were allowed to 'contract out'. This meant that they could if they wished, refuse permission for their payments to be used as contributions to Labour Party funds.

Army Reform

The poor showing of the British army during the first stage of the Boer War and the fears of the growing instability in Europe, made the British government conscious of the need to re-organize the army. The work was in the hands of **R. B. Haldane,** Secretary for War, who produced his plans during 1907–8. An **Expeditionary Force** of 160,000 men **(later called the British Expeditionary Force or B.E.F.)** was created for possible use in Europe at short notice. A volunteer force of part-time, trained men was brought into being to be ready for full-time service in an emergency. This force was known as **The Territorial Army** (or popularly as the 'Terriers') and stood at 276,000 men in 1910. Officers Training Corps (1906) and a General Staff, prepared for co-ordination and direction of armies in the field, was also created. The battledress of the British army was changed to **khaki** (an Indian word meaning muddy) which was an effective camouflage. **Khaki** had been worn in India and South Africa for some time and the famous scarlet coat had last been worn in battle in 1885. Haldane's changes meant that the Army was ready to fight on the Continent if the need arose.

Trade Unions, 1910–13

The years immediately before the outbreak of the First World War saw a short revival of trade which coincided with an upsurge of **Trade Union militancy.** The boom in industry was not matched by any wage increases and the Unions, anxious to press their members' claims with vigour, turned to strikes. The Unions involved, the **Transport Workers** (who included dockers), **Miners and Railwaymen** were capable of paralysing the country and in these years they came to appreciate fully their power. Late in 1913 under the direction of the Miner's leader, Robert Smillie, the three unions agreed to form the **Triple Alliance** which would work together and, when necessary, strike together. Through the nationwide strike, such as that of the Miners in 1912 which lasted for five weeks, the Unions came to appreciate their strength and ability to put pressure on the country and government. The government did its best to arbitrate between employers and Unions and when required, to send troops to areas where public order was threatened. The war intervened and temporarily halted the growth of Union militancy, but it would re-appear in the 1920s.

Conclusion

The Liberal government of 1906–14 had made considerable progress in dealing with the problems of poverty and insecurity among the poor. It had begun a process by which the government took on responsibility for the basic standard of living of the poorest members of the community. This would be continued after the war by both Conservative and Labour administrations. The Liberals had also defended and upheld the supremacy of the elected House of Commons over the House of Lords through the Parliament Act. They had placed the army and navy in readiness for the European conflict which began in 1914. As a price of their survival and success they had granted Home Rule to Ireland and made concessions to the Labour Party and Trade Unions.

Chapter 10
Foreign Affairs, 1865–1914

Introduction

In 1865, the year of Palmerston's death, Britain was still 'the workshop of the world', a great manufacturing and trading power with world-wide interests. The security of Britain and the protection of her vast international trade were guaranteed by the Royal Navy. During the next thirty years Britain increased her overseas possessions and became the world's greatest Imperial power, drawing strength and authority from the ownership of her Empire. The gaining of overseas territories and in particular Britain's joining for the 'scramble for Africa' led her to clash with other powers such as France. For a time Britain remained aloof from Europe and kept up what, in the 1890s was called 'splendid isolation' but by 1900 this attitude was seen to be dangerous and unrealistic. So in the years leading to the outbreak of war in 1914, Britain attached herself to one of the two European alliance systems, that between Russia and France.

This was a **period in which Europe changed dramatically**. In 1866 the army of Prussia defeated the Austrians at Sadowa and made the way clear for Bismarck, the Prussian chancellor, to unite the states of northern Germany. In the Franco-Prussian War of 1870–71 France was crushingly and decisively beaten by Prussia and her allies and the new German Empire was founded. The old pattern of European states was completely changed. France, hitherto the first military power in Europe (or so she claimed), was humiliated and left with a burning desire for revenge. A new state, the German Empire, had come into being with a population of 41 millions and a rapidly expanding industrial output. Germany, under Chancellor Bismarck, now dominated the affairs of Europe whilst France and Austria took second place. Bismarck wanted order and stability in Europe, the isolation of France and a period of peace in which the new Germany could grow in economic strength. To this end he set up the Dreikaiserbund (League of Three Emperors) in which the Emperors of Austria, Russia and Germany agreed to consult each other and settle their differences peacefully.

Britain had played no part in these events. She had all but turned her back on Europe. There were politicians, especially in the Liberal Party who argued that Britain should keep clear of European affairs which were of little concern to her. Thanks to Free Trade and the strongest navy in the world, Britain could safely keep herself aloof from European problems. The holders of such views were sometimes called 'Little Englanders'. They also felt that Britain should keep clear of Imperial adventures which cost money and often lives. John Bright, a Liberal M.P. and staunch 'Little Englander', warned that if Britain followed the policy of Imperial expansion she would go the way of the 'conquering Roman Empire' towards eventual destruction and ruin. **Gladstone's foreign policy during his first ministry (1868–74)** followed Little Englander lines. In 1870 his government did not object when Russia broke the Black Sea clauses of the Treaty of Paris and introduced warships into the Black Sea. He allowed the claims of the United States government for damages done by the Confederate warship Alabama to be settled by an international court and in 1872 paid up the £2,000,000 which had been agreed as damages.

If Gladstone was willing to take a 'back seat' in international politics, **Disraeli, the Conservative leader, favoured a more active policy.** Speaking in 1872 at the Crystal Palace, Disraeli asked his audience if they wished Britain to 'be a great country, an Imperial country, a country where your sons, when they rise, rise to paramount positions, and obtain not merely the esteem of their countrymen but command the respect of the world.' Two years later in 1874 Disraeli became Prime Minister and was free to promote policies which asserted British power in Europe and added to the Empire. From this time on, **the Conservatives stood for Imperialism and an active, forward foreign policy.**

The Eastern Question, 1875–78

Disraeli was anxious to show that Britain was a force to be reckoned with in European affairs. He was mistrustful of the way in which Europe had come to be dominated by Germany, Austria and Russia through the Dreikaiserbund. Disraeli's chance to demonstrate Britain's authority came in 1875 with the revival of the **Eastern Question.** He followed Palmerston and based his policy on the belief that the security of the Turkish Empire was essential for the protection of India. He claimed that 'Constantinople is the key to India' and was determined to uphold the Turkish empire against all comers and in particular Russia.

The crisis in the **Near East began in 1875** with a rebellion in the Turkish Balkan province of Hercegovina which spread to neighbouring lands. The Austrian foreign minister, Count Andrassy consulted with his German and Russian colleagues and sent a note (the Vienna or Andrassy note) to the Turkish government which suggested reform. Disraeli immediately announced that Britain regarded Turkish affairs as of direct concern to her and wished, in the future, to be consulted over them. Disraeli agreed with the first note but when the three powers sent a second and stronger note (the Berlin Memorandum, 1876) to the Turks, he called it bullying. To show his concern he ordered a squadron of **British warships to Besika Bay, close to Constantinople. Britain was now openly committed to backing Turkey against the three major powers of Europe.** Disraeli suspected, with some justification that Austria and Russia may have been anxious to profit by Turkish embarrassment and annex her territories. The revolt in the Balkans had spread during 1876 and involved a rebellion in the Turkish province of Bulgaria. The Turkish suppression of the uprising was typically brutal and cruel. News reached Britain and the rest of the world of the **Bulgarian atrocities** in which Turkish troops had killed over 12,000 men, women and children. There was an angry outcry in Britain, and **Gladstone** returned from retirement to whip up support for the persecuted Christians of the Balkans. His pamphlet, *The Bulgarian Horrors and the Question of the East*, sold 40,000 copies in a few days and the movement of support for the Balkan Christians became a national crusade. The answer to the Eastern Question was, in Gladstone's view, the breaking up of the savage and inhuman Turkish administration and its replacement by self-governing, free states. Disraeli, who had supported the Turks and ignored their cruelties, was embarrassed, but soon he was able to raise the Russian bogey for the Russian government was planning a war on behalf of the Balkan peoples.

In Russia a powerful and influential pressure group called the Pan-Slav movement had been pressing the Czar's government to go to war with Turkey on behalf of the suffering Christians in the Balkans. By the beginning of 1877 the **Russian government had been steamrollered into war.** To try and stop the war, a conference had been held at Constantinople where Lord Salisbury represented Britain, but the Turks would not compromise. In **April 1877 a Russian army invaded the Balkans.** The war went slowly for the Russians but by the beginning of 1878 they had overcome Turkish opposition, liberated large areas of the Balkans and had reached Adrianople on the shores of the Straits. **In Britain alarm and fear had been aroused by Russian aggression and wide areas of public opinion came round to Disraeli's view.** In **January 1878 British warships anchored off Constantinople** within sight of Russian troops and war fever was raging in Britain. Music-hall audiences sang, 'We don't want to fight but by Jingo if we do, we've got the ships, we've got the men and got the money too.' Russian success had frightened Austria who Disraeli gambled would support Britain if war broke out.

The crisis came to a head in March 1878 when Russia and Turkey signed the **Treaty of San Stefano.** This forced Turkey to hand over large areas of the Balkans which would be turned into an independent Bulgaria. In the eyes of both Britain and Austria, the new 'big' Bulgaria would be a puppet of Russia and a threat to both nations. British and Austrian hostility to the treaty increased the threat of a wider European war which Bismarck wished to avoid at all costs. He called the **Congress of Berlin (1878)** where the great powers could discuss the problem, negotiate and find a settlement. **Disraeli represented Britain** and the terms which obtained were described by him as 'peace with honour'. Bulgaria was reduced in size and territory returned to Turkey who promised reform, as was usual at such conferences. The provinces of Bosnia and Hercegovina were placed under Austrian rule which displeased their inhabitants and led to further serious problems in thirty years' time. Britain received the eastern Mediterranean island of **Cyprus** which strengthened her influence in the area. The Balkan nationalists had suffered a setback and uprisings and terrorism continued in the area.

Disraeli had, through his intervention in the Balkans, broken the understanding which had existed between Russia, Austria and Germany and showed that Britain was still a force to be reckoned with in Europe.

Isolation, 1879–1904

Britain had got its way at the Congress of Berlin and had, for a time, frustrated Russian ambitions in the Balkans. One result of the Congress was the creation of a system of alliances between the major European powers which divided Europe into two camps. In **1879 Germany and Austria-Hungary signed the Dual Alliance which in 1882 became the Triple Alliance when Italy** joined. The Triple Alliance powers agreed to fight together if attacked by Russia. **Russia,** to a large extent isolated by this alliance, turned to **France** and in 1892 signed the **Dual Alliance** with the French (it was only made public in 1897). Britain had no part in these two alliance systems. Her governments, both Conservative and Liberal, saw no advantage in tying Britain permanently to either of the groups. Yet whilst Britain was not part of the pattern of alliances, she was anxious to co-operate with members of the power blocs when it was in her interest to do so.

This was a period when the European powers were expanding and annexing territory, particularly in Africa and Asia (see p. 92) and **Britain wished to maintain her position as the leading Imperial power.** This objective brought Britain into conflict with France and Russia both nations seeking new territories. British governments were deeply suspicious of the activities of the French in Africa and the Russians in the Far East, both areas where Britain had territories and interests. It was therefore British policy in this period to keep a careful check on the Russians and French and where possible to hinder or scotch their ambitions. An indication of the fears of British governments was the decision in **1889 to maintain the 'two power standard' of ships in the Royal Navy.** This meant that the full strength of British waships would always be double that of the combined Russian and French navies.

Russian ambitions collided with British interests in two areas, the Balkans and China. In 1885 Russian troops crossed the Afghan border at Pendjeh and aroused the old bogy of a Russian threat to India. Gladstone considered sending British warships through the straits into the Black Sea to menace the coast of Russia but was warned off by the major European powers. The Russian demonstration at Pendjeh came to nothing (see p. 101) but in 1887, Gladstone's successor, Lord Salisbury, made an agreement with Italy and Austria-Hungary for joint naval action if Russia dared to threaten the eastern Mediterranean.

Russian ambitions in China proved a more serious threat to what Britain considered as her interests. The crumbling and weak Chinese Empire was unable to resist the pressures of the European powers at the end of the nineteenth century. **Britain, which had large and profitable commercial interests in China, wished to preserve the Chinese empire by means of the 'open door' policy.** This allowed for all foreign powers to gain trade in China through free competition, an arrangement which suited Britain since British business interests were by far the largest. Since the early nineteenth century, Russian armies had been moving across central Asia, overcoming the local tribes and conquering land. In the 1890s Russian influence had reached the Chinese border and the British believed, with good reason, that Russia was greedy for Chinese territory. In 1898 the Russians obtained Port Arthur on the Chinese Pacific coast. The British were alarmed and looked about for friends to help them resist the growth of Russian influence in China. They could find no assistance from the European powers. (In 1900 Chinese nationalist fanatics, known as Boxers, began attacking Europeans and besieged the European embassies in Peking. This affront to European power led to an army, with contingents from all the powers, relieving the legations and exacting retribution on the Chinese.) This co-operation did not last and Britain, without allies, was faced with finding a way to halt Russian expansion. The answer was the **Anglo-Japanese alliance of 1902.** By this agreement Britain promised to fight alongside Japan if the Japanese were attacked by two nations. Japan, like Russia, was anxious to gain territory in China and had already been in conflict with the Russians over Korea. The issues between Russia and Japan could only be settled by war but the Japanese were wary of Russia's ally, France. Now that Japan was allied to Britain, she need not fear the intervention of the French navy and the way was clear for an attack on Russia. Britain had gained an ally which would protect her interests in the Far East and the defeats inflicted on Russia by the Japanese in the Russo-Japanese War of 1904–5 crippled Russian power in China.

Tension between France and Britain centred on clashes of ambition in the Mediterranean and Africa. The French bitterly resented the British occupation of Egypt in 1882 (see p. 102) and British naval power in the Mediterranean. Diplomatic efforts were made by the French to prise the British out of Egypt but with no success. A further source of friction between France and Britain was the **Fashoda incident of 1898.** A small force of French colonial troops under Colonel Marchand had crossed from west Africa to the Nile valley, and after this long and arduous journey had established themselves at Fashoda on the shores of the Nile in southern Sudan. Here they were found by Kitchener's forces, which had just marched south from Egypt and defeated the Dervish army at Omdurman (see p. 103). The French claimed the southern Sudan for themselves, the British disagreed. Lord Salisbury stated 'We claim Sudan by right of conquest' and the French grudgingly and angrily backed down. Unable to challenge the

Royal Navy in the Mediterranean and therefore incapable of supporting their claims in the Sudan with force the French renounced all interests there (1899). The French back-down was a triumph for the British and for 'splendid isolation', supported of course by the Royal Navy. **Yet it was increasingly obvious that Britain could not 'go it alone' in the world and that to maintain her world power and protect her trading and colonial interests she needed permanent friends.** This truth had been apparent in the Far East where the Japanese alliance had been signed as the only way of keeping the Russians in check. The Boer War (see p. 108) had revealed Britain's lack of firm friends for she had been universally condemned and criticized throughout Europe. In the early years of the new century, the British government was under pressure to find reliable and lasting links with other European powers. The choice was between Germany and her allies, Austria-Hungary and Italy on one hand, and the Dual Alliance of Russia and France on the other.

Ententes with France and Russia, 1904–7

In 1898 the British government had toyed with the idea of an alliance with Germany but negotiations had broken down. For some time there had been signs of **growing Anglo-German rivalry** and the British government became suspicious of the motives of Germany's rulers. Germany had always been a European power with interests confined to the continent of Europe but after the accession of Kaiser Wilhelm II in 1888 and the dismissal of Bismarck in 1890 Germany's ambitions began to expand. In short, **Germany wished to be a world-power with international influence like Britain.** Since 1881 Germany had shown a friendly interest in Turkey and in 1898 the Kaiser had visited Constantinople where he announced himself the friend of the Islamic religion. Shortly after, German engineers began to build a railroad across the Turkish empire, financed by German money. When completed the **Berlin-Baghdad railway** would bind Turkey closer to Germany. A further sign of German dreams of world power was the **Navy Law of 1898** which planned a fleet whose size might rival Britain's. Germany had already clashed with Britain in 1896 when the Kaiser sent a telegram to President Kruger of the Transvaal, congratulating him on the defeat of the Jameson Raid (p. 108). These events alarmed British politicians and the British public. At the same time that Germany was developing ambitions for world power her economy was growing and her share of world trade increasing. Britain's share of world trade had fallen from 38% in the early 1880s to 29% in the early 1900s whilst Germany's had risen from 17% to 20%. In trade as in international diplomacy Britain was coming to regard Germany as a rival.

To guarantee herself against German expansion, **Britain sought the friendship of France.** Between 1903 and 1904, the British foreign secretary, Lord Lansdowne, negotiated with the French foreign minister, Delcassé. The outcome was the **Entente Cordiale** of 1904. The Entente ('understanding') settled all the outstanding disagreements between Britain and France and had been marked by a successful royal visit of Edward VII to Paris in 1903. Britain's position in Egypt was accepted by the French, and Britain promised to let France have a free hand in Morocco and where necessary support French influence there. For the future both countries promised to co-operate in the conduct of foreign affairs. The British also agreed to withdraw warships from the Mediterranean and station them at bases on the Scottish coast to meet the growing challenge of the German navy. In return the French fleet in the Mediterranean was increased. In the event of war with Germany, the British fleet was expected to protect the northern coasts of France.

The Entente was strengthened in 1906 when the Liberal foreign secretary, Sir Edward Grey, agreed to senior **British army officers having secret military discussions with the French**. The object of these discussions was the sending of a British Expeditionary Force to France to fight alongside the French army in the event of a war with Germany.

Having established warm relations with France, Britain sought to patch up her differences with France's ally, Russia. **The Anglo-Russian Entente (1907)** settled differences over Tibet and Afghanistan on the frontiers of India and agreed to the division of Iran into areas of Russian and British influence. **The ententes with France and Russia ended British isolation from the European powers.** Britain had not joined the Dual Alliance and had not promised to fight for either France and Russia in the event of a war with Germany. Still the naval agreements and the military conversations with the French army indicated that the British government contemplated fighting Germany. Britain now had two partners within Europe with whom she would co-operate and with whose interests she would identify.

The Road to War, 1904–14

The test of Britain's new-found friendship with France came when the Germans tried to overthrow French influence in Morocco. In 1905 the Kaiser had visited Tangier and announced that Germany was prepared to claim interests there. Morocco's future was discussed at the **Algeçiras Conference (1906)** where Britain stood by France and the Germans, supported only by Austria, backed down. **In 1911 the Germans again asserted their claims in Morocco and challenged the French by sending the gunboat 'Panther' to Agadir harbour.** They demanded the Congo as compensation for allowing France to control Morocco. Britain again supported France and Germany backed down. The firm attitude of the British government was made clear by the Chancellor of the Exchequer, David Lloyd George, at a speech in the Mansion House when he stated that Britain would not shrink from war if her 'interests were vitally affected'. It was clear that Britain would not stand by and let Germany bully France over Morocco and nor would it permit Germany to establish influence in the Mediterranean. German naval expansion added a further bitterness to Anglo-German relations during this period. In 1904 the British had begun building a new battleship, **H.M.S. Dreadnought,** which was launched in 1908. Mounting ten heavy guns, Dreadnought could outsail and outshoot any existing battleship. To keep command of the seas, it was necessary for the British to build more and more of these revolutionary warships. In 1908 the Germans embarked on plans for building 'Dreadnoughts' which frightened the British. Spurred on by fears of how many new battleships the Germans were building, **the government rushed into a naval building programme with the intention of matching every five German Dreadnoughts with eight British.** The British public, fearful of the growth of the German navy, pressed for more ships and national feeling was further stirred up by rumours of German spies and wild tales of Zeppelins (German airships) flying over British soil. Erskine Childer's thriller, *The Riddle of the Sands,* published in 1903 told of a secret German invasion plan. **The naval race and fears of German ambitions widened the gulf between Britain and Germany in the six years which led up to the First World War.**

The Outbreak of War, 1914

The crises over Morocco in 1905 and 1911 did not lead to war for Germany was not willing to fight on behalf of her claims. The crises had demonstrated to her the new partnership between Britain and France and increased her fears of encirclement. She and her ally, Austria-Hungary, found themselves surrounded by Britain and France on one side and Russia on the other. In the years before 1914 all powers had taken steps to improve the efficiency and strength of their armies, none more than Russia. After her defeat at the hands of Japan, Russia had begun re-arming and re-organizing her army and navy in such a way that by 1917 she would have superiority over the Germans. This development frightened the Germans who had planned, in the event of war, a swift and devastating attack on France, followed by a knock-out blow against Russia. This plan allowed for the fact that Russia would need much longer than France to prepare her armies for battle. As the Russians improved their armed forces, her slowness could no longer be taken for granted. From 1912 onwards the German generals argued that the sooner war came, the better their chances of victory.

At the end of June 1914 **Archduke Franz Ferdinand,** heir to the Austro-Hungarian throne, and his wife were assassinated by a Serb terrorist in Sarajevo. This was one more incident in a terrorist war between Serbian nationalists and the Austro-Hungarian authorities. The terrorists received aid and encouragement from the kingdom of Serbia, which had the protection and friendship of Russia. The Austrian government, with the backing of Germany, demanded the right to enter Serbia and crush, once and for all, the terrorist cells and threatened war if the Serbs did not agree. Serbia looked to her guardian, Russia, and defied the Austrians. Austria prepared to invade Serbia and Russia mobilised her armies to defend Serbia. The moment had come for Germany to challenge Russia which had not yet completely reformed her armies. The Germans demanded that the Russians ceased mobilisation for if she continued, her armies would have the advantage over those of Germany. Russia refused and Germany ordered mobilisation. France now had to fulfil the terms of her alliance for Russia was at war with both Germany and Austria-Hungary. She mobilised her armies ready to march into her lost provinces of Alsace and Lorraine.

So far Britain was not involved. On 1 August, as the French army began to mobilise, crowds gathered outside the British embassy in Paris shouting 'Vive l'Angleterre', believing that Britain would join France against Germany. In London the French ambassador, faced with Sir Edward Grey's remarks about possible British neutrality, asked if Britain had forgotten 'honour'. **The events in Europe had so far not touched Britain.** The war had started because of Austria's desire to teach the Serbians a long overdue lesson, Russia's need to stand up for Serbia and Germany's wish to strike at Russia before she became too strong. None of these matters was of immediate concern to Britain although she had promised to defend France's unprotected Channel coast against the German navy. On 3 August Germany announced that her army wished to march through neutral Belgium as part of **Schlieffen Plan.** This plan, devised in 1905, intended that a million German soldiers should march through Belgium, outflank the French forces on France's border and march on Paris. If the plan worked France would be defeated in one decisive blow. To strike this blow **the Germans had to march across Belgium, whose neutrality had been guaranteed by all the great powers, including Britain, by the Treaty of London in 1839.** The German government scorned the treaty as 'a scrap of paper' and expected little or no opposition from the Belgian government. **The news of Germany's demand to enter Belgium and the crossing of the Belgian border by German troops made the British government insist that Germany withdrew and respected Belgian neutrality or risk war. The Germans refused this British ultimatum and on 4 August war was declared.**

The **German invasion of neutral Belgium had been the reason why Britain declared war.** In the months that followed the outbreak of war, British propaganda portrayed the British as standing up for the rights of small nations and defending international treaties. Belgium was shown in *Punch* as a small boy standing up to a bullying German with a cudgel, and the British public was fed on horror stories of the German advance over Belgian soil and of the atrocities of the German Uhlans (lancers) who spared neither women or children. Britain was fighting a holy war, a crusade, against a brutal, bullying foe.

Truth is the first casualty of war and whilst it is true that Britain declared war to defend Belgium, **there were other deeper reasons for British entry into the war.** A German victory over France like that in 1870–71 would lead to an increase in German economic power through the annexation of French land. Already Germany was outpacing Britain in international trade and the German desire for 'world power' was a direct challenge to Britain and her empire. The growing German navy at its base in Kiel on the North Sea coast directly threatened Britain and British sea-power. In spite of the surface friendship which Britain and Germany publicly showed in the years before the war, British governments were suspicious of German motives. The power which dominated Europe, would, it was feared, come to dominate the world and replace Britain. For this reason the British had cultivated the friendship of France, secretly planned to fight alongside her armies and, in 1914, to go to war with her against Germany.

Chapter 11
The First World War

Introduction
The First World War was a **total war.** It involved not only armies, navies and air forces but also the entire civilian populations, both men and women. **The whole British population was organised to fight the war;** men volunteered for the armed services and then were conscripted and women took their places in the factories and farms. To equip the mass armies with the most modern weapons, the government was forced to supervise and in some cases take over industrial production completely. The shortage of food which followed unrestricted submarine warfare in 1917 led the government to introduce food rationing. War made unavoidable other limits on personal freedom such as internment of enemy aliens, censorship of the press and the control of industrial manpower.

The First World War was not only a test of courage and endurance for the fighting men, it was also a test of the technology and industrial strength of the nations involved. To win, governments had to transform nations into fighting machines designed to bring the maximum of human and industrial resources to bear on the war effort. The weapons of war dictated the form of the fighting, a struggle of men and machines which brought, inevitably, mass slaughter. By the autumn of 1918 the armies of Germany and her allies, Austria-Hungary, Turkey and Bulgaria were close to collapse and by 11 November they had all surrendered. Britain and her allies, France, Italy (which had entered in 1915) and the United States (which had entered in 1917) had won. **Britain alone had suffered 750,000 dead.**

The War on Land: the Western Front
When Britain declared war on 4 August 1914, German armies had already entered Belgium in accordance with the Schlieffen Plan. This plan had intended that a million German soldiers should march through Belgium and northern France with the result that the French would be outflanked and trapped. At first the plan was successful, in spite of valiant Belgian resistance. The **British Expeditionary Force,** under Sir John French, had been sent to Belgium in the second week of August in order to assist the

French and hold back the German advance. On 22 August British forces engaged von Kluck's 1st Army at **Mons** and thanks to their rapid rifle fire briefly halted the German advance. Their numbers were insufficient to hold back the Germans for long, and in the next thirteen days the British fell back 200 miles. The French too were in retreat and their main forces, on the eastern border with Germany, had also been driven back after terrible reverses. At this critical stage in September the advantage passed to the British and French whose forces were able to outflank the Germans and defeat them on the Marne. The next few months saw a series of struggles in northern France and Flanders in which both sides tried to establish defensive lines. After a savage fight, the British took Ypres and by Christmas the front had become stable. The outcome of this campaign was the establishment of two lines of trenches, one allied and the other German, which stretched from the North Sea to the Alps. The remainder of the British Expeditionary Force occupied the northern end of this line in Flanders. Unable to secure victory by open, mobile warfare, the two sides dug in and faced each other across No Mans Land.

Trench Warfare

From the winter of 1914 until the end of the fighting, **trench warfare dominated the western front**. The creation of this system of static warfare had been a direct result of the fighting in the first few months of the war. The firepower of infantry, armed with rifles and machine-guns, backed up by artillery which fired long range high explosive shells, exposed troops in the open to devastating fire. Casualties were correspondingly high; the French army suffered 300,000 killed in the first five months of the war. To avoid such casualties there was no alternative but to seek cover and dig trenches. The war, which some optimistic generals and politicians had predicted would last six months, had turned into a seemingly endless struggle between mass armies holding strong and apparently unassailable defensive positions. **A new problem faced the commanders, how to secure a 'break through'.** Both German and allied generals were to devise a series of schemes for weakening, attacking and overwhelming the elaborate system of trenches and pierce the enemy's line In turn there was an obvious need to strengthen the trench systems by laying barbed wire and making the trenches resistant to heavy and often prolonged shellfire. New weapons therefore appeared. In 1915 the Germans introduced poisoned gas but this did not prove decisive and was soon copied by the allies. In 1917 the allies introduced armoured tanks, cumbersome monsters on caterpillar tracks, but their potential was not fully realised until the very end of the war. Each side increased the number and power of their guns for **it was firmly believed the intensity and weight of artillery fire could be the key to success in any offensive.** In 1915 frontal attacks by the allies had been beaten back by machine-gun fire so it became necessary to destroy machine-gun nests as a preliminary to an attack by infantry. To this end the British stockpiled nearly 3 million shells in preparation for the attack on the Somme in 1916 The shock of such fire was met by the Germans who simply dug deeper trenches; the machine-guns were not wiped out as the British soon learnt to their cost.

Measure and counter-measure tended to balance each other out and casualties mounted steadily. After 1915 British newspapers deliberately suppressed publication of casualty lists for fear of undermining morale at home. The new type of warfare demanded new and massive armies, drawn from the civilian populations of the fighting nations.

Mass Armies

When, in August 1914, Field Marshall **Kitchener** had been made Secretary for War, he prophesied that the war would be long and in consequence called for a mass volunteer army. His call, made more urgent by the losses of the British Expeditionary Force, is best remembered through his own stern, moustachioed face and pointing finger on the recruiting posters. His appeals and perhaps the poster stimulated a marvellous response. **Between September 1914 and March 1916 2.5 million men came came forward of whom 600,000 joined by the spring of 1915.** The great industrial centres of London, the Midlands, Lancashire, Yorkshire and the North East produced the greatest numbers of men. Many came to the recruiting offices on the understanding that those 'who joined together served together' and so the **'Pals Battalions'** came into being. Men, who in peacetime shared occupations and interests, joined up in groups – the shop assistants of Newcastle and Gateshead together formed the 18th Northumberland Fusiliers and there were battalions of miners, railwaymen and clerks. The enthusiasm and patriotism which created and inspired the volunteers of this new army were remarkable and moving, yet the volunteers of what was called 'Kitchener's Army' were insufficient and by March 1916 a reluctant government introduced **conscription.** From then on men were ordered to join the armed forces and those who evaded this call or refused on private grounds were imprisoned. The new volunteer army was trained and ready to fight in an offensive which the army's General Staff had planned for 1916. It was to occur on the Somme River.

British Offensives

The Somme, 1916

During 1915 the British and French armies had launched a series of offensives against various points on the German line. Gains had been few and losses very heavy. In December 1915 Sir John French, discredited after the failure of the Loos offensive, was replaced as Commander-in-Chief by **Sir Douglas Häig.** The new commander in France and Flanders was a competent general, but his decisions aroused much controversy. Determined in his belief that war would only be won by the defeat of the German army on the western front (a view which was eventually to be justified), Haig masterminded a series of offensives in 1916 and 1917. With the French commander, Joffre, Haig had intended to launch attacks on the German line in northern France which would coincide with French offensives. The British attack was planned to occur on the River Somme. The French schemes came to nothing for their army was the victim of a sustained and ferocious German offensive at Verdun in February 1916. The intensity of the German attack made the need for a British offensive a matter of urgency for the French hoped that it might relieve the pressure on their forces.

The Somme offensive opened with a fortnight's shelling of the German trenches which, it was hoped, would remove the barbed wire entanglements and destroy the machine-gun nests. On 1 July 1916 the British forces moved forward for the attack, each man leaving his trench burdened with 60 lb of supplies and equipment. Immediately the attacking units came under murderous machine-gun fire and soon they found their way barred by barbed wire. The preliminary shelling had not been as effective as the planners had hoped. Many shells had been defective and the Germans rightly suspecting that the bombardment was the beginning of a full scale assault, had dug in deeper. The disastrous first day, with astonishing casualties, set the pattern for the remainder of the offensive which was called off, after very limited gains, on 1 November. In the space of a few months, the British army had suffered 400,000 dead and wounded.

Passschendaele

The failure of the Somme offensive was the beginning of a series of crises for the allies. During the winter and spring of 1916–1917, **the morale of the French army slumped** and widespread unrest among its soldiers led to a series of mutinies. **The Russian Revolution of February 1917** and the calamitous Brusilov offensive of the summer signalled the collapse of the Russian army. After the October Revolution, the new **Bolshevik government made peace with Germany** at Brest Litovsk (December 1917). Germany was now free to move great numbers of troops from the eastern to the western front. The **entry of the United States into the war** in April 1917 was a welcomed compensation for these set-backs for it marked the start of a full flood of American money and material into Europe. The Americans however needed a year in which to raise and train an army of a million men which was promised to the allies for the late spring and summer of 1918.

The French commanders, unsure of the loyalty of their own troops, favoured a cautious policy of limited offensives during 1917. Haig, in spite of doubts and misgivings in the British cabinet, proposed a further offensive during the summer. This came to be known as **Passchendaele** (or the Third Battle of Ypres) and was fought, often under appalling conditions, in Flanders. Heavy and continuous shellfire had shattered the drainage system of this low-lying area and after heavy rainfall the battlefields were changed into water-logged morasses of mud. Movement was limited – photographs and newsreels show horses trapped up to their bodies and men often fell into the mud and drowned. The offensive failed although in November over 300 **tanks** broke the German lines at Cambrai. The chance was missed for the British lacked infantry reserves to exploit the advantage.

Haig believed, perhaps optimistically, that the British offensives of 1916 and 1917 had undermined the morale of the German army. Whilst there was some truth in this opinion, the British had suffered heavy losses and the troops had been severely shaken. During 1917 and 1918 there were several incidents which showed that unrest existed within the army including a brief mutiny at Etaples. The losses were made up thanks to the flow of conscripted men. **In January 1918 the British army in France totalled just over 1 million men, only slightly less than its numbers in January 1917.**

1918

Since its attack on Verdun in 1916, the German army in the west had remained on the defensive. The release of troops from the Russian front in 1917–18 increased the manpower of the German forces and made possible an offensive in the west. Other considerations influenced German military thinking. The expected arrival of massive American reinforcements during 1918 would tip the balance heavily in favour of the allies. Inside Germany the growing effects of the allied naval blockade, war-weariness and food shortages during 1917–18 had encouraged unrest, especially among the working classes. Aware of events in Russia, the rulers of Germany became increasingly fearful of revolution. **The offensive planned for March 1918 was to be Germany's last attempt to secure final victory.**

The offensive, known as **Operation Michael** and directed by General Ludendorff, included a massive assault on the British held trenches in northern France. Alerted by the heavy concentration of German troops, armaments and supplies, the British took measures to strengthen their own trenches during March. On 20 March the first wave of the German attack began and within two days the British line had been breached. **British and French forces withdrew under the intensive attack but their retirement never became a rout.** Within a week the allies had regrouped and the German offensive began to run out of steam. The struggle lasted until July and at one stage the Germans came within 30 miles of Paris. The well-conducted defence of the British, French and United States armies (by June there were over 1 million Americans in France) held off the Germans. **The German army had shot its bolt and failed to win the breakthrough and victory.** In July Ludendorff privately admitted that victory had eluded him and that defeat would shortly follow. **It was now time for the allies to counter-attack and on 8 August the big push started.** Lessons had been learnt from earlier offensives. The massive opening bombardment was dispensed with and in its place came the creeping barrage of carefully directed shellfire behind which the infantry could advance, so allowing the enemy little time to recover. As a spearhead for the infantry massed tanks were used, including the recently developed small 'Whippets'. By the end of October, the Germans were retreating, unable to stem the allied advance. In Germany latent unrest had exploded into violence on the streets and the sailors at Kiel had mutinied. **Unable to fight on, the Germans asked for and were granted an armistice on 11 November. The war was over.**

Conclusion

The **Western Front had been the most important theatre of the war. It was there, as Haig had anticipated, that the German army was beaten and with it the German nation.** The British army had played a crucial role in the fighting on this front. At great cost to itself it had contributed to the weakening of the German forces in the terrible offensives on the Somme and at Passchendaele. At the same time it had taken pressure off the exhausted French especially at the time when the French army was on the verge of breaking. In 1918 it had held out against the German offensive and played a leading part in the counter-offensive which had brought Germany to its knees. That the British army did all this is to a large extent a consequence of the bravery, fortitude and dogged determination of the British soldier. Russian morale broke, that of France nearly collapsed and finally in 1918, so did the German. The British army did not suffer such despair.

Victory also came from the British administration and government which transported, fed, clothed and armed the fighting men. In the spring of 1918 the German troops occupying British positions were both delighted and dismayed by the abundance of their supplies. Fed on tales of how the British were suffering and only too aware of how they and their families were, the discovery of British plenty helped to undermine the morale of the German soldier.

Lesser campaigns

Gallipoli

The stalemate on the western front and the inability of the allies to break the German army there forced generals and politicians to examine alternative means by which Germany could be beaten. During the winter of 1914–15, **Winston Churchill,** First Lord of the Admiralty, proposed an **attack on the Straits between Turkey and the Balkans.** Such an attack, it was argued, would relieve pressure on Russia which was then fighting the Turks in southern Russia, and could easily force Turkey out of the war. If successful, the attack would have led to the occupation of Constantinople and might therefore have persuaded the Balkan states to join the allies. Churchill's plan convinced Kitchener, and by January 1915 the cabinet agreed that it should be carried out. Bold in its concept, the plan proved difficult to fulfil.

A naval attack on the Straits in March 1915 ended with the sinking of several ships, including two British battleships, by Turkish mines. Forewarned of further attacks, the Turks prepared their defences and were ready for the landing of British troops a month later. **The attack by British, New Zealand and Australian forces on the Gallipoli peninsular made little headway and soon both sides were digging and holding trenches**. In December the **decision to withdraw** was taken reluctantly by the cabinet, largely as a result of the persuasiveness of **Sir William Robertson,** the Chief of Imperial General Staff. He argued that the campaign was wasteful and took men away from the decisive area of war, the western front. The reputation of Churchill, who had resigned from the Admiralty, suffered and so did British prestige.

The Middle East

Apart from Gallipoli, the war against Turkey was carried on in Palestine and Mesopotamia. The Mesopotamian campaign, undertaken by British and Indian troops, had been designed to protect the Persian Gulf oil fields. Initially successful, this campaign ran into difficulties in 1916 when 10,000 troops were forced to surrender at **Kut.** The **Palestinian campaign** was more fruitful. Jerusalem fell to **General Allenby's** forces in December 1917 and by the end of the war, Palestine and Syria were in British hands. One rather spectacular feature of this campaign had been the Arab revolt led by **T. E. Lawrence.** Lawrence, with British backing, had encouraged and led Arab irregular forces in raids against Turkish forces and communications. Tales of his adventures made exciting reading in newspapers and Lawrence emerged as a national hero.

The subsidiary campaigns in the Middle East contributed little to the defeat of Germany. They did however take up between one and two million men and aroused French suspicions that Britain was neglecting the main centre of war and using much needed men to conquer territory for the British empire.

The War at Sea

Introduction

In 1914 the **British navy was superior in terms of ships and manpower to those of Germany and her allies.** When war broke out the Royal Navy had **three major objectives.** The first and most important was **to find and bring to battle the ships of**

the German High Seas fleet, which were, for the most part, concentrated at Kiel on the North German coast. The second was to **protect allied shipping** and ensure the safe continuation of trade on all the seas. The third was to **extinguish the trade of Germany and her allies and deny them supplies of any sort which came by sea.**

Proud of its traditions, the Senior Service was superior in the number of its ships to the German Navy. Yet as the war showed there were serious defects in the design of some British ships and gunnery left much to be desired. Nevertheless the Navy succeeded in each of its objectives, and especially by its blockade of Germany, helped to secure victory.

Naval Engagements

At the beginning of the war, the Navy was faced with the task of intercepting and destroying scattered units of the German fleet in the Mediterranean and Far East. In the first days of the war a determined pursuit of the German battleship **Goeben** did not prevent it from entering Turkish waters and helping persuade Turkey to take Germany's side. More menacing was the German Far Eastern squadron under Admiral von Spee. In October 1914 Spee's heavy cruisers engaged and defeated an inferior British squadron at **Coronel,** off the coast of Chile. The news of this defeat was a serious blow to British prestige and immediately, two battle cruisers were sent to the South Atlantic with orders to defend the naval base of Port Stanley in the Falkland Islands. In the brief battle of the **Falkland Islands** (November 1914), the German squadron was scattered and destroyed by the heavier guns of the British ships and Coronel was avenged. Other German warships were hunted down, including the cruiser Emden which had briefly and brilliantly disrupted allied shipping in the Indian Ocean. **Within a few months of the outbreak of war, all German surface vessels had been driven from the seas.**

There remained the High Seas Fleet at Kiel on the north coast of Germany. In terms of battleships, the British outnumbered the Germans by seven to four and therefore the German command was forced to be cautious and avoid a general engagement. In spite of this the Germans were able, during 1914 and 1915, to make a number of lightning raids across the North Sea and shell British coastal towns, including Scarborough and Hartlepool. Public opinion was enraged and pressure was put on the Royal Navy to intercept the raiders. At the battle of the **Dogger Bank**

(1915), a German force was engaged and some damage was inflicted on it before it hurried back to Kiel.

For nearly a year after the fight at the Dogger Bank, the German authorities did not commit their Fleet to action. This policy was reversed early in 1916 and the Germans again contemplated making quick raids on the British coast. The outcome of this decision in favour of a more aggressive naval policy was the **battle of Jutland,** fought on 31 May–1June **1916,** the only major sea battle between the main British and German fleets. The British were forewarned of German preparations at the end of May, thanks to the **Admiralty's possession of German naval codebooks** which made it possible to decipher German wireless messages. In the knowledge that the High Seas Fleet was making ready, the Grand Fleet, under the command of Admiral **Sir John Jellicoe,** left its anchorages in northern Scotland. Preceded by screens of scouting cruisers, the main battle fleet sailed eastwards, hoping to find and engage the Germans. Contact was first made during the afternoon of 31 May, when **Sir David Beatty's** battle-cruisers engaged Admiral Hipper's battle-cruisers, supported by the battleships of the High Seas Fleet under Admiral Scheer. The British came off badly from this fight. Three battle-cruisers, the Queen Mary, Indefatigable and Invincible were blown up and others were severely mauled by the accurate German fire. 'There seems to be something wrong with our bloody ships today,' remarked Beatty, a comment which could have been extended to British gunnery which was less effective than the German. Beatty's plan was to draw the German ships towards the approaching British battlefleet. To an extent he was successful, but when the Germans came into contact with Jellicoe's battle-ships, they shied away. Rather than risk a duel in which his own ships would have been outnumbered and outgunned, Scheer, manoeuvering his ships with great skill, turned back for Kiel and safety. The British pursued into the night. Throughout the dusk and darkness, there was confusion and muddle with many small engagements between British and German vessels. By dawn it was clear that the Germans had got away and Jellicoe's fleet turned back for its bases. Who had won? The Germans claimed a victory for they had inflicted great casualties in both ships and men. This was indeed true but the British claimed that they had gained their objective and driven the Germans back to port. This was also true and the British claim to victory was given greater force by the fact that the German fleet remained in port, never to emerge until the war was over.

Jutland had shown the German command that a decisive naval victory over the British was an impossibility. In the light of this knowledge, **the Germans turned to unrestricted U Boat warfare as the only way to injure British seapower.**

Blockade and U Boats

One of the first tasks of the Royal Navy had been the imposition of a **tight blockade on Germany and her allies.** All ships, including those of neutral countries, were stopped and if they were carrying goods for Germany, they were seized. By this means German seaborne trade was brought to an end and Germany was denied raw materials and food which she had previously imported. Likewise all German exports ceased. The consequences of the blockade were often exaggerated. Yet whilst it would be wrong to say that its effects were enormous, **it did contribute to shortages, especially of food.**

Germany's answer was to strike at British trade through the use of **U Boats.** In 1914 Germany possessed 24 submarines but by 1917 she had over 100, including newly developed types capable of sailing over 10,000 miles. The value of U Boats was quickly shown in 1914 when one torpedoed three British cruisers and a mine laid by another sank the battleship Audacious. The most important work of the U Boats was against merchant ships and this was soon realised. By following what was called **'unrestricted U Boat warfare',** the German navy believed that it could retaliate against the British blockade and strike a deadly, even lethal, blow against Britain's trade. 'Unrestricted' submarine warfare meant that the U Boat sank a ship on sight without first finding out whether it was carrying war supplies or even whether it was British. Whilst such methods might endanger British commerce, they had the drawback of provoking the United States. In February 1915 the German government announced its intention to follow a programme of unrestricted warfare and soon after the passenger liner **Lusitania** was torpedoed off the Irish coast with great loss of life. Americans were among the dead and the United States government protested strongly. The diplomatic consequences of its decision worried the German government which, in September 1915, abandoned unrestricted warfare. In **January 1917, with an increased fleet of submarines, the Germans again declared 'unrestricted' U Boat warfare,** confident that once implemented such methods would quickly weaken the British. By April one in four ships which left British ports were sunk and in that month the U Boats sunk over 1 million tons of shipping. **In Britain wheat supplies existed sufficient for only six weeks.** The answer to these losses was the **convoy system,** by which merchant vessels travelled together in groups under the protection of warships. This was carried out at the instruction of the Prime Minister, Lloyd George, in the face of doubt and criticism from the Admiralty. The convoys were successful and losses were cut.

The Navy was able to wage war against the U Boats with two new inventions, the hydrophone (by which listeners could detect the underwater noises created by the U Boat) and depth charges, which could be launched from surface ships to explode under the water. Mines were laid in waters through which the U Boats passed and in 1918 in a raid was made on the U Boat base at Zeebrugge on the Belgian coast which partly blocked the port. The U Boat campaign had failed. As predicted it had helped to bring the United States into the war but it had not eliminated British commerce.

Conclusion

The Royal Navy played a **decisive role in the war.** It had **destroyed German seaborne trade and helped to deny the Germans raw materials and food by the blockade.** In spite of missing the chance to defeat decisively the German fleet, it had convinced the German government of the risk of further encounters, forcing the Germans to keep their fleet bottled up in harbour until the end of the war. It had also played an important part in **defeating the German U Boats** and so helped to ensure the **continuation of British imports.** Most importantly it had guaranteed the freedom of the seas for the allied powers, enabling their ships to move men, supplies and equipment as they wished.

Air Warfare

From the moment of its invention in 1904, the military value of the aeroplane was recognised. For some time before the outbreak of the war, the army and navy had developed their own flying units. In 1914 the **Royal Flying Corps** with 44 aircraft accompanied the British Expeditionary Force to France. The aircraft were used for **observation of enemy troop movements** and information gained from the air proved vital before the battle of the Marne. From then until the end of the war aircraft were widely used for observation and directing artillery fire. Early in 1915 cameras were devised for **aerial photography.** With aircraft from both sides endeavouring to spy out positions and movements of armies, it was inevitable that fights between aircraft occurred. To start with pilots fought with pistols and rifles but soon machine guns were fitted to 'fighter' planes. Command of air and with it the ability to overwatch the enemy without interruption became of great importance.

In August 1914 naval aircraft had dropped bombs on German Zeppelin sheds inside Germany and by 1915 military aircraft were bombing German railway lines in order to damage communications. **Bombing raids** had become a regular feature of fighting on the Western Front by 1918 and large numbers of Allied aircraft attacked and bombed the Germans during their advance in the spring. In April 1918 the naval and military branches of the airforce were merged as the **Royal Air Force** and under its commander, Lord Trenchard, the new force began a series of bombing raids on the German industrial centres in the Rhineland. A twin-engined bomber, the Vickers Vimy, had been developed for raids on Berlin which were planned to take place in the winter of 1918–1919. **German airships (Zeppelins)** had raided British towns and cities in 1914 and these bombing attacks continued throughout the war. Just over 1,000 civilian lives were lost but the raids enraged the British public. The ponderous Zeppelins and their successors, the Gotha bombers, forced the government to station fighter aircraft to protect cities as well as anti-aircraft batteries.

The war had been a stimulus to the development of aircraft and the development of their potential as weapons of war. When the war ended, both sides were employing aerial bombing of both military and civilian targets. The theorists of aerial warfare argued that bombing from the air as a means by which civilian morale could be weakened as well as injuring war production. Although not decisive in the war, the aeroplane had shown that in total war there could be no division between the fighting armies and civilians.

The Home Front

Political

During the war normal political life continued. The Liberal government under **Asquith** which was in power when war broke out was forced, in 1915, to enter into a coalition with the Conservatives in order to escape from criticism and ensure political as well as national unity. Described by Churchill as 'terribly weak', **Asquith's leadership was challenged by Lloyd George,** whose performance as **Minister of Munitions** revealed powers of energy and determination which won him immense popular respect. From the **end of 1916 Lloyd George was Prime Minister** at the head of a coalition of all parties, dedicated to the forceful pursuit of victory. In these political changes the press had played an important part in boosting or demolishing the reputations of public figures. As **newspapers were the only means by which the public appreciated what was happening,** their influence was enormous. Two newspaper owners, **Lord Northcliffe** who controlled *The Times* and *Daily Mail*, and **Sir Max Aitken (later Lord Beaverbrook)** who owned the *Daily Express*, were able to wield considerable powers over their readers. The population, with few exceptions, was dedicated, almost to the point of hysteria, to winning the war and therefore could be easily aroused by rumours of muddle or mistakes.

Asquith, the Liberal leader and Prime Minister, had in November 1914 created a **War Council** of whose members, with the exception of Balfour, the ex-Conservative Prime Minister, and Kitchener were Liberals. This **body was dominated by Asquith, Churchill** (First Lord of the Admiralty) **and Kitchener** (Secretary for War) and it was their influence which led to the adoption of the Gallipoli scheme. Demands for the transfer of troops from France and allegations of **shell shortages** were publicized in Northcliffe's newspapers. The Conservatives in the House of Commons, sensing the government's weakness, threatened a debate on the conduct of the war. To forestall trouble Asquith offered the Conservative leader, Bonar Law, a **coalition** and in May 1915 a cabinet was formed which included Conservatives, Unionists and one Labour M.P. There were sacrifices and one was Churchill's resignation from the Admiralty, much to the delight of the Conservatives who had never forgiven his betrayal of their party ten years before.

One figure came to the fore in the coalition, **David Lloyd George.** As Minister of Munitions and, after Kitchener's death at sea in June 1916, as Secretary for War, Lloyd George showed flair, energy and inventiveness. By contrast Asquith's performance was not impressive and during the difficult year of 1916, he attracted much criticism. A man of dynamism and determination was needed, a leader who could drive the nation forward to victory.

For some Liberals and Bonar Law's Conservatives, Lloyd George was that man and a campaign to make him Prime Minister was backed by Aitken's *Daily Express*. After a bitter squabble in the cabinet, Asquith resigned and in **December 1916 Lloyd George became Prime Minister** at the head of a coalition in which the Conservatives were strong.

Lloyd George proved to be what his supporters had hoped for and he earned the title 'The Man who won the War'. The consequences of his becoming Prime Minister were, however, unfortunate for his own party since many Liberals still supported Asquith. The Liberal split lasted after the war and contributed to the long-term decline of the party. Other factors were also weakening liberalism. The ideas of *laissez faire* were of little use in war-time for it was necessary for the government to intervene actively in industrial life in order to produce the supplies needed for victory. The needs of the war effort were reflected in Lloyd George's creation of new departments of government, staffed by businessmen and with sweeping powers to control industry. These included departments of shipping, labour and food.

Economic changes
Paying for the war effort was one of the chief responsibilities of the government. The armies and their supplies and loans to allies forced the government to raise loans including over £1,000 million from the United States. Income tax was raised from 1s 3d. in the £1 in 1914 to 6 shillings in 1918 and a tax of 80% was imposed on excess profits made by companies making war material. The Liberals were forced, reluctantly, to abandon Free Trade for the **McKenna Duties** (1915) imposed taxes on imported foreign luxury goods such as motor cars.

The **organization of industry** was crucial and, as the war went on, the government took over the direction of the railways, the coal mines and other industries involved in the production of war material. The Trade Unions were also drawn into the war effort, thanks to Lloyd George. He persuaded the Unions to supervise the bringing into industry of masses of unskilled workers whose arrival alarmed skilled men frightened that they might lose their status. All over the country committees were set up to direct and control production and farming. The demand for victory meant that people in all areas of life had to submit to government orders and controls on a scale that would have been unimaginable before the war.

Social Life

The first and most significant social change which came during the war concerned **women**. Mass enlistment caused a labour shortage and in July 1915, the suffragette leader, Christabel Pankhurst, led a demonstration of women under the slogan 'We demand the right to serve'. Her wish and those of her followers were fulfilled. **Great numbers of women took the places of men who were in the forces,** over 200,000 in government departments, a further half a million in offices and many more in factories and on farms. The war witnessed a remarkable release of women's energies into all kinds of work, paid and unpaid, which contributed directly to the war effort. In a sense the country, facing total war and the need to field and equip a mass army, could not ignore the willingness and talents of women. The long term consequences would be that women, after the war had ended, would come to expect wider opportunities and greater equality with men – after all they had spent four years doing 'men's work'.

The mass armies created for the war did much to **erode class barriers.** Troops drawn from the working classes were commanded by officers from the middle and upper classes. Social groups which often knew little of each other were thrown together in the trenches. The result, in that it can be measured, was that many men of the middle classes became aware of other classes, their habits and their problems. Suffering and fighting together the classes were mixed and some, but not all of the old barriers and suspicions began to disappear. At the same time, the new conditions of warfare demonstrated the weakness of many of the older and inflexible traditions of British life. The technical superiority of German engineering, shown at Jutland, exposed the neglect of science and technology within the British educational system. Another indication of this neglect was the need to set up the Imperial Chemical Industries with government backing in order to catch up with German skills in this field.

Conclusion

The First World War was the mainspring of many changes within Britain. To achieve victory the government and people of Britain had had to make sacrifices and adapt their lives in ways which would have surprised their fathers and grandfathers. Total war had demanded that the government should take on many fresh responsibilities including the running of industry, a measure which before the war would have been called socialist. Traditional beliefs were undermined by the war. The Liberals had to jettison some of their cherished faith in personal liberty by introducing conscription and in part abandon Free Trade. *Laissez faire* was killed by the war. There could also be no return to the pre-1914 world although many politicians hoped that this would be so once Germany had been beaten.

For the people, an ordeal was over. Women had found new opportunities which they would not give up; the class barriers had been lowered a little. A great patriotic appeal had been made thoughout the war. It urged the people to victory and it was successful. The war ended with a fresh appeal which looked to the future and the fruits of victory. In the next twenty years these fruits were to turn sour in the mouths of the eaters.

Chapter 12
The Labour Party 1880–1939

The Labour Party was effectively established in 1900 when the Labour Representation Committee made up of delegates from many Labour and Socialist organizations was set up to help representatives of the working class or 'labouring interests' to become M.Ps. In 1906 the title Labour Representation Committee was dropped in favour of **Parliamentary Labour Party** and in the same year the first sizeable number of Labour M.Ps was returned to the House of Commons (30 as opposed to 2 in 1900). 1900 then is the date at which the plant first begins to show above ground, as it were. 1906 the date at which it was clear that it was going to flourish. To understand the nature of the plant and the soil in which it took root it is necessary to go back beyond 1900, and to know something of the great influences or nutrients of the party, Socialism and Trade Unionism.

Socialism

Any political organization needs an ideology, a set of ideas or principles to guide its actions. The **idea** which was, indeed is, **fundamental to the Labour Party is socialism,** a creed which sees equality as a necessary objective in society and which sees the state as opposed to individuals as the agent and guardian of that objective. Indeed it may be said that socialism is distrustful of individualism, believing that the individual is invariably selfish, each concerned for his own welfare and unlikely to act unselfishly for the good of society as a whole. Control must therefore be taken out of the hands of individuals as much as possible, and the state, by which is meant the government, must direct and shape society so that fairness and equality can be brought about. The socialist, then, hopes for a society in which the differences of wealth and social standing no longer exist and in which the state controls the major sources of wealth on behalf of the people which it represents.

Socialism in Great Britain

Socialist ideas had been developing in Great Britain since the beginning of the nineteenth century. **Robert Owen's** ideas of a co-operative society, which he had attempted to put into practice, in New Lanark in the 1820s could be described as socialist. **Karl Marx's** works **The Communist Manifesto** and **Capital** were written whilst he was a political exile in Britain, and were inspired in part by the workings of British industry and its impact on the lives of working people. Marx was of course the greatest of all exponents of Socialism and from his writings derive all modern theories of Socialism. Socialist ideas were not immediately influential in this country. Owen's experiments came to nothing and Marx's works were not translated and published in this country until nearly 40 years after he wrote them (*Capital* first appeared in 1887).

There were several reasons for this indifference on the part of the British public to socialist ideas. First, the **religious and moral ideas** of this time were strongly individualistic. Victorians believed very much that **individual effort formed the basis of a prosperous and happy society.** Society would be prosperous because individual hard work generated wealth, happy because the religious concern which each person had for the salvation of his or her soul led to an active interest in doing 'good works', to a philanthropy which eased some of the worst aspects of poverty and suffering. Secondly, the **economic ideas of the time** were highly optimistic and **contradicted the Socialist claim that the State was needed to control the economy.** The **Free Traders** such as those who supported the Anti-Corn Law League in the 1840s believed that once all trade barriers had been removed, then national prosperity would quickly increase. With the spread of prosperity social problems would vanish and the tensions and divisions within society dissolve. The poverty which went with inequality would disappear. For those unconvinced either by the religious or Free Trade arguments a third alternative was available in the form of securing the admission of the working class to Parliament. The Chartists (see p. 35), local associations of working men active between 1838 and 1848, believed that once the labouring class gained a voice in Parliament, governments would be forced to make radical changes for its benefit.

Up to 1850 then the need for socialism was not accepted and other remedies were sought to cure poverty. In any case Marx was only beginning to develop his ideas and the nature of industrial society was just beginning to be understood. After 1850 the working class which had been continuously active in one way or another since 1815 sank back into a kind of disillusioned apathy – it was obvious in 1848 if not earlier that Chartism had failed. As for the handful of middle class intellectuals, who had been leaders of working class agitation in both the 1815–20 troubles and the time of the Chartists, they turned their energies into social reform and free trade, and in the 1860s and 1870s they placed their faith in Gladstonian Liberalism, which combined the ideas of Free Trade and religious individualism. Free Trade had produced national prosperity at least up to the 1870s and there was still the hope that religious conscience would transform society. To many (and there were many working men among them to whom Gladstone made a strong and direct appeal) Gladstonian Liberalism offered high hopes of improvement.

By 1880, however, the shortcomings of Gladstonian Liberalism were apparent. Free Trade had not created a land of plenty and there were unmistakable signs of economic stagnation and a marked decline in agriculture (see ps. 113–4). The gap between the rich and poor far from narrowing seemed rather to be widening. Gladstone's great reforming ministry (see p. 67) was past and its achievements were in the fields of administration rather than social reform (temperance and education apart and many working men felt they could well do without temperance). The focus of Gladstone's mind and as a result of his party's energies turned to Ireland (see ps. 74–5). It was against this background of disappointment that people began to incline towards socialism, though ironically it was members of the middle class, the main beneficiaries of Gladstonian Liberalism, who formed the vanguard.

Social Democratic Federation

This was the first of the socialist societies to be set up. It was formed in 1884 by **H. M. Hyndman,** a curiously aristocratic figure who had been educated at Eton and never dropped the elegance of dress he had acquired there, always appearing in a frock coat and top hat. Hyndman had read Marx's *Capital* in 1881 and the extent to which it influenced his own ideas can be seen from his own book *England for All* which appeared in the same year and which attracted some supporters to his side. The membership of the Federation in the early days was prestigious. Marx's daughter Eleanor joined as did William Morris, a notable artist, writer and designer. There were working men as well, Tom Mann and John Burns who later became influential Trade Unionists. The Federation made itself felt in many ways through the publication of many socialist pamphlets, by participation in strikes and demonstrations like that on 13 November 1887 which came to be called 'Bloody Sunday' after rioters were dispersed by police and troops. The Federation never became strongly influential however, although two of its members were asked to join the Labour Representative Committee in 1900. So it stood on a level with the Independent Labour Party and above the Fabians who were allowed one member.

By the end of 1884 some of the more prominent Federation members were beginning to disassociate themselves from the movement because they felt that it was too strongly dominated by Hyndman. Some, like Tom Mann, felt that there was no future for the organization which kept such a distance from the working class. The **membership of the Federation was predominantly middle class and Hyndman was positively hostile to the Trade Union Movement.** Yet as Tom Mann realized, Trade Unionism had a vast political potential and the S.D.F's failure to identify with it was a major source of weakness. Another weakness was the **lack of a long term plan for the conversion of Britain to socialism.** Hyndman played with the idea of violent revolution as his instigation of riotous demonstrations shows, but the Federation also contemplated more peaceful methods such as putting up candidates for elections. This proved a dismal failure in 1885. Hyndman was not a dynamic leader capable of massing working class support. He was a gentleman dilettante who played with socialism in the same way that others of his class took up polo, yachting or big-game shooting. Without Trade Union support he had no power base and after the departure of Eleanor Marx and Morris who went off to found the Socialist League, Hyndman had no prestige.

The Socialist League
The rival Socialist League did not become an important political force. Morris was an aesthete (a lover of beauty) and a romantic who passionately hated industrialism and all the ugliness which it had created. He dreamt of a blissful medieval past in which cheery craftsmen created objects of beauty with their hands. If only, he believed, the working man could cease to be the slave of a machine and become a craftsman like his ancestors then he would discover the dignity of labour and the value of himself. In a world of artists and craftsmen the false values of money and rank would vanish forever. Morris believed that industrialization and the manipulation of money had degraded the workman and made work drudgery. All this could be changed if the working

man was transformed into the craftsman of the fourteenth century, although it is highly unlikely that the inhabitants of the fourteenth century would have shared this rosy view of their world. Morris's political views bordered on the eccentric and in spite of their charm, were utterly impractical. His achievement lay in the field of design in glass and tapestry and his printed books.

The Fabians

The **Fabians** were, by contrast, **more practical and down to earth.** They were also decisive in regard to the means by which the socialist state should be brought about. The group was named after the Roman commander Fabius Cunctator who overcame his enemies by slow, gradual but effective measures. The Fabians were influenced by Marx's description of industrial society but they were most strongly affected by his analysis of historical development. Marx had argued that societies pass through three major stages and that socialism would be achieved in the third. The first phase was aristocratic in which society was dominated by the landowning classes. This group would be displaced by the middle class whose wealth was drawn from the profits of industry and who were known as capitalists (from capital or money). In Britain the aristocratic phase had been passed through and the country was, during the nineteenth century, in the midst of the second stage, that is dominated by the middle classes. Marx argued that the third and final phase would be brought about when the working classes (or proletariat) would rebel and overthrow the capitalist masters of industry. Then the socialist age would begin.

The Fabians shrank from violent revolution. They saw **their task** as one of persuading unbelievers of the rightness and inevitability of socialism. In particular **they hoped to persuade those with power to give way** in order that the new socialist age would come about as smoothly and peacefully as possible. To this end the Fabians concentrated on the production of **pamphlets** which urged the socialist view and 'permeation', winning over the minds of those in power. In the words of a leading Fabian, **Beatrice Webb,** they aimed 'to make the thinking persons socialistic rather than to organize unthinking persons into socialism'. She and her colleagues, including her husband Sidney, were against founding a separate socialist party and it was with extreme reluctance that they agreed to the forming of the Labour Representation Committee and to joining its committee. This desire to gain the ear of the powerful, their closeness with existing authorities and the high respect which they had for intellect placed them at a remove from working people. The playwright Bernard Shaw, probably their most famous member, remarked 'we were middle class all, rank and file as well as leaders'. The importance of the Fabians is hard to assess. They were theorists, hostile to attempts to give the Labour movement a political existence and their ignoring the Trade Union movement and the snobbery of some of the members kept them apart from working men. Their **pamphlets were widely** read and several working men, later prominent in the Labour Party, were members. Once the Labour Party was under way, they gave it their help, shaping its thought and one Fabian, Ramsay MacDonald, became the first Labour Prime Minister.

Trade Unionism

The Trade Unions were **working class organizations,** formed from and led by working men, unlike the S.D.F. and Fabians. By 1890 there were 750,000 Trade Unionists in Britain. 'The Labour Party was born out of the bowels of the T.U.C.' was the typical straight-forward and gutsy comment of Ernest Bevin. Between 1850 and 1880 Trade Unionism was dominated by the **New Model Unions,** associations of skilled workmen such as Engineers. All unions were represented on the **Trades Union Congress** which was liberal in sympathies. In 1874 the T.U.C. gave money to help two working class M.Ps who voted with the Liberals but spoke for themselves on Labour matters. During the 1880s the Trades Union movement changed. The **New Unionism** was the unionism of the unskilled workers such as dockers, miners and gas workers, men of a more militant spirit.

The **political importance of the New Unionism was twofold.** First the success of the 1889 Dockers Strike forged a strong sense of class solidarity and helped make working men less willing to identify with the middle class. The failure of economic methods became obvious by the mid-1890s when employers were able to fight strikes effectively and the **effects of depression made Trade Unionists of all kinds realize the need for a political outlet for their grievances.**

The Independent Labour Party

The **founder members** of this movement **were Trades Unionists.** Its roots were in Bradford where various labour and socialist groups came together to sponsor candidates for Parliament in 1891. The example was copied and by 1892 there were three 'Labour' M.Ps, including **Keir Hardie** in the Commons. On Keir Hardie's initiative the Bradford Conference was held in 1893 and attended by all groups interested, including Unions and Fabians. Their aim was a national party and the outcome was the **Independent Labour Party.** Its membership was working class and its policy was socialist. Its **successes were limited** and in 1895 all its 27 candidates were defeated.

Trades Union sympathy in a party standing for working class interests grew in the late 1890s, and in 1899 its annual congress approved overwhelmingly a scheme to this end. The Independent Labour Party had shown the way and indicated that working men could unite together for a political purpose for the first time since the death of Chartism.

Growth of the Labour Party, 1900–24

There were many strands to the Labour movement and unity of purpose had been hard to achieve. The **Labour Representation Committee** set up in 1900 with **Trades Union** backing was dogged by disunity – the Miners Federation did not join until 1908. Its aims were broadly to embrace socialists anxious for far-reaching economic and social changes, as well as Trades Unionists whose interests were often confined to matters of wages, conditions of work and relations with employers. The **Taff Vale Case** and **Osborne Judgement** (see ps. 119–120 and 122) made the Unions realize the value of a voice in Parliament. Ramsay MacDonald, the Committee's secretary, played an important part in smoothing the passage of early years and securing unity. Growth did come, in 1902 2 Labour M.Ps were elected and in 1923 there were 191, who received 4 million votes, The alliance with the Liberals in 1903 and experience in Lloyd George's ministry in 1916–8 helped the party find its feet and its members gain experience.

First Labour Government, 1924

Labour came to power in 1924 after the rejection by the voters of Baldwin's policy of Trade Protection (see p. 165). Labour gained 191 seats, the Liberals 158 and the Conservatives 258 and when **Ramsay MacDonald was given the opportunity to form a government with Liberal backing,** he jumped at the chance.

Not much was achieved in this short ministry which lasted less than six months. Some attempt was made to ease some of the cuts in respect of education and the conditions under which unemployment benefit was paid, Labour's most radical change was in housing with **Wheatley's Act (1924)** which raised government subsidies and enabled half a million new houses to be built by local authorities in ten years. In the area of unemployment Labour achieved very little in spite of talk of a programme of government financed public works.

Labour survived in power thanks to Liberal support. The Liberals were far from sympathetic to revolutionary socialism and the **Labour government's efforts to establish links with Soviet Russia lost it Liberal support** and sealed its doom. The subsequent election was overshadowed by the **Zinoniev Letter** published by the *Daily Mail* in which Zinoniev, a senior Russian official suggested that MacDonald's proposed treaty with Russia would pave the way for a British revolution. The letter was a fake and it has sometimes been thought that it turned the electorate against Labour. In fact it was the Liberals who lost more votes than Labour.

Second Labour Government, 1929–31

The **second Labour ministry** was dominated by the events which followed the **1929 Wall Street Crash** which occurred within months of MacDonald becoming Prime Minister. **American finance and business quickly fell apart** and the **repercussions were felt all over Europe.** America could no longer buy British goods and so exports fell and unemployment swiftly rose. The **Labour government was divided about solving the problem** and there were many different suggestions. MacDonald saw the problem as the breakdown of the capitalist system but he and the party rejected **Sir Oswald Mosley**'s scheme for public control of industry and planned foreign trade. Meanwhile **government expenditure went up,** especially on unemployment pay and **revenue was falling.** The answer Labour chose was the traditional one of **cuts** and in 1931 a committee under **Sir George May** was set up to find what cuts could be made. The **May Committee** reported in the mid-summer of 1931 at a time when foreigners were rapidly withdrawing money from London banks. The May Committee recommended among other things **£96 million in cuts, including unemployment pay.** The Labour cabinet could not stomach such a **betrayal of the working class** and the T.U.C. came out openly against any cuts. The cabinet split and MacDonald sought the advice of King George V, Baldwin and the Liberal, Samuel. The result was the **National Government,** a coalition with MacDonald as Prime Minister, backed by Conservatives and Liberals (see p. 169).

Conclusion

In 1931 the leader had betrayed the party even though the party had no answer to the crisis of capitalism. In twenty years the Labour party had risen to become the major radical party in British politics, replacing the divided Liberals (see p. 165). It was a party of the working class, a child with many fathers – Trade Unionism, Fabianism and the Social Democratic Federation. Its experience of government had been limited, in 1924 by the need to hold Liberal support and in 1929 by the unexpected demands of the financial crisis. These circumstances prevented it from fulfilling the dreams of its founders; they would have to wait until 1945.

Chapter 13
The Inter-War Years, 1918-39

Introduction

The general election of 1918 saw the victory of Lloyd George's coalition, which had campaigned with the slogan 'a land fit for heroes to live in'. A wonderful promise which appealed to the voters, it proved impossible to fulfil. In its place the people of Britain faced a series of economic crises, a long depression and widespread unemployment. None of the political parties found an effective remedy for the sickness which affected British industry, so from 1921 to 1940 there was never less than 1 million without jobs. Yet whilst successive governments could not end the depression or restore full employment, each attempted to reduce the personal hardship which went with it. The work begun by the Liberals between 1906 and 1914 was continued and social services were added to and expanded into new areas such as housing. The inter-war years saw the acceptance, by all political parties, of the principle that it was the government's duty to provide welfare services.

Lloyd George's Coalition, 1918–22

Riding on the wave of success after Germany's defeat, Lloyd George called a **general election at the end of 1918.** Candidates who supported the coalition were given a letter signed by Lloyd George (contemptuously called a **'coupon'** by Asquith) and the result was a sweeping victory for the Coalition. After the 'coupon election', Lloyd George turned to the business of building a new Britain, the **'land fit for heroes to live in'** which he had promised. **The Housing Act (1919)** was the first step and it aimed to provide cheap housing for the poor. Local authorities were given a subsidy by the government so that they could build houses which were to be rented cheaply. The scheme ran into financial difficulties and by 1923 was all but dropped. Nevertheless the Act admitted that government had a responsibility to provide adequate housing and was a further extension of the idea of state-backed welfare services. The **National Insurance Act (1920)** extended the 1911 National Insurance Act (see p. 124) to all workpeople earning up to £250 a year (except farm workers and domestic servants). After 12 weeks contributions, a man could expect 15 shillings (75p) a week in unemployment pay and a woman 12 shillings (60p). Twelve million men and women were affected by this act which, when unemployment increased in the 1920s, took some of the edge off bitterness and resentment.

Industrial and economic problems

Immediately after the war ended, there was a boom. The government was able to organize the **demobilization** of the armed forces on the principle 'first in, first out' and by 1919 80% of men in the services had been discharged. They returned to a country which seemed prosperous and in which industry was flourishing. **By the winter of 1920–21 the boom was over and trade slumped.** There were several reasons for this sudden change. There had been over-production and business men had over-estimated the world market for British goods. Before 1914 Britain had exported textiles to the Far East but by 1920 China and Japan were producing their own textiles at prices which undercut British exports. The world demand for such basic exports as coal and ships had also declined. Old problems which had existed prior to 1914 returned. British goods were not competing and in many areas Britain's trading rivals had used the opportunity of war to take over British markets.

The **first consequence of the trade slump was unemployment;** by June 1921 over **2 million were without jobs**. The areas which suffered most were in the North since the **old industries** such as **textiles and ship-building** were the hardest hit by falling world demand.

Coal-mining was also in the doldrums and here the problem was made worse by the struggle between the miners and coal owners. A government enquiry, called the **Sankey Commission,** had examined the state of coal mining but its members failed to agree about its future. In their report (1919) a small majority of the commission argued for nationalization but the government rejected this suggestion. It did however pass the **Coal Mines Act (1919)** which limited a miner's working hours to seven at the coal face. The mines remained under government control until March 1921 when they were handed back to their pre-war owners. The owners first act was to demand a reduction of wages which in their eyes was the only way to keep the industry profitable. The Miner's union strongly objected and the owners replied with a closure of all the mines – a lock-out. For the miners the struggle with the coal owners was a way of life and they had the backing of the railwaymen and transport workers. The **Triple Alliance** of pre-war days had been resurrected (see p. 125) and the other two unions promised to strike in sympathy with the miners. The government, faced with the prospect of a wide-scale strike which would effectively bring all industry to a standstill, opened negotiations with the unions. On **'Black Friday'**, 15 April 1922, the railwaymen and transport workers backed down, leaving the miners unsupported and isolated. They were left with no choice but to accept the owners' terms and return to work in July. The fight between the owners and the miners was not over, the resentment remained and would soon break into an open struggle. **Lloyd George lost his working class support.**

The Fall of the Coalition, 1922
Late in 1922, the **Conservatives,** inspired by Stanley Baldwin, decided to **withdraw their support from Lloyd George.** They were discontented with his concessions in **Ireland** (see p. 88) and his bungling over the **Chanak incident** (see p. 175). His pledge of the 1918 election had not been fulfilled – the 'land fit for heroes' had not materialized. The man who had won the war had been unable to win the peace and so he resigned. His achievements, in peace and war, had been considerable but he divided his own party into his own and Asquith's followers. **From 1922 onwards the Liberal party was a declining force in British politics. Its place had been taken by the Labour Party.**

Bonar-Law and Baldwin, 1922–3

Lloyd George was followed as Prime Minister by **Bonar Law,** the Conservative leader. After his retirement through ill-health in 1922, the party leadership and post of Prime Minister was filled by **Stanley Baldwin. Baldwin's answer to the depression was to end Free Trade and introduce duties to protect British industry.** He fought a general election in 1923, calling for popular support for protection, but was defeated. The Conservatives won 258 seats in the Commons, Labour 192 and Liberals 157. The Labour leader, Ramsay MacDonald, was asked to form a government (see p. 160).

Baldwin's Second Ministry, 1924–9

In the **General Election of 1924 the Conservatives gained nearly half the national vote and 419 out of 615 seats in the House of Commons.** The Prime Minister, **Baldwin,** was a solid, respectable pipe-smoking figure who wanted **industrial peace at home** and an **end to the politics of the class struggle**. In matters of **social and welfare reform**, his government's policies followed the pattern which had already been established by the Coalition and Labour administrations. Much of the social reform of this ministry was the result of the work of the Minister of Health, **Neville Chamberlain,** the son of Joseph Chamberlain. **The Pensions Act** (1925) introduced contributions for Old Age Pensions which were to be given to women at the age of 60 and men at 65. In 1928 payment of unemployed benefits (the dole) was allowed to men who had never worked and therefore paid no contributions. Another major change brought about by Baldwin's ministry was the **Local Government Act (1929).** This abolished the old Poor Law Unions and brought the care of the poor into the hands of County and Borough Councils. The local authorities were now in charge of education, public health, roads, housing and local planning. The rates on farmland and industrial property were reduced and local authorities were compensated for loss of income by government subsidies.

The government created the **Central Electricity Generating Board (1926)** which organised national power supply and established the national grid. The **British Broadcasting Corporation** was brought under government control in 1927 with a monopoly of wireless broadcasting. This measure meant that there would be no rash of commercial stations as in the United States and no commercial sponsorship of programmes. Both measures showed how far Conservative thinking had changed in thirty years for here was a Conservative government setting up national corporations by which the government directed and controlled industry. The old principles of *laissez faire* were almost totally abandoned.

Industrial and economic problems
The major problem which faced Baldwin's government was industrial stagnation and its consequence, unemployment. The government believed that revival would depend on the increase of exports.

To promote industrial revival and to make the currency stable, Churchill, the Chancellor of the Exchequer, brought Britain back on the **Gold Standard** in the **1925 Budget.** The sense of this measure was hotly debated then and later. On one hand the Gold Standard (by which the value of the pound sterling was backed by gold) reduced the costs of imported raw materials and food, but on the other, it forced up the price of British goods exported abroad. Whilst there was an increase in wages and production during Baldwin's period as Prime Minister, the restored Gold Standard did little to encourage exports. A further help to exports was thought to be the reduction of production costs, which in effect meant lower wages. In 1925 Baldwin voiced the opinion that, 'All workers of this country have got to take reductions in wages to help put industry back on its feet'. If wages which were already low were further cut, then this would reduce demand at home for many would be too poor to buy manufactured goods. These arguments avoided the main problem which was and continued to be the lack of demand for the products of Britain's older industries, coal, textiles and ship-building. The industrial expansion and rising prosperity of this period was concentrated in southern England and in such growing business as car manufacture. In terms of the value of production the motor industry overtook cotton during the 1930s.

General Strike, 1926

Perhaps the greatest difficulties to be suffered by an old industry were endured by **coal-mining.** These problems led to the General Strike of 1926. From 1924 the British **coal industry had been losing to its Polish and German competitors** and the **coal owners' answer to the problem was to suggest lower wages and longer hours for the miners. The miners union naturally rejected these proposals** and the owners then replied with a **lock-out** in the hope that the miners, deprived of work and wages, would give way. Under the threat of a mass lock-out in June 1925, the government offered a subsidy to the mining industry to be paid over the next nine months. During this time the government-appointed **Samuel Commission** were to undertake an enquiry into the industry and make suggestions for the government to consider.

The **Miners Union had the backing of the Trades Union Congress** (representing all Trade Unions) which had taken over negotiations on their behalf. **The T.U.C. was willing to call upon all its members to strike if the miners' case was rejected.** Aware of this the government made preparations for a General Strike which might inevitably follow any deadlock in bargaining with the miners. In March 1926 the **Samuel Commission reported** to the government and suggested that the royalties (revenues) from the mines should be nationalized and recommended improvements in conditions of work for the miners. This was cold comfort for the miners for the Commission also proposed a reduction in wages. The owners stood by their old demands, longer hours and lower wages. The miners' leader, A. J. Cook, spoke for all his men with the demand 'Not a penny off the pay, not a minute on the day'. The government and the general council of the T.U.C. continued to negotiate but with no result and on 1 May 1926 the miners were locked out of the pits. The hand of the T.U.C. was now forced and it went ahead with plans for a General Strike although still negotiating with the government. These talks broke down when printers at the *Daily Mail* refused to print the newspaper's editorial which called for patriotic solidarity. **From 3 to 12 May there was a General Strike but its effect on the country were not as crippling as the Unions had hoped.**

The **government plans** for the distribution of goods worked and there was a widespread response to appeals for volunteers to drive trains and buses. In spite of the warlike tone of Churchill's official government newspaper, the *British Gazette*, there was very little violence between the strikers and the police. The T.U.C. kept its lines open to the government and a compromise was reached through **Herbert Samuel.** In return for calling off the strike, the Unions were promised a National Wages Board which would organise the cuts in miners' pay whilst the industry would be re-organized along the lines laid down by the Samuel Commission. The **miners** stubbornly refused the settlement and **stayed out on strike for a further six months. In the end they accepted longer hours and lower pay.**

The General Strike was over and the government could claim a victory for what Baldwin regarded as wisdom and commonsense. The **Trade Disputes Act (1927)** made it illegal for Trade Unions to call sympathy strikes (which meant strikes in support of men in other unions) and strikes intended to 'coerce' the government. In 1927 the government, at the opening session of Parliament, drew attention to 'encouraging signs of improvement in trade and industry' and looked forward to a return to normal conditions. Baldwin was accused of inactivity by his opponents, which was to a certain extent true. Baldwin was following a policy of not promising changes which he and his government could not bring about. During the 1929 election the Conservatives campaigned with slogans such as 'Trust Baldwin' and 'Safety First'. Baldwin had broken the General Strike, his government had introduced important social reforms and whilst industry in the north was idle, there were signs of a national recovery.

The National Governments, 1931–9

From the financial crisis in the summer of 1931 until the outbreak of war, Britain was ruled by 'national' governments. These were strongly backed by the Conservatives with some Labour and Liberal support and were widely and popularly supported by the public in the general elections of 1931 and 1935.

Ramsay MacDonald was **Prime Minister from 1931 to his resignation in 1935, Baldwin from 1935 to 1937 and Chamberlain from 1937 to 1940.**

Industrial and Economic Problems, 1931–9

The National Government had been created to deal with **the financial crisis which had occurred in the summer of 1931.** Its first actions were designed to ensure British financial stability. **Immediate cuts were made in public spending** so as to balance the budget. The salaries and wages of men and women employed by the government were cut by 10% (15% in the case of teachers) as was unemployment pay (the proposal which had originally divided the Labour cabinet). One sudden and unexpected result of the cuts was a strike of sailors aboard Royal Navy ships which was known as the **Invergordon Mutiny.** The dispute was quickly settled but the news of the incident further undermined foreign confidence and there were hasty withdrawals of foreign money from London. The next step taken by the National Government was **the abandonment of the Gold Standard** by which the pound was devalued by a third which automatically reduced the cost of British exports.

After these measures, MacDonald called a **General Election,** in which **National Government supporters won a sweeping victory** with over 14 million votes and 554 seats in the House of Commons against Labour with 51. This was what was called the 'Doctor's Mandate', a phrase used at the time which suggested that the government would act as a doctor, treating and curing the sick British economy.

The first answer of the National Government to the economic difficulties which faced the country was Protec-

tion. The introduction of duties on foreign goods appeared the only way to save and help British industry. The doctrines of Free Trade which had for nearly a hundred years been accepted by British governments and people were swept aside. **A tariff (duty) of 10% was imposed on foreign imports in the 1932 budget.** A Tariff Commission was created with powers to raise tariffs above this level if such action would assist particular British industries. Within a short time, three-quarters of the goods imported into Britain carried tariffs of between 10 and 20%. Raw materials and food were, however, not included and the products of the Empire were also exempted. The government hoped to persuade Commonwealth governments to join an Imperial Free Area (like that planned by Joseph Chamberlain in 1903), (see p. 115) and an Imperial Conference was called at Ottawa to discuss the plan. The **Ottawa Conference (1932)** was not successful for the Commonwealth governments were unwilling to allow British goods to compete freely with their own products and the British government refused to tax imported foreign food.

At home, the government took steps to assist agriculture by giving **subsidies to farmers** to encourage them to grow certain crops. By 1936 over £40 million was being given to British farmers and special marketing boards had been set up to control the sale of certain commodities such as potatoes and milk. By these measures it was hoped that food production would be increased and the need for imported food reduced.

By **1934 there was a recovery in industrial production** and the government drew strength and confidence from the apparent fact that its measures were working. The cuts made in unemployment pay and government salaries were restored and income tax was reduced. The number of unemployed had fallen to about one million and in southern England there was economic growth and prosperity. Home consumption rose, thanks to high wages and low prices. This was especially noticeable in housing with growing numbers of private houses being built, particularly around London. A journey along one of the suburban train lines or ring-roads still reveals masses of red-brick or mock-Tudor semi-detached houses built during this period. Whilst some cried out against the swallowing up of the countryside, the new houses reflected part of the dreams of English people in the 1930s. They remain a token of the prosperity which spread throughout southern England.

There was also another England, revealed in J. B. Priestley's

English Journey (1933) of industrial towns with closed shipyards, mills and factories, the England of the nineteenth century industrial revolution. Recovery had not affected these parts for the products of their industries were no longer required by foreign buyers. There were towns, like Jarrow in Durham, where two-thirds or more of the workforce were without jobs. From time to time men from these towns would form up and march south to London to show their conditions and misfortune to the government. The **'Hunger Marchers'** protests helped persuade the government to set up a fund for the relief of **'Special Areas'** of high unemployment (1934). The success of this scheme was very limited. The measures of the National Government were unable to reduce the number of the unemployed to below one million and it remained at this figure until 1940.

The economic problems of the 1930s and the apparent inability of the established political parties to solve them effectively, led many people to turn to new political movements of the extreme left and right. **Sir Oswald Mosley,** one of the most outstanding Labour M.Ps in the 1920s, had broken with his party in 1930 after its refusal to consider his plans for government investment and control over industry. In 1932 he founded the **British Union of Fascists.** Its members wore a uniform with a black shirt and like their Italian counterparts, they held marches and open-air rallies. Faced with Fascism on their own doorsteps, left-wingers in Britain did all they could to break up Mosley's meetings and the Fascists retaliated with equal and often greater violence. The nuisance value of the Fascists was so great that in 1936 the government passed the **Public Order Act.** This made illegal the wearing of political uniforms and gave the police the power to ban political marches.

A further domestic problem troubled the National Government in 1936, the **Abdication Crisis.** The new king, **Edward VIII,** was determined to marry Mrs. Simpson, an American woman who had been divorced twice. This plan was unacceptable to the government and a great many of the king's subjects for a number of reasons. Edward VIII was Head of the Church of England which at this time did not approve of divorce, the Commonwealth governments were uneasy about Mrs. Simpson as a possible Queen and many British people thought that the King should overrule his private feelings out of a sense of duty. In short, as Mr. Baldwin told the King, the country would not accept Mrs. Simpson as a royal consort. Edward, faced with the alternative of marrying the woman he loved or the crown, chose to abdicate in December 1936. He was made Duke of Windsor and left Britain to marry Mrs. Simpson. His younger brother, the Duke of York, became George VI.

Conclusion

From 1936 onwards the government's time was increasingly taken up with the conduct of foreign policy (see pp. 176–82). The drift towards war had begun and efforts were made to prepare Britain for the coming struggle. Arrangements were made for air-raid shelters to be manufactured and distributed and Air Raid Precaution services set up. The Ministry of Health undertook plans for the mass evacuation of children from large cities in anticipation of air-raids. Re-armament was stepped up, providing a new boost for industry.

The inter-war years which had begun with plans for a better Britain ended with preparations for war. Throughout this period Britain had faced serious economic problems, the result of the decline of old, basic industries. In consequence the northern parts of Britain suffered decay and unemployment for which there seemed no remedy. **The fruits of prosperity and the expansion of new industry were confined to the Midlands and the South.** The governments of Britain during the 1920s and 1930s had followed the path of the pre-war Liberal government by continuing to expand the provision of welfare services and state help for the poor. The direction of industry by the state, originally the product of war-time necessity, survived the war and became normal policy. State subsidies for sick industries, direct government intervention in industrial disputes and state ownership were policies adopted by all parties. Many measures which, before the war, would have provoked fierce controversy were passed through Parliament with little or no debate; as Mr. Baldwin remarked the differences between the parties were often very slight or non-existent.

Chapter 14
British Foreign Policy, 1919–39

Introduction

The World War over, the British people and their leaders wished to restore peace and security to Europe and see that they were preserved. For the next twenty years the objective of British foreign policy was the maintenance of peace throughout the world by means of international co-operation and negotiations. To this end Britain was a member of the **League of Nations** which had been founded in 1920. The League was not a success. It was unable to resist or stop the warlike and bullying policies of Japan, Italy and Germany. Unable to uphold peace, Britain was forced to face reality and in the late 1930s began to prepare for war with Germany.

The Problems of Peacemaking, 1919–22

Between 1919 and 1920 the allied powers signed a series of peace treaties which laid down terms to Germany and her allies. The most important of these was the **Treaty of Versailles** between the allies and Germany. It was negotiated and signed during the summer of 1919 and aimed to make Germany incapable of waging another war. Britain was represented by the Prime Minister, Lloyd George, who had expressed himself in some sympathy with popular demands for a harsh treaty which had been expressed in such slogans as 'Squeeze Germany until the pips squeak'. In private the British government was less willing to allow Germany to be crippled or left with a burning desire to avenge humiliation. The French thought otherwise. Clemenceau, the French spokesman at Versailles, like the rest of his people mourned over a million casualties and wished to avenge the loss of Alsace-Lorraine and the heavy payments extracted from them by the Germans in 1871.

The French view prevailed and Germany was ordered to pay over £6,000 million in **reparations,** sums of money which were to be paid to the allies to meet the costs of the war and to show publicly German 'war guilt'. The British reluctantly agreed although the Treasury estimated that Germany could only afford less than half the agreed sum. Germany's ability to pay was further lessened by the loss of territories on her eastern border and the Saar industrial area.

As a guarantee of future peace, Germany's armed forces were drastically reduced, her navy was handed over to Britain (the fleet sank itself at Scapa Flow) and her western border province, the Rhineland, was made a de-militarized zone. In so far as it was possible the treaty had satisfied France's desire for revenge and guaranteed France's security against future German aggression.

Britain was given the right to administer the old German colonies, such as Tanganyika, and the threat of the German navy had been removed. There was criticism of the treaty in Britain, particularly from the economist, **J. M. Keynes,** whose book **The Economic Consequences of the Peace** argued that Germany could not stand the strain of paying reparations. Britain was therefore sympathetic to the **Dawes Plan (1924)** which moderated the scale of German payments. Later many British politicians would sympathise with German efforts to reverse some of the treaty's provisions.

Two problems left by the peace treaties concerned Lloyd George's coalition, those of **Russia and Turkey.** The 1917 Bolshevik Revolution and subsequent Communist government had shocked Conservative and Liberal opinion in Britain although many Labour party members were sympathetic. There had been **allied troops in Russia since 1917,** sent there to protect supplies of arms from falling into communist or German hands. With the beginning of a civil war between the Communists and counter-revolutionaries (the Whites), British and allied forces had co-operated with the Whites. **Intervention in Russia continued during 1918 and 1919 and was enthusiastically backed by Churchill who was filled with a deep loathing of all that communism stood for.** The British forces did little to influence the outcome of the war and British policy was criticized by Labour sympathisers. Lloyd George did not share Churchill's zeal for the anti-communist cause and in **1920 the cabinet ordered the withdrawal of British troops and warships.**

The **Treaty of Sevrès (1920)** had been made between the allies and Turkey and was followed by a Greek invasion of Turkey. In the war that followed, Mustapha Kemal (later known as Kemal Ataturk) drove out the Greeks and his troops moved towards the Straits. This area had been declared a de-militarized zone but was occupied by British troops. When these were confronted by Turkish troops at **Chanak** (1922), a war seemed likely, the more so since Lloyd George was passionately pro-Greek and anti-Turk. Unsupported by other European powers, Lloyd George stepped down and his mishandling of the incident helped to bring about his downfall.

Britain had played a significant part in the process of post-war peacemaking although she had been unable to soften the vengeful demands of the French. It was hoped that the weakening of Germany would ensure future peace and Britain was no longer threatened by the German navy. At the same time Britain had acquired former German colonies and control over parts of the Turkish Empire (see p. 174). For future peace and security, British hopes were to rest with the League of Nations.

The League of Nations, 1920–33

The **League of Nations** was the creation of Woodrow Wilson, the United States President and its representative at the Versailles conference. By the terms of its Covenant, each member nation of the League promised to co-operate for the achievement of international peace and security through collective action. If one country went to war, then the League nations would act together against it. Britain was a founder member of the League in 1920 but in that year the American Congress refused to join and the League was left without the powerful backing of the United States.

The League suffered another weakness. In theory all the members would take action together against a country which went to war, but there was no agreement as to what form this action would take. In 1924 the Labour and Conservative governments refused to approve of League proposals for action against aggressive nations on the grounds that such actions would prove unworkable. This was so and when put to the test the League proved unable to obtain international co-operation.

Disarmament was one important aspect of the League's work. In Britain it was hoped, both by Labour and Conservative governments that a reduction of arms would lead to international peace. At the **Washington Naval Treaty (1922),** Britain, the United States, Japan, France and Italy agreed to stop building battleships during the next ten years and to limit the numbers of ships in their navies to fixed proportions. For every five British battleships there would be five American and three Japanese. This treaty marked the end of the British policy of making sure that the Royal Navy had a superiority over foreign navies. This treaty was regarded as the beginning of international disarmament. The Labour and Conservative governments between 1925 and 1933 reduced expenditure on the army, navy and airforce and the French followed suit. The **League of Nations Disarmament Conference (1933)** failed to get an agreement between the nations. Thereafter, as international tension increased so did national armaments.

At the same time as reducing armaments, British foreign policy aimed at gaining international co-operation towards peace. The **Locarno Pact (1925)** was designed to prevent any war between France and Germany over their joint frontier. The Germans confirmed the frontier which had been drawn at Versailles and Britain and Italy promised to fight against whichever nation violated the frontier. Britain also signed the Kellogg-Briand Pact (1928) which outlawed war as an instrument of policy.

Throughout the 1920s **British governments were in support of agreements to bring peace and order to international relations.** They were also willing to assist plans for disarmament and **give their backing to the League of Nations**. Behind the actions of the British government was a wish to avoid war through international discussions and agreements. On the surface this policy appeared successful but once challenged by Italy and Germany in the 1930s, it quickly fell to pieces. Ruthless leaders would not let their nations be bound by treaties and the League was shown to be without the power to check aggressive nations.

The Road to War, 1933–9

The year 1933 marked a turning point in British foreign policy. By that year two new leaders had appeared in Europe who were prepared to ignore the League of Nations, build up their armed forces and when necessary, resort to war in order to get what they wanted. The first was **Benito Mussolini,** the Italian Fascist dictator, who had seized power in 1922 and who openly proclaimed his dreams of restoring the old glories of the Roman Empire. More menacingly he hinted that Italy had been cheated of her just deserts at the Treaty of Versailles. In Germany **the Nazi party and its leader, Adolph Hitler,** thrived and grew strong on resentment against the Treaty of Versailles and promised the return of Germany's past power and glory. Hitler went beyond demands for the return of land lost at the Treaty and spoke of a 'greater Germany' whose frontiers would include all German speaking people. **In 1933 Hitler took over the government of Germany** and was free to fulfil the promises he had made to the people of Germany. Europe was now transformed. Two warlike states, led by dictators, were prepared to make their demands and use every kind of force to secure them.

Britain and the Dictators, 1933–8

Background

Once he had control of Germany in 1933, Hitler withdrew the German representative from the League of Nations disarmament conference. Within months he began to re-arm Germany secretly, in defiance of the Versailles Treaty which limited the German army to 100,000 men. In 1935 Hitler revealed the existence of his growing air force (the Luftwaffe) and in the same year the army commander, Von Blomberg, announced to an appreciative audience of war veterans that 'The world has been made to realize that Germany did not die of its defeat'.

Before looking at **Britain's policy towards Nazi Germany,** it is important to **examine the thinking which shaped that policy.** For many years public opinion had believed that the building up of arms contributed to war. This had been so, it was thought, in the years up to 1914. For this reason the **Labour Party** had been strongly opposed to spending money on arms and one of its most prominent leaders, **George Lansbury,** was an open pacifist – one who believed that war was wrong in any circumstance. Pacifism was strongly felt in many quarters in Britain. In 1933 the Oxford Union (the University debating society) had voted in favour of the motion 'This House would not fight for king and country'. An opinion poll, organised by the pacifist **Peace Pledge Union** in 1934 revealed $11\frac{1}{2}$ million votes in favour of international disarmament and support for the League of Nations. Pacifism drew strength from public knowledge of the realities of war expressed in plays like *Journey's End* or novels like *All Quiet on the Western Front*. The development of aircraft since 1918 had led to **alarmist and often exaggerated fears of the consequences of bombing from the air.** Speaking in a Parliamentary debate in 1933 Churchill had spoken of an expected 40,000 dead in a week if London was bombed. No one contradicted him and the Prime

Minister, Baldwin, remarked that 'The Bomber would always get through'. There was in the Britain of 1933 a genuine revulsion against war, a fear of its consequences and a desire to avoid it. There was also a tendency to under-estimate Hitler and disbelieve the more frightening or outrageous of his threats. In 1934 *The Times* commented 'There is more reason to fear for Germany than to fear Germany'.

Certainly the British people were quickly made aware of the full horror of the Nazi regime with its murders, persecution of the Jews and Concentration Camps. There was also a small body of opinion which saw much to admire in Hitler and Mussolini and praised their achievements. Yet during the 1930s few people in Britain could not have been unaware of the evil and malignant nature of Nazi rule. By contrast public opinion was probably slow to awake to the seriousness of Hitler's threat to the rest of Europe.

The National government of Baldwin and his successor, Neville Chamberlain, (who became Prime Minister in 1937), understood that public opinion would not favour immediate re-armament. Yet Baldwin and his cabinet were deeply concerned about British air power. From 1933 **Britain began enlarging and re-equipping its air force** and this programme resulted in RADAR and the supply of Hurricane and Spitfire fighters to the Royal Air Force by 1939. Baldwin stated to the House of Commons in 1933 that 'this country shall no longer be in a position inferior to any country within striking distance of our shore'. So while British politicians were attempting to come to terms with Hitler in Europe, they were encouraging a programme of re-armament of the air force.

The size of the German air force and the fear which it created (by 1935 it possessed over 1,000 aircraft and by 1939 800 long-range bombers) **did influence the policies of Britain and France.** There was also, in Britain especially, **a feeling that Hitler and Germany had some justice on their side when they demanded back losses suffered at the Treaty of Versailles.** There was also a feeling in many Conservative circles that Hitler could be contained and that eventually he would turn Germany against Communist Russia. Since 1917 there had been great suspicion and fear of Russian communism among the middle and upper classes in Britain. Hitler had loudly spoken of his hatred for communism and it was possible that if satisfied in Europe, he would attack Russia. To put it crudely, some people in

Britain hoped to see Nazi Germany and Communist Russia at each others throats, a struggle which might destroy both ideologies.

The Labour party and the left wing in Britain thought otherwise. Nazism and Fascism were the enemies of socialism, whether it was the Labour party variety or the Communist variety. In Britain the left wing came to realize that Europe was facing a fight between the two sets of political beliefs and this was fulfilled when the **Spanish Civil War** broke out in 1936. On one side was the left wing Republican government which was enthusiastically supported by Communists and the British Labour party, and on the other was General Franco's Nationalist party and its supporters including Spanish fascists (Falangists). Germany and Italy sent troops and aeroplanes to help Franco but the British and French governments refused to intervene. This non-intervention policy did not stop thousands of republican sympathisers in Britain and elsewhere from enlisting in the Republican International Brigade. The struggle in Spain was between rival political beliefs and systems, and for the left it was a forerunner of a greater conflict which seemed inevitable.

For the **governments of Baldwin and Chamberlain, the main objective was keeping the peace in Europe.** In practical terms this meant **negotiating with Hitler and Mussolini** and attempting to come to an agreement with them. This policy came to be known as **'appeasement',** in other words giving way to the demands of the dictators. To an extent this was true, but it should be remembered that few people in Britain would have supported an alternative, defiant policy. This would have been called 'warmongering' and would have been widely opposed. Gradually as the nature of Nazism was fully revealed in all its grisly details and the extent of Hitler's ambitions were appreciated, the British people realised the war would be inevitable. They did not welcome this fact but thanks to the preparations of the government, the country was not unprepared or undefended in 1939.

Abyssinia and the Rhineland, 1935–6

The first challenge to the peace of Europe came from Mussolini, who for some time had planned to seize the African state of **Abyssinia** (Ethiopia) and add it to the Italian Empire. He was of course risking a clash with the League of Nations which would condemn such aggression but he was made bold by the League's recent failure to stop Japanese attacks on China. Mussolini's risk paid off, for the League, whilst condemning Italian aggression and proposing economic sanctions, did not cut off Italy's vital supply of oil. The British government lacked the power to intervene effectively and, going behind the back of the League, the British Foreign Secretary, Sir Samuel Hoare, made an agreement with Pierre Laval, his French counterpart. The **Hoare Laval Pact (1936)** gave Italy a part of Abyssinia, an arrangement which aroused public anger in Britain and forced Hoare's resignation. Meanwhile the Italians had taken the whole of Abyssinia. The **League had been shown to be ineffective** and the attempt by Britain and France to obtain a private deal with Italy appeared as profitless bungling. Italy's success in challenging the League was quickly followed by **Hitler's occupation of the de-militarized zone of the Rhineland in 1936.** As the German troops crossed the Rhineland to take up their positions opposite the border with France, the alarmed French government turned to Britain for support and help. Britain was not sympathetic to the French. It was argued that the Germans had a good right to occupy what was their own territory, or, in the phrase used at the time, take over 'their own back-garden'. The British people shared the attitude of the government and the French, deprived of British support, were left to stand by and let the Germans go ahead. Hitler's bluff had not been called (at the time he was not strong enough to take on both Britain and France) and his appetite was whetted for further easy gains.

Mussolini's successful defiance of the League, his occupation of Abyssinia and the lack of Anglo-French solidarity over the Rhineland marked the end of international efforts to resist aggression and keep the peace. **Hitler now felt free to carry through his programme to unite all German speaking peoples in one state.**

Munich, 1938

In March 1938 **Hitler's troops occupied Austria** (Anschluss) and later in the year he turned his attention to **Czechoslovakia.** In the Czech province of **Sudetenland lived a sizeable number of Germans whom Hitler wanted in the German state.** Faced with German threats, the Czech President Beneš looked to France, the ally of Czechoslovakia. The French, internally divided and frightened of the growing power of the German air force, turned to Britain. The British Prime Minister, **Chamberlain,** was anxious to avoid war which was still feared by the British public and he knew than any firm line would not be supported by the Commonwealth. Early in September he flew to Germany and had **discussions with Hitler at Berchtesgaden** but these talks ended in deadlock. Later in the month, he flew to **Munich** where he, Hitler, Mussolini and the French Foreign Minister, Daladier, had further talks. The result was the **Munich agreement** by which the Czechs handed over territory to Germany, thereby satisfying Hitler. War had been averted and Chamberlain was given a rapturous welcome in Britain where he announced 'Peace in our time'.

Churchill, a critic of Chamberlain and the policy of 'appeasement', described the Munich agreement as 'a total and unmitigated defeat'. His views were not shared by the British people who had spent September 1938 preparing for war. Their mood changed in **March 1939 when Hitler broke the agreement and seized the whole of Czechoslovakia.** It was now obvious that Hitler would not be bound by any agreement and that he would never be satisfied until all of Europe was at his feet. **Both the government and the people of Britain realized that war was inevitable and unavoidable.** The policy of 'appeasement' was dropped and Britain prepared to face up to Hitler.

The Outbreak of War, 1939

The **first steps** taken by the government **to prepare for war** were the doubling of size of the Territorial Army and the introduction of conscription. **Britain already possessed an ally, France, and both countries signed treaties with Poland, Rumania and Greece which promised them help if they were attacked by Germany.** It was now clear that if Hitler continued his policy of aggression in Europe (Poland was planned as the next victim) he would have to face war with Britain and France.

The **two allies hoped to include Russia in their alliance** and negotiations were opened with the Russians. Chamberlain was unhappy at having to seek the friendship of communist Russia and he admitted 'a most profound distrust of Russia'. The talks continued during the summer of 1939 in an atmosphere of suspicion and it became apparent to the Russians that the British and French had no plans to defend Poland, in spite of the promises they had made to come to her aid. Meanwhile the Russians had also been negotiating with the Germans and as a result signed the

Russo-German Non-Aggression Treaty on 22 August. This treaty ended all chances of an alliance between Britain, France and Russia. Hitler was now free to launch his planned attack on Poland.

On 1 September 1939 the Germans swept into Poland with tanks and bombers. **Britain was forced to fulfil the terms of her guarantee to Poland** but first the government played with the idea of negotiation. The mood of the country was different from what it had been at the time of Munich and Chamberlain's address to the House of Commons on 2 September was greeted with stunned horror. He still shrank back from war and as the Labour M.P. Arthur Greenwood, rose to speak, a voice cried 'Speak for England'. After years of giving way to a ruthless and greedy dictator, the people of Britain had come to realise that there could be no more surrender. **Chamberlain demanded that the Germans withdrew from Poland or face war with Britain. They did not and on 3 September, war was declared.**

Britain had gone to war because it was no longer possible to come to terms with Hitler. He was determined to bully his way to the domination of Europe, his word could never be trusted and where threats failed, he used force. In Churchill's words, 'Once again we must fight for life and honour against all the might and fury of the valiant, disciplined and ruthless German race'.

Conclusion
For just under twenty years, successive British governments had attempted to secure the peace of Europe through the League of Nations and later, treaties and agreements. From 1933 they had to deal with Germany and Italy, neither of which had any desire to keep their word. At the time of Munich the British people still feared war, but this mood evaporated as the reality of Hitler's aims became clearer; as long as he existed, there could be no peace in Europe.

Chapter 15
The Second World War

Introduction

The Second World War was a **total and universal war.** The armed forces of Britain and her allies fought campaigns in Europe, Asia, Africa and the Mediterranean Sea, and in the Atlantic, Indian and Pacific Oceans. Britain, with the Commonwealth and Empire, mobilized 12 million men and women for the war effort. In Britain the entire population was either directly or indirectly involved, for victory demanded the fullest use of every national resource.

Fighting against Britain were the Axis powers: Germany, Italy, which entered the war in June 1940, and Japan, which joined the conflict in December 1941. Britain's **major allies** were **France, defeated and occupied in 1940, Russia, invaded by Germany in the summer of 1941, and the United States, which joined the war in December 1941 – although she had been supplying Britain with arms and equipment for the past two years. Victory was achieved in 1945** with the unconditional surrender of the Axis powers. Britain had suffered 450,000 casualties, many of them civilian, and the Commonwealth and Empire a further 120,000.

For what had Britain been fighting? Quite simply **Britain's war aim was the overthrow and destruction of Nazi Germany.** Nazism was recognized as a vile and malevolent creed which imposed a cruel tyranny upon all who stood in its way. Its destruction was Britain's objective and this was publicly and officially announced after the Anglo-American conference at Casablanca in 1943. The achievement of this objective required courage, skill and determination. The cause was a good one and for this reason the war may be said to have been a truly just one.

Europe, 1939–42

The Fall of France, 1940

Hitler's war began on 1 September 1939 with the invasion of Poland. Three weeks later Poland was partitioned between the Germans and the Russians. For the next two, Germany held the military initiative and took the offensive, seeking by war to produce a Europe submissive to Hitler's will. In these campaigns, Britain and her allies were forced to play a defensive role.

In **1939 British land and air forces had been sent to northern France** where they held a defensive line just opposite the Belgian border. The strategy employed by Britain and France was defensive and based upon the **Maginot Line.** This was a continuous bulwark of steel and concrete, bristling with guns which faced the German frontier. The French commanders placed all their faith in this defensive line for it was argued that no attacking force could break through it. The Germans had no wish to do so and so the war became a waiting game, a period of inactivity which was nicknamed 'the phoney war'.

During this period British morale was boosted by the sinking of the German pocket-battleship **Graf Spee** which had been attacking merchant shipping in the South Atlantic and Indian Oceans. In December 1939 the Graf Spee was cornered by a squadron of cruisers and forced to run for the neutral Uruguayan port of Montevideo. There she was scuttled, for her commander was frightened by the rumour of a powerful British force in the offing.

In **April 1940 Hitler began his offensive in Europe** and the phoney war ended. He ordered a series of whirlwind campaigns which resulted in German control over most of western Europe within four months. The first blow fell against **Norway** which Hitler needed to secure the safe transport of Swedish iron ore and as a source of bases for his navy. The German onslaught was carefully planned, sudden and effective. The allies were taken by surprise and their naval and military response was muddled and bungling. **Early in May British and French forces had to abandon Norway to Nazi occupation.**

The **Norwegian campaign's most important political result was the fall of Chamberlain.** For some time M.Ps and the public had been growing restless about his conduct of the war and there was a growing demand for a coalition government. A House of Commons debate on 7-8 May was marked by savage criticism of Chamberlain, and over 100 of his Conservative supporters deserted him. Chamberlain felt that he had no option but to resign as Prime Minister. His earlier connections with appeasement and his uncertain approach to the problems of modern war made him an unsuitable war leader. **On 10 May Winston Churchill became Prime Minister,** an office he held until the General Election of 1945. He headed a **coalition ministry** of Conservatives, Labour and Liberal politicians. **He controlled war strategy** with the assistance of a naval, military and air force staff and was responsible for all major decisions.

In **Churchill** the British people had found a leader who could express their sense of unity and purpose. His wireless broadcasts with their rich and evocative language seemed to embody the will to victory and the common detestation of the enemy. **His firm understanding that Britain could only win the war in alliance with the United States and with the help of her vast resources was probably his greatest contribution to victory.** From the beginning of the war he cultivated a cordial friendship with the American President Roosevelt and this proved invaluable as the war progressed. As a strategist some of his judgements have been subject to criticism, in particular his obsession with an offensive against Germany from southern Europe. He was also at times overbearing and impatient of the advice of some of his commanders, whom he often treated in a high-handed manner. On balance, his stubborn determination and sense of purpose made him the most suitable and inspiring war leader the country could have found.

f19On the day that Churchill became Prime Minister, Hitler launched the campaigns that ended in the Fall of France. German forces simultaneously attacked and overran Denmark, Belgium and the Netherlands, and massed Panzer (tank) divisions cut across northern France. By-passed, the Maginot Line was useless. The German tactics were known as **Blitzkreig** (lightning war) and they depended for their success on surprise and the concentrated use of tanks, backed up by motorized infantry and dive bombers. The speed of the German advance and the power of their concentrated tank divisions caught their opponents off balance. The Panzer thrusts through the Ardennes split the French armies and left them and their commanders bewildered. Unable to adjust to the novelty and daring of the German attack, **French morale slumped and French forces disintegrated.**

he British Expeditionary Force was isolated and pinned down in an area around the Channel coast port of **Dunkirk.** Saved by a brief lull in the German attack and helped by fog and rain which made conditions difficult for German dive bombers, **the remnant of the British army was evacuated from Dunkirk.** Over 300,000 men, minus their equipment, were carried across the Channel by Royal Navy vessels, and by south coast yachts, pleasure steamers and fishing boats whose owners had responded to BBC wireless appeals. A further 200,000 British, French and Belgian troops were safely ferried from other French ports. **France soon surrendered but the British had saved much of their army.**

185

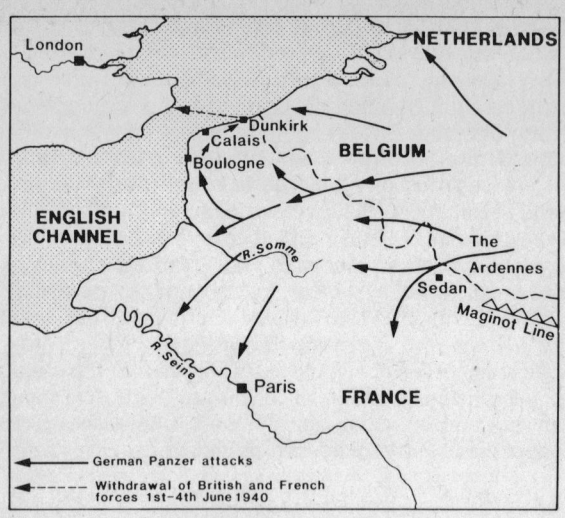

Fall of France, 1940

The Battle of Britain, 1940

The fall of France meant that Hitler now dominated the whole of western Europe and that Britain stood alone. He had mistakenly expected that Britain would sue for peace, but once he realized that this was impossible, he gave orders for **Operation Sealion, the invasion of Britain.** This operation would begin with the destruction of the RAF for the **Germans needed complete control of the air** if their forces were to cross the Channel safely. To achieve this end, the German Luftwaffe **collected 800 medium and long-range bombers with 800 supporting fighters** at airfields in northern France and Belgium. To meet this threat the RAF's Fighter Command could muster just over **800 Hurricane and Spitfire fighters,** numbers which were increased by the steady flow of new aircraft from the factories. Yet whilst the factories could produce 500 new planes a month, the RAF was worried by the **shortage of trained pilots** to fly them. Better armed and more manoeuvrable than their adversaries, the British fighters were superior in combat. They were well supported by the 51 **RADAR stations** around Britain's coastline. These enabled Fighter Command to have ample warning of the weight and direction of the German attacks.

The **Battle of Britain began in July 1940 and lasted until the middle of September.** It was in three phases, each dictated by the strategy of the German command. The first began with an unsuccessful attempt to secure air superiority over the Channel; the second centred on German attempts to destroy airfields in southern England; and the third, which began in early September, consisted of night raids on London combined with less severe bombing of airfields. The move of target priority from the airfields gave Fighter Command a much needed breathing space. For Londoners the night attacks meant something in the region of eighty consecutive nights of bombardment or, as it was called, the Blitz.

During the fighting the **RAF were able to inflict heavier casualties on their opponents** although the loss of British pilots was heavy. After the **intensive battle on 15 September, the Luftwaffe abandoned any hope of gaining air superiority over England.** On 17 September Hitler postponed Operation Sealion – the plan was finally abandoned only in 1942. Nevertheless **Britain was saved from invasion.** The RAF had lost 650 planes, the Luftwaffe 1,100.

German bombing of Britain continued. The raid on Coventry on 17 November marked the beginning of a series of heavy raids on provincial towns and cities. This attack lasted until the middle of 1941 by which time the German aircraft were needed for the attack on Russia. During 1942 there were a number of raids on British towns and cities in retaliation for the bombing of Germany. These were known as Baedeker raids and the targets included a group of historic towns such as Exeter. German bombing caused grievous loss of life and destruction of houses and factories, but aerial bombardment did not create civilian demoralization and unrest as had been predicted before the war. Quite the contrary proved true, for those who had endured bombing showed every sign of even greater determination.

The Battle of the Atlantic, 1940–5

From the Battle of Britain until Hitler's invasion of Russia in June 1941 Britain fought alone. Her government was faced with two major problems. The first was equipping her forces and paying for supplies; the second was the maintenance of sea power.

American Assistance
The Lend Lease Agreement was the answer to Britain's first problem. Since 1939 the United States government had allowed Britain to buy war supplies as long as they were paid for in cash.

By the end of 1940 money was fast running out. Roosevelt was, however, very willing to extend credit to the British. He likened America's position to that of a man whose neighbour came to him asking for a hosepipe to stop his house from burning down. Behind this comparison lay the fact that America sympathized with Britain and was willing to do all she could to prevent the whole of Europe falling under Nazi rule. By the **terms of the Lend Lease Agreement of March 1941 the United States supplied Britain with the weapons of war and the flood of aid gradually increased.** By the end of 1943 the United States was supplying 77% of all escort vessels and nearly all the transport planes and landing craft needed by the British. By 1945 Britain had received £6,756 million in supplies, although by the agreement she had contributed large sums to the United States in such ways as building camps and airfields in Britain for use by the United States forces.

Control of the Atlantic

The solution to the problem of sea control was less easy. For American supplies and fuel to reach England and for the transport of troops and supplies to the theatres of war, Britain needed control of the seas. The Germans, through their surface ships and **U Boats, were determined to cut Britain off from supplies and drive her ships from the seas. The Battle of the Atlantic** was the struggle against the U Boats. The continuous sinking of British ships was made worse by the inability of British shipyards to replace lost merchant vessels in sufficient numbers. There was also a shortage of escort vessels before 1943 and it was only in July 1941 that the Royal and Canadian navies could offer complete protection for convoys right across the Atlantic. Even then, many convoys were rationed to two sloops or destroyers. During 1941, 1,229 merchant ships were sunk, and in 1942, 1,664, many of them in the unprotected waters of the Caribbean. The Germans stepped up their programme of U Boat building so that submarines lost were quickly replaced.

The response to this desperate situation was twofold. **More escort ships were built and equipped with better detection devices and more effective depth charges. Long-range aircraft,** Sunderlands and Liberators, were employed, until by 1944 the whole Atlantic was open to aerial surveillance — one aircraft actually captured a U Boat on the surface! By the summer of **1943 the battle was being won**. The extra escort ships meant that squadrons could go into action and hunt the U Boats. By the end of the war 700 had been sunk out of a total fleet of 1200. **This** success meant that the growing flow of men, equipment and fuel from the United States could travel safely, both to Britain and the Mediterranean. The German surface vessels were also accounted for. The heavily armed battleship **Bismarck** broke into the Atlantic in 1942, sunk the battlecruiser Hood but was crippled by an attack of torpedo bombers from HMS Ark Royal. She was finished off by British battleships. Her sister ship **Tirpitz** was sunk by Lancaster bombers in Trondheim fjord on the Norwegian coast. The pocket battleship Scharnhorst was also sunk by HMS Duke of York off the same coast. Depleted, the German surface navy ceased to threaten Allied convoys after 1943.

The Mediterranean and North Africa

Introduction
In **June 1940** Mussolini's **Italy entered the war.** Mussolini's aim **was the ending of British power in the Mediterranean and Middle East and its replacement by an Italian Empire embracing all the lands bordering on the Mediterranean and the Red Sea.** The first stage on Mussolini's road to the new Italian Empire was the invasion of Greece and an attack on Egypt. To support his armies Mussolini possessed a **fleet** which appeared powerful, at least on paper, and which seriously **endangered British lines of communication in the Mediterranean.**

In June 1940 the British had shelled and put out of action the captured French fleet at Mers-el-Kebir on the North African coast, preventing it from reinforcing the Germans or Italians. The torpedo bomber attack on the Italian fleet at **Taranto** in November 1940 disabled three battleships, and in 1941 the Italian navy suffered a further heavy blow at the Battle of **Matapan,** where it lost three cruisers. These successes gave only limited security to Britain, however. Oil tankers from the Persian Gulf and Iraq could not use the Suez Canal and had to be re-routed around the Cape of Good Hope. German and Italian convoys could still cross the Mediterranean and bring supplies to their forces in North Africa until mid-1942.

Britain was involved in two land campaigns against the Italians in North Africa and Greece. The **Italian invasion of Egypt** which threatened the Suez Canal **was successfully deflected by General Wavell.** In the winter of 1940-1 he counter-attacked and **drove the Italians back into Libya.** Further advances were prevented by German intervention in Greece and Churchill's decision to divert troops from North Africa to assist the Greeks. The **Greek campaign** in the summer of 1941 ended with a British withdrawal and the German airborne invasion of **Crete** where the British suffered heavy losses. Churchill's decision to involve British forces in Greece has aroused controversy. He had weakened the North African army and gained nothing but it was claimed that the gesture towards the Greeks earned United States approval, for its people felt strongly for the Greeks in their struggle against Germany and Italy.

The Desert War

The years 1941-3 saw a series of advances and retreats across the North African desert. The Italian and **German forces under Rommel** sought to **occupy Egypt and take the Suez Canal.** This would have destroyed British power in the Middle East. Beyond this, their forces would be in a position to make further advances towards Iraq and Iran and so **jeopardize Britain's oilfields.** Axis planners also considered combining this thrust with an advance of German forces southwards through Russia towards the oilfields. So the British were defending not only the Suez Canal but their vital sources of oil too.

An offensive named Operation Crusader in the late autumn of 1941 highlighted **British weaknesses in North Africa.** British tanks and equipment were found to be inadequate and the abandonment of the operation paved the way for Rommel to mount a series of offensives in 1942. General Auchinleck, the British commander, realized that Rommel's forces could only be beaten when the British had numerical superiority in tanks and artillery, and to this purpose he began to stockpile supplies for a future offensive.

The **successful accumulation of supplies depended on them being safely convoyed through the Mediterranean. The key to eventual British victory therefore depended upon keeping the Mediterranean open.** A naval struggle developed in 1942 with Axis bombing of **Malta,** Britain's vital staging post, and submarine and air attacks on convoys. The same problem that dogged Britain also troubled the Axis powers, who depended on fuel and supplies carried by ship. The British therefore attacked German and Italian shipping in the hope of cutting Rommel off from desperately needed oil and armaments. The **campaign was successful and by August 1942 Rommel was receiving only 25% of the supplies he needed** and his forces were frequently running short of oil.

In spite of heavy losses, **the British were able to build up substantial reserves of fuel and equipment**. The new commander of the North African forces (the Eighth Army) **General Montgomery** was able to halt Rommel's advance at Aam Halfa in the summer of 1942. By October the British had taken the **offensive at El Alamein**. Thanks to a two-to-one superiority in tanks and Montgomery's careful planning, based on excellent intelligence of the enemies' movements and forces, the Alemein offensive was a success. German and Italian units began to fall back, pursued by the Eighth Army.

The **Alamein offensive coincided with Anglo-American landings on the western coastline of North Africa** at Algiers and Oran. These landings, known as **Operation Torch,** had been undertaken by British and American forces at the request of Churchill. With Anglo-American forces advancing from the west and the Eighth Army from the east, **the Axis armies were trapped, and by May 1943 what remained of them had surrendered. The North African campaign had ended with the removal of all Axis forces from the area.**

The Invasion of Italy
The final stage in the battle for control of the Mediterranean began with the relatively easy occupation of **Sicily** in July 1943, an operation which encouraged schemes for landings on the Italian mainland. The fighting potential of Italy was broken and Mussolini was forced to resign. In September 1943 Allied forces landed at **Salerno** and **Taranto** on Italy's southern coasts and then in the following year at **Anzio** on the coast close to Rome. The Allied invasions forced **Italy's surrender in September 1943** and a month later the new Italian government joined the Allies.

Germany had reacted promptly to the fall of Italy and her forces had occupied the southern and central parts of the country. They fought defiantly and their resistance slowed the Allied advance. In June 1944 Rome fell but it was only in April 1945 that the northern Italian cities were in Allied hands. The Italian campaign drained German troops from other theatres of war but contrary to early Allied hopes, proved a difficult struggle.

New Allies

During 1941 the course of the war had changed radically. On 22 June Hitler launched **Operation Barbarossa, the invasion of Russia** which had always been his most deeply held ambition.

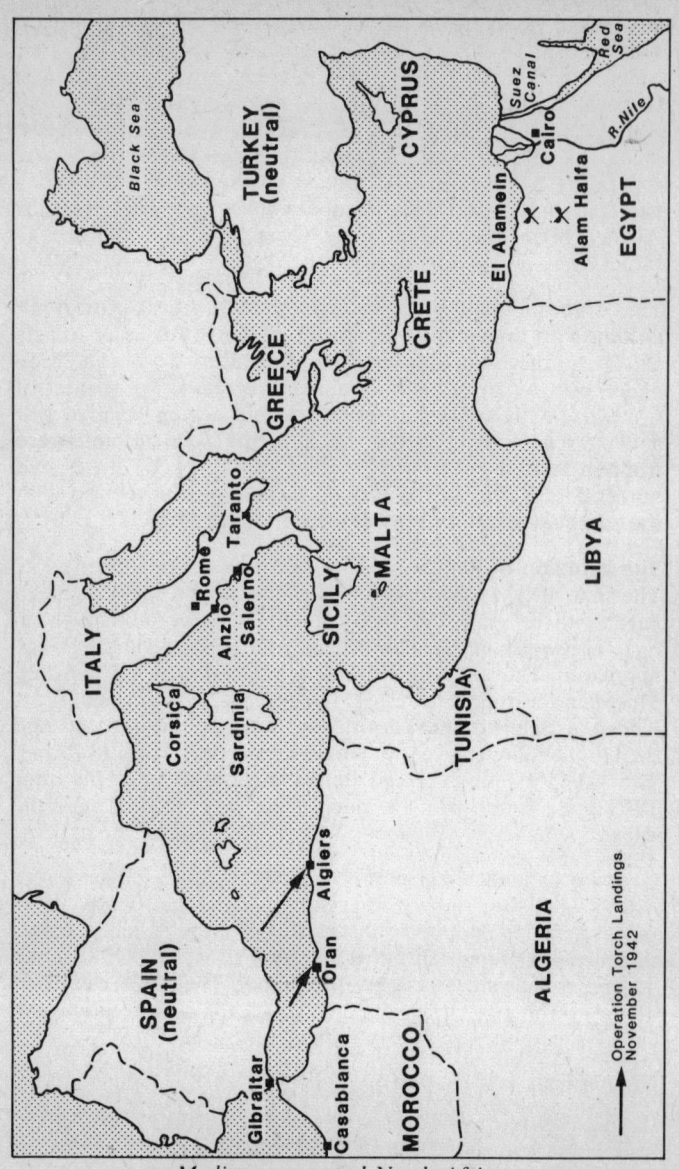

Mediterranean and North Africa

The greater part of the German army and airforce was concentrated for this campaign, which in its scale surpassed all others during the war. Hitler dreamt of a vast German Empire created out of the heartlands of Russia. The initial successes of the Germans were astonishing but the Russian winter of 1941-2 halted their advances. On 7 December 1941 the Japanese attacked the American Pacific base at **Pearl Harbor** in a bid for control of the Pacific and four days later Germany and Italy declared war on the United States.

From now on Britain's war effort was part of a larger one co-ordinated by the Allied command. The impact of the United States entry was decisive, for now the whole weight of American manpower and industrial resources was placed behind the Allies. A growing stream of equipment, men and oil crossed the Atlantic.

The **Americans accepted that the defeat of Germany was their first priority.** Early in 1942 President Roosevelt summed up the Allies' position: 'The whole question of whether we win or lose depends upon the Russians. If the Russians can hold on this summer and keep three and a half million Germans engaged in war, we can definitely win. Once we lick the Germans, with the help of England's Fleet we can defeat the Japanese in six weeks.'

The defeat of Germany meant thae invasion of western Europe. This was America's overiding objective. Churchill was less warm to this plan. He argued for the offensives in North Africa and won, operations there postponing the invasion of France for over a year. Later he pressed for other operations in the Mediterranean and southern Europe but was overidden by the United States. Although there was every effort to promote harmony at all levels between politicians and generals, the British and Americans often failed to see eye to eye on matters of overall strategy. With some little justification, the Americans suspected that the British were dragging their feet over the invasion of France. It was also inevitable that the Russians called strongly for operations in Europe to relieve pressure on their forces in the East.

Europe, 1942–5

The final defeat of Germany could only be secured by the defeat of her armies in western and eastern Europe. This became the Allies' objective. The defence of Stalingrad (1941-2) and the great tank battle at Kursk in July 1943 marked the end of the German offensive in Russia. Thereafter the Russians counter-attacked, pushing the Germans back in southern and eastern Europe. The decisive initiative had passed from Germany to the Allies, whose turn it now was to attack German forces everywhere. **The Allied offensive in western Europe took two forms, the bombing of Germany by the British and American air forces (1942-5) and the invasion of France, Belgium and Germany in 1944-5.**

The Bombing of Germany, 1942–5

Before the outbreak of war the British government had appreciated the potential of strategic bombing. The relentless bombing of an enemy's industrial areas was a way in which he could be defeated. Denied war equipment, the enemy would be forced to surrender, or so it was argued. Such an offensive required long-range, well armed bombers capable of carrying heavy bomb loads. In 1938 orders had been laid for the building of four-engined, long-range bombers (Halifaxes, Stirlings and Lancasters) and these were being supplied to the RAF by 1941-42.

At this stage in the war the **supporters of strategic bombing argued that it would win the war by the destruction of Germany industry.** Less optimistic views were expressed by some officials who claimed that intelligence reports and experience showed that industrial targets could not be bombed with sufficient precision to have the desired effect. **Air Marshal Harris,** who commanded Bomber Command, and **Lord Cherwell,** Churchill's scientific adviser then proposed a new **offensive aimed at German towns and cities.** The destruction of houses, homelessness and demoralization would, they argued, undermine and finally destroy Nazi Germany. This prediction was accepted and whilst attacks continued against industrial targets, operations began against centres of population. **Massed night raids** were flown against German cities and in May 1942 the first 'Thousand Bomber' attack was made, with Cologne as the target. Hamburg suffered likewise shortly after. The offensive was kept up throughout 1943 and 1944 in spite of heavy losses which in that year totalled 10% of all aircraft involved. By the end of the war 55,000 aircrew had lost their lives over Germany.

The **United States Airforce joined the offensive,** operating from bases in eastern England. During 1943 they flew daylight sorties against industrial targets with the intention of crippling German aircraft and fuel production. They too suffered heavy losses even though their B. 17 (Flying Fortress) bombers were well protected. Casualties were so high that at one stage operations were suspended until the arrival of long-range fighters. **The long-range Mustang fighter** was able to offer the bomber squadrons effective protection against the Luftwaffe whose opposition was soon eliminated.

Throughout 1944 the RAF and USAF delivered round-the-clock raids against Germany, hitting cities, towns and factories. What were the consequences of these raids? Historians disagree. The prophesy that Germany would be undermined was false; civilian morale did not break. It remained as firm as it had been when Britain was bombed. The damage to German industry is hard to assess accurately. The German war machine was at its fullest production in 1944 and the structure of the Nazi state had not encouraged efficiency. German industry had to be manned by millions of slave workers forcibly recruited from all over occupied Europe. What is certain is that **German industry was dislocated and production was hindered,** but the damage was less severe than the supporters of the bombing had predicted.

The Invasion of France, 1944-5

Since Russia's entry into the war, her leader, Stalin, had appealed for an Anglo-American invasion of western Europe so that his own hard-pressed forces could be relieved. The cry of 'Second Front Now' was widely taken up inside Britain, where there was strong sympathy for the Russians. At the **Casablanca Conference in 1943 Roosevelt and Churchill committed themselves to the invasion of Europe.** Command of the Allied forces was given to the American General **Eisenhower** and planning was well underway during 1943. The invasion posed many problems for the Allied staff. The first was that of intelligence. There had been raids on the French coast at Dieppe and St. Nazaire during 1942 and experience gained on these occasions was augmented by other sources. Aerial reconnaissance and the French resistance provided detailed information about the coastal defences of what the Germans called 'Fortress Europe'. Devious schemes were devised to make the Germans believe that the landings would take place at Calais and not, as was intended, along the Normandy coast.

The German defences were the next problem. To overcome this the Allies mustered 7,500 aircraft and 1,200 warships with which to pound the German defences and disrupt communications inland. Technical devices, known as 'funnies' and including mine-destroying tanks were developed to overcome early problems when landing. After the landings, success depended upon the Allies ability to pour over more men, equipment and fuel, so that the advance inland could proceed. For this purpose great, concrete floating harbours, called **Mulberries,** were built and floated across the Channel. Thus an artificial port was established at Arromanches through which men and equipment could flow. Oil was supplied by underwater pipelines, of which 25 were laid under the Channel. Code-named **Pluto,** these pipelines ensured the supply of fuel for the Allied advance.

The D Day invasions took place on 6 June 1944. Landings occurred at five beaches along a forty-mile stretch of the Normandy coastline. 70,000 troops formed the first wave of the assault and 20,000 paratroopers dropped inland to seize essential communication links and prepare the way for the advance inland. Air and sea superiority ensured that after initial hitches the beaches were secured and within a day Anglo-American forces were moving inland.

Reinforcements followed to strengthen the Allied battle-line. The well planned offensive succeeded and within two months of the first attack **over 2 million British and American fighting men** were on French soil with their equipment. German resistance was stubborn but by 20 August the enemy had been driven from Normandy and Free French forces soon liberated Paris.

General Montgomery commanded the forces in northern France and his army fought its way over the Belgian border and in September liberated Brussels and Antwerp. He persuaded his Commander-in-Chief Eisenhower to permit a paratroop and glider landing at **Arnhem** in September 1944. The overall objective was a thrust across Holland and then onto the North German plain. After courageous assaults, the Allied forces were unable to gain an advantage and the operation was abandoned.

Germany was now on the defensive. Still, Hitler was determined to do what he could to hit back. The **Ardennes offensive** of December–January 1944-5 was undertaken with the intention of throwing back the Allied advance. **This failed and it marked the last effort of Germany to take the offensive.**

The V bombs were another means by which Germany attempted to strike back. The first, the V1, was a flying bomb which was capable of flying at over 400 m.p.h. and which was launched against London and other English targets from bases in northern France. It was stopped by anti-aircraft fire and fighters. Over 5000 were launched and did considerable damage before their bases were overrun by the Allies. The V2 was a rocket which flew at over 3000 m.p.h. and over 1000 were fired against London where they created considerable havoc and loss of life. **Both weapons had come into Germany's armoury too late to effect seriously the outcome of the war.** Their development had been held up by heavy RAF raids on their research station at Peenemündë in 1943.

1945
From January 1945 Germany was collapsing. On all sides she was under attack from enemies with superior numbers and firepower. In April the Russians began their attack on Berlin. The British and Americans, fighting on German soil, had their strategy directed by political decisions. In November 1943 the Allied leaders, Churchill, Roosevelt and Stalin, had met at Teheran (in Iran) and had there discussed plans for the future of Europe after Germany's defeat. Germany would be split into three zones, each occupied and governed by one of the three powers. Berlin was to lie within the Russian or eastern zone, and the city would also be divided into three zones, each under the control of the authorities of each power. Eisenhower was therefore unwilling to advance too far and restrained his commanders.

The German Surrender and the Aftermath of War
Montgomery's British forces, with those of the American General Omar Bradley, crossed the north German plain where, early in May, they received the unconditional surrender of their German opponents. With his nation in ruins around him and with Russian troops fighting in Berlin itself, Hitler shot himself. His successor, Admiral Doenitz was left with no alternative but to surrender. On 7 May Germany's surrender was accepted. **The war in Europe had ended.**

As the Allied armies marched into Germany, they came face to face with the vile reality of Nazism. The **concentration camps,** like that at Belsen were opened up. Through newsreel films the people of Britain and the world finally saw the grim horror of Nazism. As early as 1942 the Allied leaders had pledged that those responsible for **'war crimes'** were to be hunted down and brought to trial. Included in this category were the leaders whose decisions and policies had been responsible for the war and the deliberate cruelties of Nazism. **A war crimes tribunal at Nuremburg in 1946** tried the surviving major Nazi leaders, many of whom were sentenced to death or terms of imprisonment. Other criminals were investigated, tried and punished by the authorities in the zones of occupation between 1946 and 1949.

The Far East and the Pacific War, 1941–5

Introduction
On 7 December 1941 the Japanese launched a surprise attack on the United States base at Pearl Harbor. Other attacks were launched against the **British colonies of Malaya, Hong Kong and Burma,** as well as the Philippines and Dutch East Indies (Indonesia). **Japan,** which had been at war with China since 1929, **aimed at securing by force the economic and political domination of south east Asia.** Here she hoped to find markets for her manufactured goods and much needed raw materials such as rubber and tin from Malaya and oil from the Dutch East Indies. Moreover the Japanese claimed that they would be liberating Asian people from European colonial rule and that the Japanese 'Greater East Asia Co-Prosperity Sphere' would bring justice and prosperity to the conquered nations.

Distracted by the war in Europe, the colonial powers of Britain, France and the Netherlands were in a poor position to resist Japanese aggression. The **major hindrance to the Japanese bid for power was the United States Pacific Fleet – hence the attack on Pearl Harbor.** It was not a total success. Sufficient American warships were available to the United States to take the offensive in 1942.

South East Asian Campaigns, 1942–5
British possessions in South East Asia fell quickly to the Japanese. **Hong Kong** fell in December 1941 and at the same time Japanese troops landed on the northern coasts of Malaya. Their objective was **Singapore,** the expensively fortified island base at the tip of the Malay Peninsula. Moving swiftly through the jungle, the Japanese forced the British back until they were besieged within Singapore. The island base was the greatest strongpoint of British-held south east Asia but its defence was ineptly handled. **In February 1942 the commander, General Perceval, surrendered and 130,000 Commonwealth troops were taken**

prisoner, many to die later as the result of brutal treatment at Japanese hands.

The fall of Singapore was a signal catastrophe and a blow to British prestige in Asia. It followed closely the sinking of two British capital ships, **the Repulse and Prince of Wales,** both torpedoed by Japanese bombers off the Malay coast. They had been sent to the Far East by Churchill, who believed that their presence would intimidate the Japanese. Like many others he seriously underestimated his enemy.

Burma was invaded from Thailand in December 1941 and soon the British colony was in Japanese hands. A further threat came from a **large Japanese naval force which entered the Indian Ocean, bombed British bases in Ceylon** and sank an aircraft carrier and two cruisers.

After these initial successes, the Japanese paused for two years. During this time, **Allied troops and ships in South East Asia** were placed under the command of **Admiral Mountbatten** and reorganization was soon underway. Small British units called **Chindits,** trained in jungle warfare under the command of General Wingate, operated behind the Japanese lines in Burma with some success.

India was attacked by the Japanese in the spring of 1944. The Japanese had recruited a renegade Indian nationalist leader with some troops raised from prisoners of war in the hope that they could win Indian sympathy. The invasion was beaten back at the **battles of Imphal and Kohima**, where British and Indian troops were supplied by air. After losses of 53,000 the Japanese withdrew. The **reconquest of Burma** followed and by April 1945 the capital city, Rangoon, was retaken.

By this time, Japan was close to defeat. United States and Australian forces had slowly but decisively forced the Japanese back in the Pacific. The sea battles of Midway (1942) and Leyte Gulf (1944) ended Japanese sea power and gave control of the Pacific back to the United States. The reconquered islands of Guam, Iwojima and Okinawa gave the Americans bases from which to launch punishing raids against Japanese towns and cities. **Faced with defeat, the Japanese resisted with fanatical bravery.** The demands for unconditional surrender made by the Allied leaders at Yalta in July 1945 met

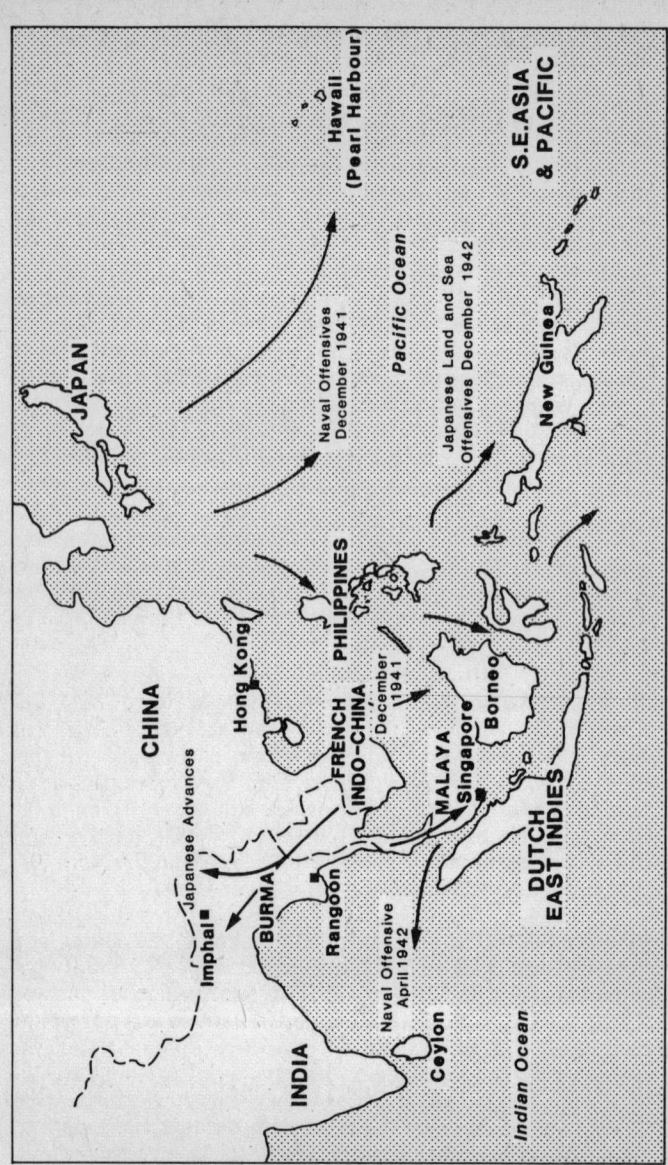

Far East and Pacific War

with a discouraging Japanese response. The Allies were faced with the prospect of a long campaign with inevitably heavy losses on the Japanese mainland.

In a final attempt to force the surrender of Japan, the United States government with the full knowledge of the British government dropped two **atomic bombs** on the cities of Hiroshima and Nagasaki. (British scientists had been working on an atomic bomb in 1940 when Churchill had the project transferred to the United States. British and American scientists had perfected the bomb by the end of 1944.) The loss of life from the atomic bomb attacks, although less than that of the continuous bombing raids of the previous six months, **persuaded the wavering Japanese to surrender. On 14 August 1945 the war in the Far East had ended and with it the Second World War. The victories of the United States in the Pacific theatre of war had been the major instrument of Japan's defeat.** One consequence was that Australia and New Zealand looked to the United States as their protector, especially after the fall of Singapore. Japan over-extended its armed forces in 1941-2, an error which led to its eventual defeat by numerically superior and better equipped armies, navies and air forces.

Britain had been humiliated by early Japanese successes and her prestige was irreparably damaged. Anti-colonialist movements were encouraged. Further damage to Britain's **position as a colonial power in Asia came from the strong feeling of the Americans that they were not fighting a war just to restore colonies to European powers.** Their attitude did much to accelerate the granting of independence to India and the break up of the French and Dutch empires in this area. **The war against Japan marked the end of Britain as an imperial power in the Far East.**

The Home Front, 1939–45

Introduction
The defeats of Germany and Japan had in part been made possible by the mobilization and organization of the population and resources of Britain. Total war demanded complete organization and direction of every national asset and the scale of this operation was greater than it had been in the First World War. What was called 'war socialism' not only transformed British life and industry, it also led to wide social changes.

Industrial and Food Production

To equip its forces, the British government had, during the course of the war, to **take over and co-ordinate the running of all kinds of industry and transport.** New ministries of Supply and Aircraft Production had to be set up to direct these vital activities. The **Board of Trade was given the mammoth task of supervising all retail trade throughout the country.** To fill these new ministries and others which were forced to expand as they took on new responsibilities, experts from beyond the ranks of the civil service had to be recruited. University lecturers, teachers, businessmen and Trade Union leaders were called in under the principle that the **fullest use must be made of all available talent.** Ernest Bevin, the Trade Union leader and Labour M.P., ran the Board of Trade, and the newspaper proprietor Lord Beaverbrook controlled Aircraft Production and then Aircraft Supply.

Manpower needed to be deployed effectively. A balance had to be achieved so that everyone was usefully employed. **Women** between 18 and 50 were registered and by 1942 could be directed to where they were needed either in offices, farms or factories. Women became used to a wider variety of work and working after marriage, starting trends that would last after the war. Thanks to economic planning and the direction of industry by government planners, production responded well to the demands of the war. In 1940 Britain was producing 83% of all the munitions needed by her armies and in 1942 sufficient rifles had been manufactured for the next ten years. Coupled with the supplies brought from the United States under Lend Lease, **Britain's own production ensured that her forces eventually possessed the weight and superiority of armament and transport that was necessary for victory.**

Food supplies were a problem. Much needed to be imported and paid for abroad and to reduce this amount the government, through the **Local War Agricultural Committees** encouraged the expansion of food production. New land was broken for ploughing and new methods encouraged for increasing yields. A less welcome measure was the direction of farmers as to what crops they should grow. The result was that cereal and potato production rose by a half during the war and the **overall efficiency of British farming improved so that foreign imports dropped.** Food and other commodities were rationed. **A**

fair and flexible system of rationing was adopted with great success. Some foodstuffs such as butter were the subject of a fixed ration; others such as meat were rationed by price – each week, you could either make several purchases of cheap meat or else concentrate your allowance on a costly joint. Most food was rationed by a points system by which items were assessed as being worth a number of points. With each person allocated a set amount of points, they could use them as they wished for such items as sweets, biscuits and jam. Pensioners, industrial workers and children were given special allocations, and infants and schoolchildren were allowed free cod liver oil (for vitamins) and orange juice. Clothes and household goods were also rationed on the points system and the government created 'Utility'goods – specially designed and priced furniture and basic, well made clothes. **Prices fell during the war and the food expenditure of the average man and woman increased.** People were better fed than ever before, on a plain but nutritious diet.

Planning for the Future

Total war on the scale waged between 1939 and 1945 required **national unity and a sense of purpose.** But what of the years after victory? What would be its fruits? Government propaganda declared that there would be a fairer, juster society. The **Beveridge Report**, which was accepted by the government in 1943 thanks to Labour insistence, called for a universal system of social relief. The report called for a new system of national insurance by which contributions from employees, employers and government would provide funds for the relief of poverty and all its attendant misfortunes. The establishment of the **Ministry of Town and Country Planning** in 1943 was seen as the first stage towards a fair and rational rebuilding of the towns and use of the countryside. The **1944 Education Act,** devised by **R.A. Butler,** created a new educational system. Up to 11, children would be taught at Primary Schools and then, depending upon an examination, would proceed either to academic grammar schools or to technical or modern schools where the bias would be towards practical subjects. The act also raised the school leaving age.

Planning had been seen as instrumental in securing success in war. Its application to the problems of peace and the reconstruction of the nation was seen as both desirable and necessary. A new and juster society was considered to be the rightful and well earned reward of all who had fought.

Conclusion

The Russian leader, Stalin, remarked that during the war Britain had given time, the United States money and Russia blood. This was in part true. Between the fall of France and Hitler's invasion of Russia, **Britain alone defied Germany and kept the war going.** That defiance contributed to the final victory.

Until 1942 the balance of strength had been in Germany's favour. Afterwards the manpower and resources of the Allies ended German superiority. Nevertheless with all their resources, human and physical, the Allies needed three years in which to defeat Germany. In this time Britain was unable to match the resources of the two superpowers in terms of men and equipment. Her position meant that her forces were smaller. Still they played an important part in the campaigns in Europe, North Africa, the Mediterranean and the Far East. **The RAF made the German invasion of Britain impossible,** it assisted in the bombing of Germany and the consequent damage of German war production, and it played a key role in winning the vital battle of the Atlantic. **The Royal Navy kept open the Atlantic and Mediterranean** and so made certain Britain's own survival and the eventual land victories in North Africa and western Europe. **The Army's part in winning the war was played in North Africa, Italy and western Europe.**

It must be remembered that Britain's forces included soldiers, airmen and sailors from the Commonwealth. Soldiers from Canada, South Africa, Rhodesia and India fought in the North African campaigns alongside Australians and New Zealanders. In the Far East, the Indian, Australian and New Zealand armed forces played a significant part in air, sea and land fighting. West Indians came to Britain to join the forces, especially the RAF, and native troops from the King's African Rifles fought in North Africa and the Far East.

The participation of these gallant fighting men was a reminder that Britain was an imperial power. By 1945 this power was no longer a reality. The United States and Russia dominated the world, Britain's wealth was all but spent, her trade was shattered and her industries were exhausted. The cost of victory was the end of Britain as a world power, the prize was the extinction of Nazism and all its evils.

Chapter 16
The Labour Governments, 1945–51

Introduction

The **General Election of June 1945** resulted in a massive Labour victory. Labour won 12 million votes and secured 393 out of 640 seats in the House of Commons. The Conservatives polled 8½ million votes and lost 203 seats; the Liberals were left with just twelve seats. Labour's success owed much to the dismal record of the Conservatives. The voters remembered well the 1930s and the reputation of the Conservatives had been indelibly stained by industrial stagnation, unemployment, appeasement and unreadiness for war. Churchill (who had been a Conservative renegade in the 1930s) could not by his popularity erase the memories of his party's failings. By contrast Labour offered an inspiring and tempting vision for the future which matched the mood and aspirations of a war weary people. The Labour pamphlet *Let us Face the Future* offered the voter the chance to taste the fruits of victory and, in the words of Labour's slogan, 'Win the Peace'. Inequalities and injustices would be swept away and there would be a better life in a fairer and more humane country.

Labour took power with the intention of rebuilding war-broken Britain, of restoring its wealth and transforming it into a just society. The revolution succeeded but its leaders were also brought face to face with problems beyond their control, economic crises and the Cold War. Practical men as well as idealists, Labour's leaders were forced to reshape many of their ideas and adjust their plans in response to unforseen circumstances.

The Economy

During the war an American Treasury official had claimed that Britain was 'busted'. In essence this was so and it was the first and pressing need of the Labour Prime Minister, **Attlee,** and his colleagues to **repair the economy.** This task was huge. In 1945 war damage was estimated at £3 billion, £1 billion had been lost in foreign investments and the British government owed £3.3 billion abroad. The basis of Britain's wealth was her foreign trade and this had been so disrupted that exports were merely a half of what they had been in 1939. Here lay the source of the first major problem, for Britain needed to export manufactured goods to earn the money with which to pay for her imports. High amongst these was food, vital for the nation's survival. Labour therefore needed to swell exports to a level where they could exceed imports. To achieve this, war-damaged industries needed to be re-equipped, and this in turn required cash investment.

Cash was Britain's greatest need in 1945. Her need was made more desperate by the end of the Lend Lease arrangements, which meant that from August 1945 all imports of food had to be paid for in ready cash. **The sudden disappearance of United States credit forced the government to seek a new loan.** The economist J. M. Keynes led a delegation to the United States to negotiate the fresh credit arrangement. **He obtained a $3750 loan from the United States and a further $1250 from Canada which were to be advanced over the next four years.** It was hoped that during this time the British economy would begin to flourish and that recovery would be sufficiently advanced by 1951 for repayment to begin. To ease the pressure, the total of the Lend Lease debt was reduced to $650 million. The **Marshall Aid plan,** devised in 1947, offered further assistance to Britain and the government received a further £681 million between 1948 and 1951. This plan had been part of the American response to the fear of communist Russia's efforts to subvert western Europe. American money, it was argued, had to be used to help the free nations of Europe to strengthen their economies and so remove the sources of unrest which communism hoped to exploit. The 1945 loans were subject to terms dictated by the Americans and these permitted the free import into Britain of United States goods and fixed the value of the pound at 4.03 cents, which was high and harmful to Britain's trading position.

The American and Canadian loans, gave considerable assistance to Britain, enabling it to invest in industrial renewal and purchase much needed materials, including food, from abroad. But they did not prevent a **series of financial crises.** The bitter winter of 1946-7, coal shortages, the costs of occupying Germany and feeding its people (£5 million a month in 1946) and international food shortages put fresh demands on Britain's limited reserves. **Faced with a drying up of the funds provided by the loans, the government was forced to impose a series of controls and to tighten rationing.** Bread was rationed (1946-8) as were potatoes, while the allowances of other commodities were reduced. Powdered egg, a wartime staple, disappeared altogether, much to the despair of many housewives. Whalemeat and the distrusted snoek (a predatory South Atlantic fish) were offered by the government as the means with which to augment a stringent diet, but neither was warmly received. The unsold and unloved snoek was later resurrected as cat food, or so it was said. Against this background of **austerity,** the country was exhorted to work by such billboard slogans as 'We work or want'. In 1949 the fear of dwindling reserves of dollars and the brief United States recession forced the Chancellor of the Exchequer, **Sir Stafford Cripps,** to **devalue the pound.** Before devaluation the pound was worth 4.03 dollars; after, it was worth 2.80 dollars. The cost of British exports fell by 30% and this provided a needed boost to exports although many other countries followed suit and devalued their currencies. By this time Marshall Aid was flowing into Britain and the additional dollars staved off further tightening of rations. The export drive was slowly paying off. In 1947 annual exports stood at £900 million, twice the 1938 level and by 1950 exports actually surpassed imports in value.

Labour's domestic economic policy was inevitably tied to the wider problems of international trade and credit. Hugh Dalton, Chancellor of the Exchequer from 1945 to 1947, and his successor, Sir Stafford Cripps, both produced **budgets which were designed to encourage stable prices, low costs of food (thanks to subsidies), the reduction of income tax and a low bank rate (2%) which would encourage investment.** The conservation of currency was seen as essential and so in 1947 high taxes were levied on tobacco, allowances for travel abroad were pared to the bone and American films were taxed, much to the irritation of film-goers devoted to Hollywood's products.

There was **high employment and cheap food** (which cost £500 million a year in subsidies in 1949) but rationing and controls limited the range of personal spending. To meet public demand and thwart controls, a new race of busy black-market traders came into being, known as spivs. They tricked the government and gave people what they wanted — at a price.

By 1950 the economy showed signs of recovery. Clothes rationing had ended in 1949 and the points system was abandoned a year later. The **import-export balance had swung in favour of exports** but this achievement was short lived as a result of the new pressures created by the outbreak of the Korean War in 1950. The country was well on the road to recovery and during the 1950s rationing was ended and a sudden and spectacular boom in consumer spending began.

Nationalization

Nationalization of certain key industries was a central feature of Labour's economic policy. In essence nationalization meant that an industry was taken over by the government and subsequently run by it through the agency of a cabinet minister. The minister could appoint the senior management of the nationalized industry and could intervene directly in its business affairs if and when he felt the national interest demanded. In business terms a nationalized industry was expected to break even or make a profit although its power to raise money for investment was regulated by the government. In some cases nationalized industries made losses which the government could make up from public funds. The argument for using public money in this way was that nationalized industries such as the railways were essential for the economic well-being of the country.

Labour's arguments for nationalization were social as well as economic and rested upon the assumption that certain industries such as transport were so vital to the country that they could only be run satisfactorily by the government. Further, the nature of the services of such an industry fulfilled a social need and this justified public control and public subsidy. The enemies of nationalization then and since have pointed out that such a policy could and did lead to the giving of public money to subsidize inefficiency. On the other hand Labour claimed that its actions were in the country's interests, as when it insisted on coal prices being held down. After all, coal and in fact all energy were vital for industry.

Labour's programme of nationalization began immediately it came to power. **In 1946 the Bank of England was nationalized** and in the same year the **Coal Industry Nationalization Act** placed the coal mines in public hands. The mine owners were given £164 million in compensation for their losses. Here the arguments in favour of nationalization were based upon the shakiness of the coal industry, which had suffered from outdated methods and a lack of investment since the First World War. Once nationalized, the coal industry, under the direction of the National Coal Board, began a series of schemes for the reduction of manpower and the introduction of mechanization. The **Electricity and Gas Industries were nationalized in 1947 and 1948,** each under the direction of national boards which overlooked the regional gas and electricity authorities. As part of the wider plans for energy, the Labour government began investment and development programmes for **atomic power.**

Transport nationalization was undertaken in 1946 when all large road haulage firms, all canal and waterway companies and the regional railways were brought under national control. Here the industries were in a miserable condition and the railways in particular required (and still do require) subsidies from the government.

The **Iron and Steel Bill of 1949,** which aimed to nationalize these industries, provoked stiff Conservative opposition and widespread complaints from the companies concerned. They argued that the industry was healthy and that government control would undermine profitability. The bill was passed but under the shadow of Conservative pledges that if and when their party returned to power, the iron and steel industry would be handed back to private ownership. The expectation that the sugar industry would be nationalized led to the threatened companies sponsoring an extensive advertising campaign in which their champion, 'Mr. Cube', proclaimed the blessings of private enterprise. All this assisted the Conservatives in the election of 1950.

Labour's nationalization programme created an economy which was neither capitalist nor socialist, in which private and public ownership existed side by side. The debate over whether state ownership is advantageous to the country still continues. The successes of nationalized interests can be set alongside their shortcomings and the balance must depend upon personal political bias. For those in 1945 who believed that nationalization would lead to miracles, the subsequent performance of some nationalized industries was a disappointment. For the employees of such concerns, nationalization did not open a new era of relations between workers and management.

Whilst Labour's economic policies produced a national recovery, they often led to short-term crises and a series of shortages. Austerity, shortages, controls and scrimping, while necessary, did not win public approval as was witnessed by the regular by-election defeats suffered by the government. This reaction was also seen in the results of the 1950 and 1951 general elections. Taking a broader picture, the Labour measures had encouraged and underpinned the national prosperity of the 1950s.

Social Policies

In 1945 the Labour Party had called upon the voters to support the fulfilment of the **Beveridge Plan** which was widely proclaimed as the party's chief aim. A poster of the election showed a smiling British soldier, tin hat on head, clearly looking towards the future. For his sake the voter was called on to vote Labour. The point was clear: the war was over and the fighting man deserved the fruits of victory for himself and his family. Chief of these was a juster and more humane society from which sickness, oppressive poverty and insecurity had been driven out. The Labour Party and the Trades Union Congress were pledged to create this society which was as much the realization of traditional Labour dreams as the fulfilment of Beveridge's proposals. The **National Insurance Act of 1946** was the first stage of the plan. It created a nationwide system of social security for all men and women. Under the control of the Ministry of National Insurance and run through its local offices, the new scheme offered unemployment pay, cash payments for those off work through illness, maternity allowances, retirement pensions and funeral allowances. The money was drawn from a central fund financed by the weekly contributions of workers and their employers with additional sums provided by the government. From 1946 until 1966 the weekly contributions made up between 73 and 93% of the costs of the new services. Additional assistance came through the weekly payments made to mothers for their children under the **Family Allowance Act of 1945.**

Equally far-reaching in its effects was the **National Health Act of 1946** the creation of the passionate and volatile Aneurin Bevan, the Minister of Health. The act provided for free medical, optical and dental treatment for all. Local and charity hospitals were placed under the control of the Ministry of Health, which also took on the responsibility for the establishment of local clinics and health centres. The plan won the co-operation of the specialists and surgeons (whose private practice was not affected) but provoked the suspicion and hostility of the doctors. Their organization, the British Medical Association, led a rearguard action against Bevan's proposals which was marked by a number of vinegary exchanges between Bevan and the Association's leadership. The doctors finally relented and by 1948, 90% had integrated their practices within the scheme. In its first years the National Health Service cost £400 million a year. It was serving 95% of the population and the fact that it was needed was demonstrated by the 8½ million men and women who sought dental treatment during its first twelve months of existence.

Housing was seen by Labour as another urgent problem to be tackled on a national scale. Slum clearance and the replacement of war-damaged property forced the pace for the building of new homes. By 1950 Labour boasted that it had built over 500,000 new houses although it had hoped for more. The party's critics condemned its emphasis on council housing and neglect of private building. Blame was also placed upon the mesh of restrictions which the Conservatives alleged had led to the shortfall on the housing programme.

Foreign Affairs, 1945–51

The **Cold War** between the United States and Soviet Russia dominated international relations between 1945 and 1951. Bickering between the two great powers began within months of the war ending and the roots of discord lay in United States fears of Russian ambitions. In 1945 when the Russian leader Stalin had been at Potsdam, near Berlin, an American diplomat asked him how it felt for a Russian leader to be standing in a place which had been the heart of German militarism. Stalin replied that Czar Alexander I had ridden through Paris. This had been in 1814 but the thoughts which lay behind the Russian leader's comment were alarming. The Russian grip on eastern Europe, the Russian-inspired overthrow of the Czech government in 1948 and the blockade of the Allied zones of Berlin in 1948-9 added to American fears. Churchill had pointed out in 1946 that an Iron Curtain had fallen over Europe, and to the east of it Russia set up puppet communist regimes and suppressed freedom with a mailed fist. To the west there were signs that Russia lay behind communist subversion in France and Italy. Looking back it is possible to question whether Stalin wished to undermine western governments or whether he was as ambitious as his enemies suspected, but at the time his behaviour provoked justifiable fears.

The United States reaction to Russia's aggressiveness was the **Truman Doctrine of 1947** by which President Truman pledged his country's backing to those who resisted communism. This defensive posture was supported in the same year by the Marshall Aid programme, giving economic help to western Europe.

The Labour government and its energetic and determined Foreign Secretary, Ernest Bevin, supported the United States. As a junior partner in the anti-communist front, Britain did what it could to resist communist subversion in Greece and Turkey, but in 1947 the costs of such preventive measures proved too much for the ailing British economy. Responsibility for these two countries was passed on to the willing shoulders of the United States. Britain also assisted the United States in the **Berlin Airlift of 1948-9.** The Russians cut off all land supplies to the Allied zones in Berlin through a mixture of bloody-mindedness and a wish to overawe the Berliners. In response the USAF and RAF began a massive air ferry to carry all the necessary fuel and food for the survival of the inhabitants of the Allied zones. The RAF carried 30% of all these supplies.

The increasing international tension and the government's willingness to share its burden of European defence forced the introduction of **conscription for 18 year olds (National Service Act, 1948).** The cost of arms expenditure increased so that by 1948, 7% of the government's income was being directed towards defence.

Bevin added his weight to the proposals for the creation of a permanent European alliance, NATO (North Atlantic Treaty Organization) which was formed in 1949. By this agreement the United States, Great Britain, Canada, France, Belgium, Holland, Luxembourg, Italy, Norway, Iceland and Portugal pledged themselves to joint action if any one of them was attacked. For over two years the Labour government had been secretly backing the development of a **British atomic bomb.** Russia had produced and tested its own in 1949 but then and for the next twenty years the United States possessed a superiority in such weapons. American nuclear superiority was the basis of NATO's defence against Russia. As well as playing a central part in the making of a European defence system, the Labour government backed the United Nations and the United States in the **Korean War (1950-3).** British troops joined the United Nations forces which stemmed and drove back the communist North Korean invasion of South Korea. Attlee also threw his weight behind President Truman when he was confronted by the American commander, General MacArthur, who pressed for an attack on communist China. The Labour government was committed, like the President, to a defensive containment of communism, not an offensive war. **The American alliance and the resistance of communist aggression were the main planks in Labour's foreign policy.** In terms of ideology the British labour movement was democratic with a strong faith in individual freedom. Russian communism was crudely authoritarian. Whilst many British socialists could sympathize with the aims and successes of communism, they found it hard to stomach its methods.

Commonwealth Affairs

From the 1930s the Labour Party was committed to Indian independence and in **1945 Attlee announced his government's immediate intention to give self-government to India.** The fulfilment of the promise was placed in the hands of Lord Mountbatten, whom Attlee appointed as Viceroy. His was a task made difficult by the **Moslem League.** Under its leader, Jinnah, the Moslem League had, since 1940, argued for the creation of a separate Moslem state of Pakistan. It was impossible, claimed Jinnah and his supporters, for Moslems to live safely within a state with a Hindu majority. Religious strife had always lain beneath the surface of Indian life and by **1946 reconciliation had proved impossible.** Religious rioting, massacre and counter-massacre spread from Calcutta to ravage a great area of northern India. **Partition was agreed upon and in 1947 India and Pakistan became independent amidst religious strife which Mountbatten and the British forces could do little to stop.** Labour had begun the policy of granting self-government to the colonies, a process which would be followed by the Conservatives and extended to Africa.

In **Palestine,** Arab–Jewish strife had intensified during the early 1940s when the problem was exacerbated by the influx of Jewish refugees from Europe. Since 1944 the Jewish extremists of the Irgun group led by Menachim Begin (at the time of writing Prime Minister of Israel) had been waging a murderous terrorist campaign against the British. **Unable to control Palestine, the government announced its intention to withdraw in 1948 and passed the problem to the United Nations.** As the British Army pulled out it left behind chaos and uncertainty for the Arab neighbours of Palestine announced their intention of eliminating any Jewish state which was formed. The new state, Israel, survived the Arab assault but has not yet found a means by which it can live in harmony with its Arab neighbours.

Conclusion

In the 1950 General Election Labour's slogan 'Fair Shares for All' failed to electrify the voters although the party kept the support of 46% of the electorate. In spite of this the party had a majority of six and **in 1951 the Conservatives returned to power with a small lead over Labour. Labour had achieved two major successes, the creation of the welfare state and the laying of the foundations of national economic recovery. It had attached Britain firmly to the cause of the United States** within Europe and the wider world. By this means it had helped in the process by which Russia had been checked. **It had also begun another equally important process, the granting of self-government to the colonies.**

It had hoped to do more. The idealism of the 1945 election programme had aimed at the creation of a more just and more equal society in which the suffering created by poverty was banished. Through planning and nationalization the Labour government had hoped to regenerate industry and create the wealth which could be tapped for its great social schemes. Labour had also to govern and this meant facing up to practical problems, many of which were beyond Britain's control and often not of Britain's making. **Before and after the war Britain was a debtor nation, needing to borrow money for its survival.** This meant that its government had to abide by the terms of those from whom it borrowed. The growth of international tension forced the government into a position where it had to increase expenditure on arms. The clash between Labour's ideals and practical realities came in 1950 when defence costs forced the government to impose charges for medical prescriptions, glasses and dental treatment. Bevan resigned rather than see what he considered an assault on the principles of his National Health Service. The more pragmatic Emanuel Shinwell remarked that false teeth were of little value if your head was blown off. By a mixture of the idealistic and the practical, Labour had led Britain in its recovery from war and made it a fairer, more humane society in which to live.

Key Terms

Act is a law which has been passed by a majority of votes in the **House of Commons** and the **House of Lords** and has been given the customary and automatic approval of the reigning monarch.

Bill is the name given to an act before it has been approved by Parliament and made law.

Cabinet is the collective name for the leading ministers in the **government** (Prime Minister, Foreign Secretary, Home Secretary &). They meet regularly to discuss policy and must be members of either the **House of Commons** or **House of Lords**. To survive as a government, the cabinet must have a majority of supporters in the House of Commons.

Coalition is where a government is formed in which the **cabinet** includes members of two or more political parties.

Commonwealth covers all self-governing **territories**.

Dominion is a former British colony which has its own Parliament, administration and laws but has the reigning head of monarch as head of state (e.g. Canada and Australia).

General Election is called throughout the country for the election of a new House of Commons.

Government is the name given to all ministers. To be formed, a government must have a majority of its supporters in the **House of Commons**. Usually a government relies upon members of its own party but it can and has remained in power with support from other parties (e.g. the Liberals in 1911 survived with Irish support).

House of Commons is one of the two chambers of Parliament made up of elected Members of Parliament (M.Ps).

House of Lords is the other chamber of Parliament made up of Church of England bishops and **peers**.

Peers are titled noblemen (dukes, marquesses, earls and barons) who obtain their titles either by inheritance (from their fathers) or by the command of the reigning monarch.

Radicals men who seek to solve political or social problems by drastic and sweeping changes, often involving the total alteration of society.

Suggested Reading

General histories of this period are numerous and vary in approach and detail. Below is a selection of books chosen on the grounds that they are straightforward and easy to read.

A. J. P. Taylor, *Essays in English History* (Penguin). These include short studies of various subjects and people, including Palmerston and Disraeli.

A. Bryant, *English Saga, 1840–1940*.

R. Blythe, *The Age of Illusion*, a lively series of essays about the 1920s and 1930s.

R. Graves and A. Hodge, *The Long Week-end*, a detailed but readable survey of Britain between 1919 and 1939.

The 'Jackdaw' series of documents and commentaries are very attractive and useful. Topics concerned with this period include The Vote; 1832–1928, The Indian Mutiny, Women in Revolt: the Fight for Emancipation, The General Strike, The Coming of War 1936–39 and Winston Churchill.

Other useful books covering individual topics are:

R. Kee, *The Green Flag*, a detailed account of Irish history. A. Moorehead, *The White Nile*, (Penguin), M. Strage, *From Cape to Cairo* and J. Barbary, *The Boer War* (Puffin) all deal with various aspects of the British Empire in Africa.

C. Hibbert, *The Destruction of Lord Raglan* and C. Woodham-Smith, *The Reason Why* deal with the Crimean War.

C. Barnett, *The Swordbearers* has valuable accounts of commanders and battles in the First World War with a very good description of Jutland. J. Keegan, *The Face of Battle* includes an excellent account of fighting on the Western Front and the battle of the Somme.

Historical novels need to be handled with care as many merely use the past as a background for a romantic tale which could have taken place at any time. The Flashman series are very good as they set the adventures of the hero against real events which are very carefully and well described. *Flashman at the Charge* and *Flashman in the Great Game* are both splendid, one is set against the Crimean War and the other, the Indian Mutiny.

Examination Hints

Preparation for an exam

Knowledge and understanding of a subject is the obvious key to examination success. It is also important to **write clearly** and well in order that what you know is shown to the best effect. In a subject such as History **knowledge** comes through **reading** and **understanding through thinking about what you read.** This is not always a quick process and it would be foolish to imagine that certain success will come as a result of leaving all your work to the last few weeks or days before the exam. To put off your main work to the last moment is to gamble recklessly and probably lose.

Most schools allow three or four terms for preparing for an examination and it is important to use the time set for a subject. The making of **clear notes,** reading and writing essays are all necessary in order to build up knowledge and experience of writing.

There is no set way of studying. Most people discover their own system and try to keep to it. **It is essential to have some kind of system,** however personal, **especially in making notes.** By extracting information, thinking about it and making it into notes you are helping yourself to remember it. When you are puzzled, ask questions and listen carefully to points that are raised in discussions. A knowledge of facts alone is of little use without understanding what they mean or why they are significant. It is of little use to know all the details of the 1832 Reform Act without appreciating why it was needed and what it changed. In the same way it may be useful to know all the details of alliances and crises before 1914 but this knowledge is of little help in an examination if you have little or no idea of why Britain and other countries followed the policies they did.

How you make notes is very much a personal decision although it is important that **your notes make sense to you** and **can be used easily.** Your main source of information will be your text-book and it is important to understand how it is laid out and written. Some follow a strict chronological order so that Gladstone's second Ministry is followed by Disraeli's 1874–80 ministry and so on. Others follow themes with whole sections on the Irish problem or British foreign policy – a scheme which has been followed in this book. This means that there will be occasions when you have to look in an index to find all the references to the subjects you want. History is about human activity and human activity is very hard to fit into rigid compartments. Before an examination you will begin final revision which will be easier if you have worked carefully during the previous months. Do not be tempted to narrow your subjects down on the grounds that such a topic must come up because it did not appear in the last examination paper. You may well be right but you could equally well be mistaken. **Above all be flexible.** It is misguided to memorize set answers in the hope that set questions will appear. They may not and you may therefore be tempted to write down what you have memorized just because you know it. Material like this which bears no relation to the question asked will gain you few if any marks.

Examinations

Examination papers are in **two parts. The first consists of instructions to candidates** (the rubric) and the second consists of the **questions. Read the instructions carefully** for they will tell how long you have and which questions you may answer. Many examination papers have two or more sections and you will be told how many questions you may take from each section. If you carelessly ignore these instructions some of your answers will gain no credit at all. Note the time you are allowed so that you can plan how long you have to write each answer. If through mischance you run out of time then attempt some kind of answer in note form to give the examiner some idea of what you would have written.

The **questions must be read carefully and slowly.** Try to be as cool as possible for sometimes in panic you may misread a question and give an irrelevant or mistaken answer. Having prepared the topic, you may happily see that the First World War appears and without much heed, start writing down all you know. This will be of little use if the question is confined to the war at sea.

When **reading the questions** it is important that you **think carefully about what each one is asking for.** Here it is sensible to bear in mind the crucial words: 'How', 'Why', 'What', 'Discuss',

'Describe', 'Contrast' and 'Change'. Each word provides a clear indication of the answer that is required. The first three demand some kind of explanation whereas 'describe' asks for a straightforward account, a description of what happened. This point may best be illustrated by briefly looking at three questions on one subject:

1. Why did Britain go to war with Germany in 1914?
2. Describe the changes in British foreign policy between 1890 and 1914.
3. What were the objectives of British foreign policy between 1890 and 1914?

Each deals in a different way with Britain's relations with foreign powers but each is worded in such a way as to demand a different approach to the answers. The first centres on the outbreak of war and asks for an explanation of Britain's entry into the war against Germany. The second is wider for it asks for an account of British foreign policy with the emphasis on how it changed. Since change is mentioned and two dates are given the question assumes the foreign policy in 1914 was different from that in 1890. The dates and the suggestion of change point towards the kind of answer required. This will need some account of what British foreign policy was in 1890 as a starting point. This established you may go forward and list the changes. The third question approaches the same subject from a different angle. It wants you to show the thinking behind the policy or in other words to try and show what the government was attempting to do. All will draw on the same evidence but it will be used in different ways. In answering question 2 you could fairly write, 'in 1904 Britain settled her differences with France through the Entente and gave assurances of future support for France'. This could be contrasted with earlier suspicions and colonial rivalry. In the third question the same evidence could be used to show that by 1904 Britain was aware of her lack of friends in Europe and was anxious to secure a lasting and useful understanding with one major power.

Relevance is tremendously important. The answer should keep strictly to the terms of the question. An answer to a question about Disraeli's domestic policies should not contain an account of his conduct of the Eastern Question. This had nothing at all to do with his home policy although it would be relevant to a question on his foreign policy or could be included among his achievements.

When writing an answer it is altogether worthwhile to pause in the middle and ask yourself 'am I still answering the question or am I drifting away from the main theme?' Look back at your last few sentences and if they do not help to answer the question then you have wandered away from the subject.

Style is important. An answer should have shape, that is a beginning, a middle and an end. Points should be supported with evidence. To say that 'the Irish wanted Home Rule' is fair enough but the point is given weight by the addition of evidence about the return of Home Rule M.Ps to Parliament in the 1880s and later. The shape and direction of an answer is improved by the existence of a plan. When writing exam answers you should first construct a plan, however fragmentary or skeletal, which gives you a sense of direction.

Writing an answer, you should take care about **spelling and grammar.** Proper names should be correctly spelt and you should write in a way that makes clear what you are trying to say. Muddled thinking leads to muddled writing. The sentence 'The British were worried about the German economy' hints at what many people were feeling before the First World War. The sentence 'The British were worried because Germany's economic growth was overtaking Britain's' makes the point absolutely clear. Handwriting should also be clear; pale ink and illegibility do not help the examiner to read and assess what you have written.

Commonsense is also important as in all things. To list the death of Gordon at Khartoum among Gladstone's achievements or splitting the Conservative party amongst Chamberlain's is absurd. Such errors are the result of not having read or thought about a question. The knowledge you have of a subject deserves intelligent presentation or else it is worth little. Finally, it is always worthwhile to think for yourself and express your own views. If they are supported by evidence, then they are just as valuable as anyone else's. In conclusion, always remember **four points:**

1. Read the question carefully.
2. Keep to the point.
3. Answer clearly and concisely.
4. Write legibly.

Index